PO-5146
£45.00

404123

KV-391-011

# Appearance and Identity

## Fashioning the Body in Postmodernity

Llewellyn Negrin

746.
920
P 391
NEG

APPEARANCE AND IDENTITY
Copyright © Llewellyn Negrin, 2008.

First published in 2008 by PALGRAVE MACMILLAN® in the United States—a division of St. Martin's Press LLC, 175 Fifth Avenue, New York, NY 10010.

Where this book is distributed in the UK, Europe and the rest of the world, this is by Palgrave Macmillan, a division of Macmillan Publishers Limited, registered in England, company number 785998, of Houndmills, Basingstoke, Hampshire RG21 6XS.

Palgrave Macmillan is the global academic imprint of the above companies and has companies and representatives throughout the world.

Palgrave® and Macmillan® are registered trademarks in the United States, the United Kingdom, Europe and other countries.

ISBN-13: 978-0-230-60762-0

Library of Congress Cataloging-in-Publication Data is available from the Library of Congress.

A catalogue record of the book is available from the British Library.

Design by Scribe Inc.

First edition: December 2008

10 9 8 7 6 5 4 3 2 1

Printed in the United States of America.

Transferred to Digital Printing 2009

# Contents

# Preface

This book began its life as a series of articles that I have published over the last decade. Chapter 2—"Feminism and Fashion"—is based on a much revised version of an article, "The Self as Image: A Critical Appraisal of Postmodern Theories of Fashion," published in *Theory, Culture & Society* 16 (3), 1999: 99–118, while an earlier version of Chapter 3—"Cosmetics and the Female Body"—appeared in *The European Journal of Cultural Studies* 3 (1), 2000: 83–101. The chapter entitled "Cosmetic Surgery and the Eclipse of Identity" was originally published in *Body & Society* 8 (4), 2002: 21–42, and a shorter version of Chapter 5—"Body Art and Men's Fashion"—appears in *The Men's Fashion Reader* edited by Andrew Reilly and Sarah Cosbey, first edition, 333–46, copyright 2008 by Fairchild Publications, Inc. Reprinted by permission of Fairchild Books, a division of Condé Nast, Inc. Finally, an earlier version of Chapter 6—"Ornament and the Feminine"—was published in *Feminist Theory* 7 (2), 2006: 219–35.

I am very grateful to Rita Felski and Claire Colebrook, who commissioned the last of these articles and provided me with invaluable feedback during the course of writing it. Also, my thanks go to Andrew Reilly and Sarah Cosbey, who asked me to write on the topic of body art and men's fashion for *The Men's Fashion Reader*, and who provided me with useful feedback on this chapter. I am also appreciative of the anonymous referees who gave me insightful feedback on all of the other articles mentioned above. I have also benefited from the comments received when I presented earlier versions of some of these chapters at conferences and symposiums. In particular, thanks go to the participants at the conference *Culture and Identity: City, Nation, World*, organized by the editors of the journal *Theory, Culture & Society* in Berlin, August 1995, where I presented the first incarnation of my chapter "Feminism and Fashion," and also to the participants in the Getty Summer Institute, Department of Art History and Visual Culture, University of Rochester, New York, where I presented a paper on "Cosmetics and the Female Body" in July 1999. I am also appreciative of the feedback that my colleagues and graduate students at the University of Tasmania have given me on the various occasions when I have presented versions of some of these chapters. Thanks also to Janet Wolff, whose encouraging remarks on my initial proposal for this book spurred me on to bring this project to fruition. Finally, my greatest vote of appreciation goes to my husband, Don Cartwright, who painstakingly proofread the entire manuscript, and without whose encouragement and support, this book would never have happened, and also to my parents, Marjorie and Angelo, who have always been there for me.

# Introduction

Over the last twenty years or so, there has been a major reevaluation of fashion, both in terms of its legitimacy as an area of serious academic investigation and its significance in contemporary Western culture. Whereas, in the past, there was a largely dismissive attitude towards fashion, which was seen as a subject unworthy of consideration since it was concerned with the "trivial" realm of appearances, the last two decades have seen a burgeoning of academic studies in this area.

At the same time as the importance of fashion as a realm of serious investigation has been recognized, there has been a discernable shift away from the notion of fashion as an instrument of oppression to one that embraces it as an avenue of self expression and creativity, as is evident in a number of recent writings on fashion such as *Adorned in dreams* (1987 [1985]) by Elizabeth Wilson; *Women and fashion: A new look* (1989) by Caroline Evans and Minna Thornton; *The empire of fashion* (1994) by Gilles Lipovetsky; *Sex and suits: The evolution of modern dress* (1994) by Anne Hollander; and *Fresh lipstick: Redressing fashion and feminism* (2005) by Linda M. Scott.

In contrast to the conservatism of traditional folk costume, fashion is lauded for its openness to change and love of experimentation. As Lipovetsky writes, for instance:

> . . . Fashion is less a sign of class ambition than a way out of the world of tradition. It is one of the mirrors that allow us to see what constitutes our most remarkable historical destiny: the negation of the age-old power of the traditional past, the frenzied modern passion for novelty, the celebration of the social present. (1994, 4)

Likewise, Hollander praises fashion for the "great sartorial freedom and range" it offers, which "reflects the social freedom of the last quarter of a century, when social custom no longer offers strong guidance for appropriate dress" (1994, 191).

In a similar vein, other recent theorists of fashion, such as Kaja Silverman (1986) and Evans and Thornton (1989), have embraced the constant changeableness of fashion as something that challenges the fixity of identity. In contrast to those who condemn fashion's ephemeral nature as symptomatic of an economy of waste based on planned obsolescence, these writers argue that the process of continually changing one's appearance is liberatory insofar as it serves to "denaturalize" the body, highlighting its status as an infinitely malleable cultural construction not fixed by biology.

Reflecting this more positive appraisal of fashion, the conception of the self as masquerade has become a central feature of much contemporary discourse about the body and identity. Against essentialist conceptions of the self as something static and pre-given that exists independently of the clothes that one wears, this new notion of the self as masquerade conceives of the subject as constituted wholly through the various guises that one adopts. There is no self apart from that which is constructed through the fashioning of one's appearance.

However, in this book, the assumption implicit in much recent theorizing on fashion—that masquerade is inherently liberating through its revelation of the culturally constructed nature of identity—is challenged. As is argued, in the context of contemporary consumer capitalism, in which the constant "makeover" of the self is widely promoted by the fashion and advertising industries, such a conception of the self, far from posing a challenge to the dominant ideology, is complicit with it. While such a concept may once have been subversive in an age where identity was regarded as fixed by nature or ordained by God, now it is convergent with the imperatives of late capitalism, which actively promotes the idea of a constantly transmuting self where the cult of appearance is privileged over all other modes of self-definition.

In place of this reductionist conception of the self as image, the essays in this book argue for the necessity of recognizing the importance of other sources of identity formation in the construction of the self. The intention is not to deny that there is a place for fashion in defining who one is, but to propose that it has become overvalued in contemporary culture, and is an insufficient basis on which to ground one's identity. While the cultivation of one's appearance is an inescapable aspect of what it means to be a social being, and can indeed be pleasurable, at the same time, it becomes problematic when it assumes such an importance that it comes to substitute for other forms of self-realization. In these circumstances, rather than being liberatory, it can in fact impede emancipation by diverting attention away from other forms of social action. As the cultivation of one's looks assumes ever greater importance, aesthetic criteria come to substitute for ethical ones in the conduct of one's life so that the basis of decision making is no longer "Is this a good thing to do?" but "Does it look good?"

As long as it is assumed that there is no self apart from that which is constructed through the molding of one's appearance, fashion comes to be seen simply as a random play with signs, unrelated to anything outside itself. This is evident in the postmodern practice of pastiche, which characterizes fashion in contemporary culture where elements of past styles are "ransacked" and reassembled in an eclectic manner. While this practice has been celebrated by a number of recent fashion theorists as a form of ironic play that makes explicit the culturally constructed nature of identity, at the same time, it empties the styles it references of meaning, treating them merely as "free-floating" signifiers. Not anchored in anything outside of themselves, their "meanings" become entirely arbitrary. Since they can potentially mean anything, they ultimately signify nothing. Thus, they become blank ciphers to be playfully appropriated and recombined in random ways according to their "look," rather than their significance. In this context, the fashioning of one's appearance becomes a never-ending charade of constantly changing guises, none of which is any more "authentic" than any other.

Although, at first glance, this freewheeling play with appearance may appear liberating, insofar as it opens up seemingly endless possibilities for constructing new meanings, in contrast to the relative fixity of meaning that characterized the dress of earlier eras, at the same time, it carries with it the danger of a total dissolution of the self as one's identity becomes completely subsumed by the changing mélange of masks one adopts. Where the self becomes equated with the different guises one adopts, all that one is left with is a nihilistic experimentation with style for style's sake in which the various sartorial assemblages signify nothing beyond themselves.

As is argued in this book, if fashion is to be more than a random pastiche of aesthetic forms, then it needs to be deployed as an expression of an identity that has not been constituted solely by it. While it is true that one's appearance contributes to the sense of who one is, the self is more than the masquerade. Identity and appearance, though interrelated, are not synonymous. The reduction of identity to appearance can only be avoided if appearance is recognized to be more than simply about the creation of an aesthetic "look," but refers to a self that is not constituted solely by it. Thus, in contrast to the prevalent view of fashion as a freewheeling experimentation with different "looks" that are all equally "fake," I argue that it should seek to communicate the values and beliefs of the individual wearer. Rather than being treated merely as a form of aesthetic embellishment devoid of significance, the role of bodily adornment as a carrier of meaning needs to be recognized and more fully embraced. Only then can it serve as a genuine expression of identity rather than as a substitute for it.

As well as seeking to recover the communicative function of dress, it is also important to recognize its materiality, since clothes are not just semiotic signs whose meaning depends simply on their relation to other signs,

but are integrally related to the body that wears them, as Paul Sweetman (2001) and Joanne Entwistle (2001) point out. Contrary to the tendency in the writings of a number of recent theorists of fashion, such as Jean Baudrillard (1990a, 1993a) and Cathy Schwichtenberg (1993), where the play with signifiers of dress is presented as a disembodied process in which the body of the wearer is irrelevant, it is argued, in this book, that the body one has significantly affects the nature of one's experimentation with dress. Far from being a freewheeling process without limits, the play with appearance cannot be understood independently of its grounding in the materiality of the body. In this regard, the dream of transcending the limits of the body promoted, for example, by the performance artist Orlan in her numerous cosmetic surgery operations, and also in the treatment of gender signifiers as arbitrary signs in postmodern fashion, is problematized.

Finally, it is argued that while it is all very well to affirm the expressive possibilities of fashion, what is more crucial today is an examination of the structures of inequality, which prevent the full realization of this potential. In much of the recent writing on fashion, there has been a tendency to gloss over this as fashion's openness to change and experimentation has been celebrated. Thus, for instance, while the play with gender boundaries in postmodern fashion has been presented by theorists such as Baudrillard (1990a), Polhemus (1996), and Schwichtenberg (1993) as something that can be engaged in equally by everyone, in actual fact, the arena within which such experimentation occurs is far from being a level playing field. Gender border crossings are not completely reciprocal or interchangeable. Nor are gender signifiers of equal valence, even though they may be presented as such in the postmodern carnival of signs. Rather, such play occurs in a context that is governed by the dominance of the male principle in which menswear is taken as paradigmatic.

In light of this, the apparently greater freedom accorded to women to play with identity in fashion than that allowed to men needs to be regarded with greater circumspection than has been the case in a number of recent writings on fashion, such as those of Silverman (1986) and Young (1994). What is obscured here is the fact that, not infrequently, the fashioning of one's appearance is used as a form of compensatory solace for those who lack opportunities to realize themselves in other areas of their lives. For instance, cosmetic surgery has often been used by women in situations where they have few other means of expressing themselves (K. Davis 1995, 163).[1] While this may provide relief for those who choose this course of action, it does nothing to address the causes for women's dissatisfaction with their bodies in the first place. Indeed, it deflects attention away from these underlying causes by offering an individual "remedy" to what is ultimately a social problem.

The degree of agency exercised by individuals in the cultivation of their personal appearance is also questionable in a world where advertisers and celebrities, more than ever before, are the trendsetters in matters of style. While individuals are not just passive dupes totally manipulated by the fashion industry, at the same time, the pressures and constraints within which they make their style "choices" are considerable and should not be underestimated. Even though individuals today have a greater choice about what to wear than in eras when traditional costume prevailed, they often resort to a reliance on the ready-made solutions offered by the style leaders in the advertising and entertainment worlds. The difficulty that individuals experience today in negotiating their way through the mélange of styles offered paradoxically leads to a homogenization of appearance as they retreat into forms of dress that are less individualizing or expressive in order to avoid possible social embarrassment.

This book, then, critically examines the arguments of recent theorists of fashion who have sought to legitimize its pleasures and defend it as an avenue for self-expression and creativity. Through a series of interrelated essays that address different aspects of fashion in postmodern culture, including the wearing of makeup, cosmetic surgery, tattoos, gender-bending, and the role of ornament in dress, it is argued that the greatest concern today lies not in the failure to acknowledge the pleasures of fashion, but on the contrary, in the tendency to elevate fashion to a dominant position in everyday life where the cultivation of one's physical appearance supplants all other sources of identity formation. Once primarily the province of women, in contemporary culture, the importance of appearance in defining one's self is becoming more ubiquitous, with men, as well as women, being increasingly image-conscious. While the fashioning of one's appearance is an inescapable aspect of our identity as social beings, at the same time, the self is not reducible to the masks through which we make ourselves culturally visible.

Chapter 1—"Appearance and Identity"—establishes the centrality of appearance in contemporary culture, discussing the factors underlying this. The argument is made that the aesthetic cult of the self is a fundamentally contradictory project characterized, on the one hand, by a growing emphasis on individuality, and on the other, by a decentering of the self, in which identity is treated as something that is infinitely malleable. This manifests itself in the fact that, at the same time as we place more and more emphasis on appearance as an expression of individual identity, our outward appearance reveals less and less about who we are, as the meanings of dress become increasingly ambiguous. As is argued here, the coexistence of these two apparently contradictory trends is symptomatic of the increasing difficulty that individuals have in forging, for themselves, a meaningful sense of identity through the fashioning of their physical appearance. The more they seek to ground a sense of themselves through the cultivation of a certain "look," the more chimerical this proves to be, as one "look" is no more "authentic" than any other.

In the second chapter—"Feminism and Fashion"—the challenge mounted by recent fashion theorists against the feminist critique of fashion as oppressive of women, and its advocacy of functional modes of dress, is critically examined. It is argued that, while recent fashion theorists have revealed the naïveté of the functionalist paradigm upon which the feminist critique of fashion has been premised, their alternative conception of liberatory dress as that which highlights the constructed nature of the body is equally as problematic insofar as it leaves unchallenged the reduction of self identity to image, which the advertising and fashion industries now endorse and promote. In championing the idea of the self as masquerade, in which the body of the wearer is denaturalized, recent theories of fashion display an unwitting complicity with our contemporary culture of the spectacle that privileges the cult of appearance over all other sources of identity formation.

The third chapter—"Cosmetics and the Female Body"—continues to develop this critique of the concept of the self as masquerade, propounded by recent fashion theorists in relation to the practice of wearing makeup. Whereas, in the past, the artifice of cosmetics was widely criticized as a sign of deception and inauthenticity in which the wearer masquerades as something she is not, recent theorists have advocated a cosmetic practice that openly declares its artificial nature. In their view, earlier critiques of cosmetics have been based on a mistaken premise that there exists a "true" self, independent of the masks one assumes, when, in fact, the self is constituted by these very masks. However, as is argued here, the cult of artifice is not necessarily subversive, particularly in the context of contemporary culture where such a look is actively promoted by the cosmetics industry itself.

Cosmetic surgery is the subject of the fourth chapter, in which the recent reappraisal of the practice by theorists such as Kathy Davis and artists such as Orlan is critically examined. Against Davis' qualified defense of the practice as a strategy that enables women to exercise a degree of control over their lives, it is argued that such a practice deflects attention away from addressing the social causes of women's experiences of disempowerment. Orlan's advocacy of cosmetic surgery as a vehicle for highlighting the cultural construction of the body and for destabilizing the fixity of identity is also questioned. Her proposal is found to be problematic insofar as it shares with the cosmetic industry its instrumentalization of the body as mere matter, which is almost infinitely transformable, and also effaces the economic inequalities within which such body transformations occur.

In the fifth chapter—"Body Art and Men's Fashion"—the increasing ubiquity of fashion in contemporary culture is examined in relation to tattooing. While tattoos have been regarded as inherently antithetical to fashion because of their relatively permanent nature, they are increasingly being used and promoted as fashion items, as evidenced by their growing prevalence in advertising, and on the catwalk, as well as by their adoption by celebrities in the sports and entertainment worlds. In this chapter, the growing popularity of tattoos in men's fashion advertising is explained as a consequence of the multiple conceptions of masculinity that they have come to symbolize in recent times, as well as the promise of a unique identity that they purport to offer.

The sixth chapter—"Ornament and the Feminine"—problematizes the way in which ornament and decoration have been rehabilitated in recent feminist and fashion theory. While these recent writings have exposed the denigration of the feminine implicit in the modernist rejection of ornament, they leave unchallenged modernism's conception of ornament as decorative embellishment devoid of meaning, differing from it only by giving ornament a positive, rather than a negative, valuation. Consequently, their defense of ornament as a reassertion of the legitimacy of the feminine ultimately perpetuates, rather than undermines, stereotypical associations of the feminine with the sensuous, the superficial, and the irrational. It is argued that a more thoroughgoing challenge needs to question the way in which ornament was defined during the period of modernism, recognizing its role as a carrier of meaning.

Finally, the seventh chapter—"The Postmodern Gender Carnival"—explores the significance of the play with gender signifiers in recent fashion. It is argued that the postmodern vision of fashion as a realm characterized by the infinite commutability of the signifiers of gender obscures the continued existence of gender inequalities that significantly influence the nature of this play with gender identity. In its treatment of gender signifiers as free-floating signifiers that are detached from their association with particular types of bodies, it also effaces the corporeal nature of dress, thereby perpetuating the mind/body distinction. In contrast to the view that the gender border crossings in postmodern fashion represent a transcendence of gender boundaries, I argue that these have not disappeared, but have simply been renegotiated. Despite the increasing frequency of gender border crossings in recent times, gender distinctions have not disappeared, but continue to reassert themselves in new configurations.

# 1

# Appearance and Identity

In postmodern society, physical appearance has become increasingly central to defining personal identity, as evidenced by the proliferation of features in newspapers, magazines, and television concerned with the health, shape, and fashioning of the body, and by the advent of a plethora of products and technologies for modifying the body, such as diet pills, exercise programs, and cosmetic surgery. Individuals are now expected to undertake regimes of body maintenance designed to sustain and improve their health and physical appearance, and failure to do so is seen as a sign of moral laxity. As Mike Featherstone (1991a, 187–93) points out, in our modern consumer culture, a new conception of the self has emerged—namely, the self as performer—which places great emphasis upon appearance, display, and the management of impressions. This replaces the nineteenth-century concern with character in which primacy was given to such qualities as citizenship, democracy, duty, work, honor, reputation, and morals. Whereas previously, greater emphasis was placed on other sources of identity formation than that of personal appearance, increasingly, the self is defined primarily in aesthetic terms—that is, in terms of how one looks rather than in terms of what one does.

This aesthetic cult of the self, as will be argued in this chapter, is a fundamentally contradictory project. On the one hand, it is a project that has been increasingly seen in individualistic terms in which the fashioning of personal appearance is conceived of primarily as an expression of individual identity. In contrast to earlier epochs where one's outward appearance was taken to be indicative of one's social role or status, now it is seen, first and foremost, as a projection of one's inner self. As Anthony Giddens argues (1991, 5–8, 99–102), under the conditions of high modernity, the body has become a self-reflexive project integral to our sense of who we are. While in premodern societies, modifications and adornments of the body were governed by traditional, ritualized meanings, the body in modernity has been secularized and is more frequently treated as a phenomenon to be fashioned as an expression of an individual's identity, rather than in accordance with some traditionally given system of meaning. In contemporary culture, we have become responsible for the design of our own bodies.

However, at the same time as the aesthetic cult of the self has been increasingly conceived in individual terms, there has been a deindividualization of the self. In place of the Enlightenment notion of the self as a unified entity with a fixed essence, it is now seen as something that is fragmentary, decentered, and constantly mutating. Indicative of this is the increasing ease with which individuals adopt and discard various guises in the world of postmodern fashion, where no single style reigns supreme. Confronted with a mélange of different styles derived from a diverse range of sources, individuals today are more likely to experiment with a wide range of different "looks" as is epitomized, for instance, by the radical "makeovers" in appearance undergone by celebrities such as Madonna and Michael Jackson. Polhemus (1996) characterizes the typical postmodern fashion habitué as a "style-surfer" who treats identity as something that is infinitely malleable. Rather than regarding the various guises that one adopts as expressive of a "self," which exists independently of them, the self is defined through the masquerade—there is no self apart from the masquerade. In this sense, the self is "depersonalized," being dissolved into the various masks that one adopts.

The contradictory nature of postmodern "body" projects leads to a paradox. At the same time as the rhetoric of individualism grows ever stronger, appearance has become less expressive of the individual. The more importance we invest in reading appearances as a sign of individual character and personality, the less they reveal about individuals, as the looks we adopt become more depersonalized. While we continue to seek to discover revelations of the self in outward appearances, at the same time, the meaning of items of dress and other forms of bodily adornment have become more and more ambiguous. In postmodern culture, such items, as Baudrillard points out (1993a, 92), have become "free-floating" signifiers, signifying nothing beyond themselves. One of the significant features of bodily adornment in contemporary culture is the degree to which it has become "undercoded." That is, items of dress no longer clearly signal attributes such as the class, occupation, or ethnicity of the wearer, but have, to a large extent, been stripped of their meanings, as they are pastiched together in unexpected combinations.

As will be argued in this chapter, the coexistence of these two apparently contradictory trends is symptomatic of the increasing difficulty that individuals have in forging, for themselves, a meaningful sense of identity through the fashioning of their physical appearance. The more they seek to ground a sense of themselves through the cultivation of a certain "look," the more chimerical this proves to be, as one "look" is no more "authentic" than any other.

In what follows, I shall discuss the factors that have led to the aesthetic cult of the self in postmodern culture, before examining, in more detail, the contradictory nature of this project and the dilemmas to which it has given rise.

## The Aesthetic Cult of the Self

The problem of "identity" is one that has been with us since the advent of modernity. Indeed, the concept of "identity" only arose with the collapse of the old hierarchical social order and the disappearance of ascribed social roles. In a situation where individuals could no longer take for granted what their social roles were, the task of forging, for oneself, an "identity" emerged for the first time as an individual imperative. As Bauman writes:

> Identity as such is a modern invention. To say that modernity led to the "disembedding" of identity . . . is to assert a pleonasm, since at no time did identity "become" a problem: it was a "problem" from its birth . . . precisely because of that experience of under-determination and free-floatingness which came to be articulated *ex post facto* as "disembeddedment." (1997, 18–19)

This experience of uncertainty about one's place in the world has become more acute in postmodernity as career trajectories, durability of relationships, and one's place of abode have become increasingly unpredictable.[1] Consequently, while during the period of modernity the task was how to construct an identity and keep it solid and stable, the postmodern problem of identity, as Bauman points out (1997, 18), is primarily how to avoid fixation and keep options open.

In tackling this problem of "identity," the fashioning of one's appearance has assumed an increasingly important role. During the nineteenth century, concern with one's appearance was particularly evident amongst middle class women, *demi-mondaines* (that is, kept women) and members of the artistic avant-garde. As far as middle class women were concerned, denied other opportunities for self-realization because of their exclusion from the public sphere, they resorted to one of the few areas available to them in which to exercise their creativity—namely, the beautification of themselves and their homes. As Veblen commented in the nineteenth century, "propriety require[d] respectable women to abstain . . . from useful effort and to make more of a show of leisure than the men of the same social classes . . . [The woman's] sphere [was] within the household which she [was required to] 'beautify,' and . . . be the 'chief ornament'" (1970 [1899], 126). He goes on to point out that, in cultivating their appearance, middle-class women expressed not so much their own identity as that of their husbands insofar as a well-dressed woman was taken as a sign of the wealth and high social standing of her husband (126–27). The ornate dress of middle-class women of the time was a conspicuous demonstration of the fact that they did not have to work for a living since their husbands could afford to support them in a lifetime of "leisure." In the case of *demi-mondaines*, the cultivation of an extravagant appearance was central to the maintenance of their social position, which depended on attracting the attention and support of men of high social stature and wealth (Wilson 1987, 32–33).

Amongst the artistic avant-garde, examples of the idea of turning one's life into a "work of art" are to be found in figures such as Charles Baudelaire, Joris-Karl Huysmans, Walter Pater, and Oscar Wilde, who followed the lead of fashion trendsetter Beau Brummell from the early nineteenth century. Central to this conception of "life as a work of art" was the idea of distinguishing oneself from the "crowd" through the cultivation of a distinctive mode of dress and through the refinement of one's aesthetic taste.[2] The demonstration of impeccable taste, rather than moral virtue, became the primary means through which to assert one's identity and make one's mark. As Featherstone characterizes it

> Dandyism, which first developed with Beau Brummell in England in the early nineteenth century, stressed the quest for special superiority through the construction of an uncompromising exemplary lifestyle in which an aristocracy of spirit manifested itself in a contempt for the masses and heroic concern with the achievement of originality and superiority in dress, demeanor, personal habits and even furnishings—what we now call lifestyle. (1991b, 67)

While this aesthetic cult of the self was a relatively marginalized phenomenon in the nineteenth century, during the course of the twentieth century it has become a much more generalized occurrence with, firstly, women of all social classes and, more recently, men becoming more conscious of their appearance.[3] Underpinning the spread of this concern with appearance has been the "democratization" of fashion—a process inaugurated by the introduction of mass production in the garment industry, which enabled the rapid dissemination of the latest fashions to the broader population at affordable prices.[4] No longer the preserve of the wealthy, fashion has become a phenomenon in which all can and do participate.

As a result of the central importance now accorded to the cultivation of physical appearance, our role models today are those celebrities who are leaders in fashion rather than those who have performed heroic deeds. As Shusterman puts it:

> The celebrated figures of our time are not men of valor or women of virtue but those significantly called the "beautiful people." We are less inclined to the imitation of Christ than to imitating the cosmetics and fashion of Princess Diana; no one today reads the lives of saints for edification and example, but the biographies of film stars and the success stories of corporate millionaires are perennial best sellers. (1988, 338)

Another indication of the increased importance placed on the aestheticization of the self has been the expansion and multiplication of techniques for fashioning the body.[5] Whereas, once, the main ways of modifying the body involved the application of makeup and the wearing of certain types of clothes, the new techniques for molding the body such as diet, exercise, and plastic surgery, are more intrusive, directly intervening in the body and changing its form permanently. With the advent of these techniques, the body comes to be seen as completely malleable, able to be altered at will in accordance with one's desires. No longer is the body seen as something that is fixed by biology and as having limits that cannot be transcended. Rather, it is seen as a cultural construction that is continuously being reconstituted and remodeled. The view that is prevalent today is that we can be whatever we want to be, or so the fashion and advertising industries would have us believe. As Bordo points out (1993b, 245–46), the advent of new techniques for molding the body have generated an ideology of limitless improvement and change, defying the very materiality of the body.

This is manifested, for example, in the rise of the concept of "being on a diet." It has only been in the twentieth century that we have cultivated certain bodily regimes, such as the controlled intake of certain types of foods, as a means of reflexively influencing the project of the self. While there are examples of people going on fasts in previous eras, the reasons for this practice were religious (that is, concerned with overcoming sensual appetites in pursuit of higher values) rather than in order to attain a certain culturally desirable body shape. From this point of view, anorexia and bulimia are extreme versions of the need that people feel, in our post-traditional age, to consciously and deliberately control their bodily appearance in order to create and maintain a distinctive self-identity. As Giddens argues: "Anorexia represents a striving for control of the body in a world of plural, but ambiguous options. The tightly controlled body is an emblem of a safe existence in an open social environment" (1991, 107).

Featherstone (1991b, 67) relates the increasing importance given to the cultivation of a distinctive personal appearance to the development of modern consumer culture in which the construction of lifestyles through aesthetic consumption has become a central feature. In contrast to the early stages of capitalism, where the emphasis was on discipline and the denial of immediate gratification as encapsulated in the asceticism of the Puritan work ethic, with the shift in emphasis from production to consumption, the hedonistic pursuit of noninstrumental desires has now been given primacy.

Joanne Finkelstein and Giddens concur that the rise of modern consumerism is a significant contributing factor to explaining the centrality given to appearance as a means of defining identity in contemporary culture. As Finkelstein points out in her book *The fashioned self*, in the late twentieth century, while we are well aware of the ways in which people manipulate their appearances, we put more store than ever before on physical appearance as a true indicator of a person's character. To quote her:

> In the consumer culture of modern society, physical appearance has come to be seen as an important means for claiming a degree of social status. High fashion and designer styles in clothing, individualized fitness programs, exercise equipment for home use, private gymnasiums, diet regimens and cosmetic surgery are readily available as the means for perfecting our physical appearance. The pervasiveness of these goods and services indicates an ethos in which physical appearance is held to be of paramount importance. Indeed, appearance is often conflated with the more spiritual or abstract qualities of character: people are described as having a kind, honest or determined face as if this expresses their real character. (1991, 2)

She suggests that one of the main reasons why bodily appearance has come to be treated as a central marker of identity is that in modern consumer society, where the possession and control of goods and services are highly valued, transforming the body into a commodity that can be used for the display of coveted items is seen as a more significant indicator of who one is than what one does.

Similarly, Giddens argues that in contemporary consumer culture, "the project of the self becomes translated into one of the possession of desired goods and the pursuit of artificially framed styles of life" (1991, 198). Whereas in the past, individuals were seen to have an identity apart from the goods they possessed, in the present era, one's identity is defined in terms of the image that one creates through one's consumption of goods, including the clothes and other body adornments one wears. Today, one is defined more in terms of one's image than in terms of one's actual social position or occupation. Rather than reflecting our position in society, the way we shape and adorn our bodies is now taken to be constitutive of our identity.

Another important contributing factor to the increasing emphasis placed on the aestheticization of the self in defining identity has been the decline in the significance of external systems of meaning and authority that formerly provided individuals with a means of giving direction to their lives. As Chris Shilling suggests (1994, 2–4), the growing investment in the body as constitutive of self-identity is symptomatic of the decline of transpersonal meaning structures, such as those offered by religion or by grand political narratives. In a context where there no longer exist shared systems of meaning that construct and sustain existential and ontological certainties residing outside of the self, individuals have turned toward the body as a foundation on which to reconstruct a reliable sense of self.

Renata Salecl argues, in a similar vein, that the narcissistic investment in the body characteristic of postmodern society is symptomatic of our widespread disillusionment with, and disbelief in, the legitimacy of traditional structures of authority. As she writes:

> The dissolution of the traditional family structure has changed the subject's relation to authority, which means that the subject now appears as someone who is in a position to choose freely, his or her own identity . . . In premodern society, initiation ritual situated the subject in the social structure . . . In modern, Enlightenment society, we no longer have initiation rituals, but the authority of the law is still at work . . . In contrast, in post-modern society we have a total disbelief in authority and in the power of the symbolic order, the so-called big Other. (2001, 27–28)

She continues that:

> One of the ways in which the subject today deals with the absence of the big Other is to turn to narcissistic self-admiration. The lack of identification with some ego-ideal (a symbolic role or authority-ideal) results in the subject's identification with some imaginary role (the ideal-ego) in which the subject finds himself or herself likeable. This narcissistic search for the perfect image results in the subject's obsession with changing his or her body with the help of excessive dieting, exercise and plastic surgery. (2001, 29)

This project of defining oneself through the fashioning of one's appearance is an essentially contradictory one. Georg Simmel, writing in the early twentieth century, was one of the first to recognize this. As he argued in his essay "Fashion" (1971 [1904], 294–304), the logic of fashion, which governs the molding of appearance in modernity, is driven by the coexistence of two opposing forces: on the one hand, the desire to express one's individuality through the clothes one wears, and on the other, a desire to blend in with the crowd so as not to draw attention to oneself. With the collapse of the rigid hierarchical social order of the *ancien régime*, individuals began to think of themselves as capable of shaping their own characters in the same way that they were capable of shaping their own social and economic destiny. Using fashionable items and commodities as devices for claiming a particular character or personal identity became an increasingly common ploy. People no longer regarded themselves primarily in terms of the social roles that they occupied, as had been the case in the fixed, stratified order of feudal society, but saw themselves, first and foremost, as unique individuals with their own personalities. Whereas previously, people's private selves had been subordinate to their social roles, now the reverse was the case.

At the same time, however, there was a desire not to alienate oneself from the social group through cultivating an appearance that was too outlandish. The central dilemma then, became that of how to realize one's individuality, while at the same time, maintaining one's membership of a social group. Thus, the fashioning of one's appearance in modernity has been a precarious balancing act between individuality and conformity. As Simmel writes: "Two social tendencies are essential to the establishment of fashion, namely, the need of union on the one hand and the need of isolation on the other" (1971 [1904], 301).

These tensions have become heightened in postmodernity. Thus, on the one hand, the rhetoric of individualism concerning the fashioning of the body as the expression of a unique personality has become more prevalent, while on the other, there has been an increasing deindividualization in personal appearance. At the same time that items of dress and other forms of body adornment are conceived of and promoted as a way of distinguishing oneself from others, it seems that people are dressing more and more the same, as jeans and T-shirts, for instance, have become almost a uniform. Distinctions between work and casual clothes have lessened as have gender and class distinctions in dress. While clothing draws on a greater variety of sources than ever before, it is more homogenized insofar as there is less regional and ethnic variation between cultures and between city and country. As the pastiche of different elements that characterizes postmodern fashion renders the meaning of clothing more and more ambiguous, so it reveals less and less about the identity of the wearer. Let us examine, more closely, the two sides of this antinomy.

## Appearance as Expression of Individual Identity

One of the features of fashioning the body since the nineteenth century has been the increasing emphasis placed on appearance as an expression of individual identity, rather than of membership of a social group. As Giddens points out (1991, 99–100), whereas in premodern cultures, appearance was largely standardized in terms of traditional criteria, in the modern era, modes of dress and facial adornment have become more individualized, that is, they are seen to reflect the personality of the wearer rather than simply signaling their social identity. While modes of fashioning the body continue to be influenced by group pressures, advertising, socioeconomic resources, and other factors that often promote standardization rather than individual difference, in comparison with previous eras, individuals have more choice over what they wear.

Richard Sennett, in his book *The fall of public man*, traces the origins of this process to the early nineteenth century, where clothing became less and less a marker of one's social role or position and more an indicator of one's personality. This was a consequence of the greater social mobility experienced by people in the wake of the collapse of the old social order where social position had been determined by birth.

As he argues (1976, 64–72), in the eighteenth century, people adopted certain modes of dress in accordance with the different roles they performed and these modes of presentation of the self were understood as conventionalized masks, not to be confused with the real character of the person. The body was seen to be a mannequin—a prop for certain socially coded systems of representation—rather than being symbolic of a person's interior self. Whereas today, we distinguish between actors on the stage who don guises that are understood to be quite distinct from their own personalities, in the eighteenth century, everyone was seen to be an actor, assuming an outward appearance, which indicated their social role rather than being expressive of their personality. As Sennett writes:

> In both Paris and London in the mid-18th century, people spoke of the city as having changed the basic terms of the age-old imagery of *theatrum mundi*. Fielding in 1749 spoke of London as having become a society in which stage and street were 'literally' intermixed . . . Rousseau in 1757 wrote a treatise to show that the conditions of life in Paris forced men to behave like actors in order to be sociable with each other in the city . . . Just as the actor touched people's feelings without revealing to them his own character offstage, the same codes of belief he used served his audience to a similar end. . . . (1976, 64)

There were actual sumptuary laws that assigned to each station in the social hierarchy a set of "appropriate" clothes and forbade people of any one station from wearing the clothes of people in another rank. Although by the eighteenth century, with the influx of large numbers of people into the city, such laws were difficult to enforce as people had little means of telling whether the dress of a stranger on the street was an accurate reflection of his or her standing in society, rigid codes of dress according to occupation and status continued to be adhered to as a means of facilitating interaction between strangers in the big cities.

During the nineteenth century, however, the distinction between one's public and private personae became conflated so that one's public persona came to be identified with one's innermost self. Thus, rather than regarding clothes as a conventional mask that people donned when performing certain social roles, they came to be seen as direct expressions of the wearer's personal identity. As Sennett puts it: "The codes of belief about street appearances thus began to be fundamentally different from the belief in appearances on stage" (1976, 161). Whereas stage costumes continued to be seen as artificial guises, distinct from the identity of their wearers, street dress was now required to accurately reflect the personality of the wearer.[6]

This investment of the self in one's physical appearance has become even more pronounced during the twentieth and twenty-first centuries, as is evidenced both in the marketing of fashion items and in the way individuals speak of their body modification practices. As far as the marketing of fashion is concerned, whereas in the first half of the twentieth century, fashions were still largely dictated by the leading houses of *haute couture*, which imposed a dominant style for each season, there has been an increasing prevalence of do-it-yourself style, particularly since the 1980s, with the advent of magazines such as *i-D* and *The Face*, which have promoted the idea of "street-style" fashions rather than those originating from prominent fashion designers. The basic premise underlying these magazines is that style is an act of self-expression in which one constructs for oneself a unique "look" through the creative assemblage of a range of items derived from various sources. Rather than slavishly following fashion trends, the manufacture of the self is promoted as an exercise of individual creativity. As the editor of the magazine *i-D* declared: "I wanted to get the concept over that we don't lay down the rules about what you wear" (quoted in Kaiser et al., 1991, 173). Rather, the aim of the magazine is to reflect the range of, and to provide a voice for, aesthetic viewpoints coming from the street. Even in the more mainstream fashion magazines such as *Vogue* or *Cleo*, no single particular "look" is promoted, but rather, several options are presented, encouraging the idea that it is up to the individual to mix and match items in accordance with their own taste.

Furthermore, fashion and beauty products marketed to women are increasingly promoted not so much as a way of enhancing one's appeal in the eyes of others, but as a means of self-gratification. For instance, the central motif of one of the advertising campaigns for Oil of Olay has been "It's my Time," while advertisements for Maybelline cosmetics declare: "This time's for me."[7] Whereas in previous decades, these items were marketed primarily as a means of gaining male approval, now, concern with one's appearance is more often presented as something one does for oneself rather than in order to please men—a point underlined by the defiant pout that has become customary amongst fashion models.[8] Exemplifying this individualist focus is the following statement from fashion designer Alex Perry, who says of his latest dress suit for women: "It's not just about dressing to please men. You have to feel good about yourself and show off the bits that you're proud of" (quoted by Woolnough, 2008, 48).

There is also more attention being paid to the customizing of fashion items to mitigate the effects of standardization of clothing through mass production. Thus, for example, one can select one's own trimmings for one's Nike shoes. Another example discussed by Heike Jenß (2004) is the Viennese-based company Retroframe, which buys preselected used clothing and then remarkets it under the Retroframe label, inventing a personality for each shirt they resell. This is achieved by tagging each item with a price ticket that looks like a small identity card, purporting to identify the previous owner. However, as Jenß points out, ". . . these 'former owners' are fabricated, made up from a database of photographs, fingerprints and invented personal statements, that are assigned to 'retrofake' identities that signify each garment as real and singular" (2004, 397).

Likewise, beauty products such as lipsticks are marketed in many different shades to suit the individual. As the ad for L'Oréal Color Riche lipsticks declares: "Nude Shades created just for you! Because you're worth it. To each her own: choose the perfect lip color to match your hair color or skin tone" (*Cleo*, January 2008: 1–2). Similarly, procedures such as cosmetic surgery are promoted as being tailored to the desires of the patient. In a recent feature in *Vogue Australia*, February 2008, for instance, the copy reads: "Breast augmentation has become one of the most popular cosmetic procedures. Each breast augmentation procedure should be individualized to make it a personal, unique experience. The desired breast size and shape differs widely with each individual. Some women seek a larger breast, while other [sic] simply wish to restore the volume that was lost with breast feeding. The goal of the surgery should be specifically and precisely planned to produce an optimum result for each woman."

Likewise, individuals themselves, when speaking of their fashion choices, see them primarily as an act of self-expression. As Gill et al. found, for instance (2005, 44–49), in their interviews with young British males about their body projects, there was great value attached to "being your own man" and "being different." While the theme of "being different" was used to justify widely divergent and even opposing products, body modification, or lifestyle choices, what was common to all respondents was a desire not to be seen as a conformist. The respondents claimed complete independence and autonomy in relation to all body choices, and were reluctant to concede that their perceptions of physical attractiveness might, in any way, be influenced by marketing or advertising. They saw themselves as constructing their own identities and were critical of those who slavishly followed fashion. Adhering to a libertarian model of the self, they asserted that individuals should be free to modify their bodies in whichever way they chose, and showed little awareness of the social forces that influence people's conceptions of themselves and others.

Nowhere is this heightened sense of individualism more evident than in the growing popularity of body marking practices such as tattooing and piercing in contemporary culture. Whereas in the past, such practices in Western societies were mainly confined to marginalized or stigmatized social groups such as bikers, prisoners, or members of the military, and were adopted primarily to indicate one's membership of a subcultural group, nowadays, as body markings have become more mainstream, they are used mostly as a form of personal distinction or individual self-actualization rather than to signal group allegiance. This is seen in the growing preference for customized, rather than standardized, "flash" tattoos. As Pitts writes,

> New body projects can be distinguished from more traditional ones not in utility, severity, or pain, but in their social significance . . . In indigenous cultures, the body, especially the skin, often appears as a surface upon which social hierarchies such as age, status, and clan, are inscribed or codified . . . In contrast, the modern Western body is understood not as a collective product of inscription, but as a personal projection of the self. Bodies then become understood as exteriorizing an "inward depth" (2003, 30–31).

## The De-personalization of Appearance

Paradoxically, at the same time as there has been an increasingly individualistic focus in postmodern body projects, our outward appearance reveals less and less of who we are. For, while items of body adornment have become more personalized, they have also become more ambiguous in their meaning. As theorists such as Fred Davis (1992) and Jean Baudrillard (1993a) have noted, one of the features of fashion in the postmodern era has been the loosening of the relationship between signifier and signified in dress. Compared with earlier epochs, in contemporary culture, there is a much more tenuous link between dress and that to which it refers.

In premodern times, there was a clear and unequivocal relation between dress and that which it signified. Essentially, dress reflected social distinctions that were seen as given by nature. In this situation, one could deduce, in a straightforward manner, the status or social role of the wearer through the clothes they wore. However, with the advent of modernity and the breakdown of the apparently naturally ordained social order, it became increasingly difficult to ascertain a person's social standing from their mode of dress. Frequently, individuals would adopt the garb of those to whose positions they aspired rather than wearing clothing that reflected their actual social standing. As a consequence, the culturally mutable nature of the link between dress and that which it signified became evident.

The recognition of the essentially arbitrary relation between signifier and signified in clothing opened up the possibility of "unfixing" the meanings of dress. This is what has occurred in the postmodern era, where items of adornment are increasingly seen to signify nothing beyond themselves. Rather than reflecting the "natural" order of things, as in premodern times, or creating social distinctions, as in the period of modernity, sartorial elements are now seen as "free-floating" signifiers that are infinitely commutable since they are no longer associated with any external referents. As Baudrillard characterizes it, postmodern fashion consists of a carnival of signs whose meanings are in a constant state of flux. To quote him: "There is no longer any determinacy internal to the signs of fashion, hence they become free to commute and permutate without limit" (1993a, 87). Freed from their moorings, these signs only gain their meanings through their relation to other signs. Baudrillard refers to this as the order of simulation, where signs substitute for the real. Having lost sight of a reality that exists independently of the signs of fashion, these signs are themselves taken to be the "real." Thus, as he puts it: "In contradistinction to language, which *aims* at communication, fashion *plays* at it, turning it into the goal-less stake of a signification without a message" (1993a, 94).

Similarly, Davis argues that ambiguity is rife in the contemporary dress code of Western society, and is becoming even more so. Clothing in Western society today is much more given to "undercoding" than to precision and explicitness (1992, 7–8). While we are all familiar with the cliché that the clothes we wear make a statement about us, the nature of this statement is no longer clear. Despite attempts to treat clothing as a language, it is a much more indeterminate form of communication than is language, especially in contemporary culture, where the meanings of items of apparel are in a constant state of flux, sometimes acquiring directly opposing meanings from one context to the next. Davis cautions against ascribing precise meanings to items of dress since the very same apparel ensemble can mean something quite different from one year to the next. To quote him:

> In the symbolic realm of dress and appearance . . . "meanings" . . . tend to be simultaneously more ambiguous and more differentiated than in other expressive realms . . . Meanings are more ambiguous in that it is hard to get people in general to interpret the same clothing symbols in the same way; in semiotic terminology, the clothing sign's signifier-signified relation is quite unstable. (1992, 9)

Underpinning the indeterminacy of meaning in present day modes of sartorial presentation is the practice of pastiche, which many, such as Barnard (1996), Polhemus (1996), Kaiser et al. (1991), and Kratz and Reimer (1998), have identified as a hallmark of postmodern fashion. This involves the eclectic borrowing and juxtaposition of items of body adornment from a range of different sources. Since the 1960s, fashion has not been characterized by one dominant style that epitomizes the era, but by a proliferation of a wide variety of "looks" derived from ransacking history for key items of dress in a seemingly eclectic and haphazard manner, and the rate of turnover of these different looks has speeded up exponentially. As Kratz and Reimer write:

> In postmodern times, fashion has become more heterogeneous, more unpredictable and more ambiguous. The world is shrinking, the pace of change in fashion is increasing, and people are more aware than ever before of alternative ways of dressing and of ways of making personal statements through clothes. This means that the old hierarchy, in which the fashion industry was able to dictate new trends and each season change people's ideas about what was fashionable has disappeared. It is no longer possible to guide and direct people towards one, dominating fashion. Instead, it seems more reasonable to speak of several *fashions*; fashions that furthermore have become increasingly ambiguous. (1998, 194)

Many of these fashions have originated in the youth subcultures of the postwar period that have relied on secondhand clothes found in jumble sales and rag markets as the raw material for the creation of style. In this process of recontextualization, these items have been stripped of their original meanings. Being treated as "empty" ciphers, they have been recombined in a seemingly limitless number of ways.

"*Bricolage*" is a useful way to describe this practice.[9] As explained by Lévi-Strauss, the *bricoleur* (or "rag-bag" man) is someone who makes do with whatever materials are at hand (1966, 16–22). *Bricolage* uses the remains and debris of the past, the odds and ends that are left over. Its present constructions are always made out of things that have already been used in the past. As such, it is an open-ended process without any predetermined goal but one that is constantly mutating in accordance with what is available. In a similar way, the postmodern fashion habitué fossicks through the annals of history in a relatively random way, treating all styles as potential sources for his/her sartorial assemblages.

While Elizabeth Wilson suggests that the practice of stylistic borrowing is not specific to postmodern fashion, but is also evident in fashion of earlier periods (1990a, 224–26), what distinguishes contemporary versions of this practice from those which occurred in the past is that they are marked by an ironic attitude of cool detachment rather than one of nostalgia. Whereas past stylistic revivals in fashion were motivated by a desire to "recreate" or "recover" the original meanings of these styles, the postmodern practice of appropriation entails an agnostic stance toward the past in which all styles are seen as possible sources of borrowing.[10] Far from expressing a deep allegiance to particular past styles, the postmodern recycling of styles involves a playful game of referencing in which no one style is treated as having any greater significance than any other. Stripped of their original meanings, they are treated primarily as aesthetic forms that can be assembled in various ways to achieve a kaleidoscope of different "looks." As Jameson describes it (1983, 114), pastiche is "a neutral practice of mimicry" in which various styles are imitated in an "endless parade of difference" in a manner that is indifferent to their original significance. Clothes from all different eras are mixed together without regard for any consistency, and delight is taken in being deliberately anachronistic, recontextualizing items of dress in ways that are quite at odds with their former meanings. For example, jeans are combined with sawn-off flapper dresses or tuxedo jackets, art deco with "pop art" jewelry, and silk underwear from the 1930s with a tailored suit from the 1950s.

Barnard enlists Derrida's notion of "intertextuality" to conceptualize the radical indeterminacy of meaning that results from this process (1996, 159–60). In this conception, signs only gain their meaning from their relation to other signs. Signs are not simply present, as they mean nothing on their own. Only on the basis of their place in a chain of signifiers that are different and that are also not simply present, can signs function and be meaningful. Because the "meanings" of signs are purely relational, they are constantly in a state of flux. Indeed, their meanings may be so unstable that they can mean one thing and its opposite at one and the same time. As Barnard explains it: "[i]ntertextuality . . . determines that the meaning of an object is undecidable, that it is both produced and destroyed by its place in those systems of differences" (1996: 159).

A good example of the undecidability of meaning in items of dress is the stiletto heel, which has been seen simultaneously as an object of enslavement and of liberation. As Wright points out (discussed in Barnard 1996, 161–62), on the one hand, it has been seen as oppressive insofar as it impedes movement and produces a posture that accentuates a woman's breasts and bottom. At the same time, however, extreme stilettos have been worn as an act of rebellion against traditional notions of femininity as maternal and domestic, being symbolic of the modern woman who inhabits a world outside the home.

Insofar as the signifiers of dress are seen to be "free-floating," they are no longer regarded as reflective of the identity of the wearer that exists independently of them. Rather, the self is dissolved into the various masks that one adopts. There is no self apart from the masquerade. In this conception, the self is no longer seen as a stable and unified entity, but as something that is fragmentary, nomadic, and constantly mutating in accordance with whatever guise one adopts. There is no "real" self that exists independently of one's outer appearance, but simply an incessantly changing series of masks behind which there is no fixed core or "essential" identity.

Identity becomes a theatrical performance in which one's self is constituted by, and transformed in accordance with, the costume that one assumes. However, unlike the actor who is assumed to have an identity independent of the characters s/he plays on the stage, there is seen to be nothing more to the individual today than the "characters" s/he performs. In these performances, there is no sense that one guise is any more "authentic" than any other. Rather, the artificially constructed nature of each of these "masks" is openly embraced. As Silverman describes it (1986, 150–51), the postmodern play with appearance is characterized by a "staginess" in which the act of stylistic quotation is highlighted in a deliberate manner so that the dress ensembles appear as costumes in a fancy dress ball. It is not a naïve, but a self-conscious, revival of old styles that puts "quotation marks around the garments it revitalizes." As a sartorial strategy, it works to denaturalize its wearer's identity by highlighting the cultural construction of the body. Far from being expressive of the "true" self, appearance in postmodern culture has become a constantly shifting parade of fabricated "looks" that highlight their "fake" nature.

Efrat Tseëlon expands on this conception, drawing on the dramaturgical model of social interaction developed by Goffman.[11] In contrast to impression management theory, which is premised on a distinction between a "true" private self and a "false" public self that manipulates appearances in a deliberately misleading way, Goffman's social agent has no interior or exterior. Rather, s/he has a repertoire of "faces," each activated in front of a different audience, none of which is more "authentic" than any other. Acting is not something that is put on for certain occasions, but is inherent in the nature of social interaction. In Goffman's social world, there is no "true" or "essential" self disguised behind a "false" front. Rather, all that exists are the various public personae that individuals present in different social contexts. Instead of the "depth" model of subjectivity, where the self is seen to be composed of an inner essence and an outward appearance, the Goffmanesque self consists only of surfaces. As Tseëlon puts it: "It does not rely on a dualistic image of the self but is anchored, instead, in a metaphysics of surface: an interplay of images, of signifiers with no underlying signifieds . . ." (1992: 121). Thus, in Goffman's conception, the distinction between the "real" and the "staged" or between the "sincere" and the "inauthentic" no longer has any meaning. All behaviors are "staged" and none is any more "true" than any other.

Similarly, for the postmodern self, appearances do not mask reality but are reality. "Sincerity as congruence between the private self and the public self is meaningless within a postmodern vocabulary of selfhood," as Tseëlon writes (1992, 123).

## The Postmodern Dilemma

From the above discussion, then, it is clear that the aesthetic cult of the self in postmodernity is one that is riven with contradiction. At the same time as more and more is invested in appearance as a statement of who one is, the nature of this identity is becoming increasingly chimerical as it becomes dissipated into a series of ephemeral masks. As the rhetoric of individualism becomes more and more accentuated in contemporary body projects, so our external appearance communicates less and less of our identity. This accounts for why, despite the increased emphasis on individualism in contemporary fashion, people dress more and more the same. As Hill observes (2005, 67–72), while our epoch is supposedly one of unprecedented individualism, most people, in their everyday lives, dress in casual wear or a generic type of office dress. Everybody looks like everyone else. What is evident today is the lack of attention paid to distinguishing one's clothes from other people. While the fashions on the catwalks of leading houses of *haute couture* grow ever more spectacular and outlandish, the clothing that most people wear in their everyday lives becomes increasingly nondescript.

This can be seen in the fact that at the same time as the sources from which postmodern fashion draws are more diverse than ever before, there is less variation between nations and regions with the globalization of the garment industry. Whereas in the early stages of modernity, it was still relatively easy to discern the nationality of individuals from the clothes they wore, now there is little difference between fashions in America, Europe, and Japan, for instance.[12] Thus, at the same time as postmodern fashion has become more pluralistic in terms of the variety of cultural sources that it references, the differences in clothing between countries has lessened as Western attire incorporates elements of non-Western dress, and conversely, non-Western cultures become more Westernized in their sartorial practices. Symptomatic of this is the fact that global advertising campaigns for beauty and fashion products increasingly ignore national differences in determining the images used to promote them, as Wendy Chapkis points out (1988, 38–40). Rubinstein, for instance, stopped altering its advertisements for Latin American women in the early 1980s, and Clairol sought to market glamour "in any language." Similarly, the advertising agency Saatchi and Saatchi indicated its embracement of the concept of "world branding" in their 1982 annual report, declaring:

> Consumer convergence in demography, habits and culture are increasingly leading manufacturers to a consumer-driven rather than a geography-driven view of their marketing territory . . . Marketers will be less likely to tailor product positioning to the differing needs of the country next door and more likely to operate on the basis of the common needs for their products. (quoted in Chapkis 1988, 39–40)

Furthermore, differentiation in terms of class and gender has also lessened. As far as class distinctions in dress are concerned, whereas during the nineteenth century and in the first half of the twentieth century, there was still a clear sense of fashion originating in the upper classes and then trickling down to the lower classes, as the latter sought to emulate their social superiors, now this is no longer the case. Fashion change is just as likely to be initiated by those in the lower echelons of society, and with the acceleration in the turnover of styles, and the coexistence of several styles at the same time, class distinctions have become far less obvious.[13] A case in point is the wide uptake of jeans, which are now worn by members of all social classes, even though they had their origins as working class men's garb.

Similarly, gender distinctions in dress are far less marked than they once were. Whereas in the nineteenth century, female dress was clearly differentiated from male dress, being far more highly ornamented and colorful than male garb, where the plain and comparatively austere suit was the norm, in the latter half of the twentieth century, this distinction lessened mainly as a result of women adopting elements of male dress, particularly trousers. There has also been some movement in the opposite direction, with men now more likely to wear jewelry, and with the incorporation of more decorative elements and a wider range of colors in men's leisure and sportswear.[14]

Finally, there has been a casualization of dress that has lessened the distinctions between evening and daywear and between work and leisurewear. Hill suggests that the predominance of casual wear today is due to the fact that "the signifying power of clothing has been eroded . . . Casual wear is casual precisely because it is perceived as holding little meaning beyond being practical, comfortable and relaxed . . . People can dress however they want . . . because what people wear carries little meaning" (2005, 72).

Lipovetsky appraises this homogenization of dress in largely positive terms as indicative of the democratizing influence of fashion. In his view, the diminution of distinctiveness in contemporary dress does not signal a loss of individuality, but on the contrary, is evidence of the fact that we now dress more for ourselves rather than for reasons of status rivalry. As he writes:

> The preference for casual clothing is symptomatic of the new age of individualism . . . [It] mark[s] the rise of neonarcissism in fashion, the emergence of a personality more insistent on individual autonomy, less dependent on standards of prestigious display, less concerned with competition and obvious social differentiation in appearance . . . It expresses less a position in the social hierarchy than a desire for personality, a cultural orientation, a lifestyle, an aesthetic outlook . . . People today . . . are less anxious to signify their class position than to look young and relaxed. (1994, 123)

However, although the lessening of social distinctions in dress is undoubtedly a positive development, at the same time, I would argue that the growing homogeneity in appearance is symptomatic of the increasing difficulty that people have in constructing, for themselves, a meaningful sense of identity through their appearance. On the one hand, while individuals today are confronted with a greater choice in what to wear than ever before, since, in the postmodern era there is no longer a single mainstream style which dictates fashion trends, they find it increasingly difficult to make sense of what is on offer. [15] Items of body adornment are increasingly seen as arbitrary signs, empty of meaning, employed simply to achieve a "look" rather than to communicate a meaning. As a result, there is a disassociation between individuals and the clothes they wear. Rather than being expressive of one's identity, they appear as external masks that have been "stuck on," bearing no necessary relation to the person wearing them. In this context, the fashioning of one's appearance becomes a never-ending charade of constantly changing guises, none of which is any more "authentic" than any other.

While this freewheeling play with appearance may appear liberating insofar as it highlights the culturally mutable nature of identity, at the same time, it carries with it the danger of a total dissolution of the self as one's identity becomes completely subsumed by the changing mélange of masks one adopts. The "undercoding" of items of dress in postmodern culture, though potentially emancipatory in freeing up the fixity of meaning associated with the clothing of earlier periods, can also lead to a nihilistic experimentation with style for style's sake in which the various sartorial assemblages signify nothing beyond themselves, and in which one loses one's sense of self. Hill alludes to this when he writes:

> If anything goes, does anything really matter? . . . It is this process that we can identify at work in what people wear nowadays. If people can wear whatever they want . . . then it matters very little what people wear . . . Without norms . . . there can be little in the way of a system of values or meaning at work in what people wear. And so the meaning of clothing flattens out, it empties, it fades. (2005, 72–73)

As the experimentation with various modes of self-presentation becomes increasingly arbitrary, the more individuals in postmodernity come to resemble the "schizophrenic" subject spoken of by Jameson in his characterization of the nature of identity in postmodernity. The schizophrenic experience, as he argues, is one in which the sense of a coherent identity enduring through time is replaced by a series of discontinuous presents or moments between which there are no meaningful connections. To quote him:

> . . . schizophrenic experience is an experience of isolated, disconnected, discontinuous material signifiers which fail to link up into a coherent sequence. The schizophrenic thus does not know personal identity in our sense, since our feeling of identity depends on our sense of the persistence of the "I" and the "me" over time. (1983, 119)

In a similar fashion, the experience of the self in postmodern culture has become increasingly fragmented as individual identity is dissolved into a series of disconnected and constantly mutating guises.

Although the increasingly fluid nature of identity in postmodernity can be seen as a positive development insofar as it encourages an openness to new experience, it becomes problematic when all sense of coherence is lost. Shusterman makes a similar observation in his critique of Rorty's notion of the decentered self, which bears a close resemblance to the postmodern subject described above. As he writes:

> If we abandon the aim of a unified or consistent self-narrative for Rorty's discordant chorus of inconsistent "quasi selves" constituted by alternative, constantly changing, and often incommensurable narratives and vocabularies, with no complex narrative "able to make them hang together," then the project of self-enrichment becomes mythical and incoherent . . . A unified self is not a uniform self, but nor can it be an unordered collection of egalitarian quasi selves inhabiting the same corporeal machine. Rorty's confederacy . . . of quasi selves thus seems less the formula for a Freudian ideal of self-perfection than the recipe for a Freudian pathology of schizophrenia. (1988, 349)

Seen from this perspective, the rhetoric of individualism, which characterizes contemporary body projects, masks the deindividualization of subjects in postmodernity. The more obsessive our focus on individualism becomes in popular discourses about the body and its presentation, the less evident it is in actual social life. With the postmodern aestheticization of the self, identity has been reduced to the ephemeral world of appearances. Whereas it once was recognized that there were other sources of identity formation besides that of fashioning one's body, now, appearance and identity are indistinguishable, as the self becomes the masquerade.

Some have sought to counteract the threatened nihilism arising from the arbitrary experimentation with various "looks" by the endeavor to fix their identity permanently on their skin. Indeed, I would suggest that it is no accident that as the conception of identity as infinitely malleable has become more widespread, so, too, has the practice of body marking that seeks to fix, permanently, one's sense of identity. Body marking, as an act of self-narration or self-expression, is now seen as a means by which individuals seek to fix a sense of their identity by permanently emblazoning it on the surface of their bodies. Unlike other forms of body adornment, which can be easily removed, the permanency of tattooing is employed in order to give its wearer a coherent and stable sense of self. As Sweetman puts it, body marking is used ". . . to anchor or stabilize one's sense of self-identity, in part through the establishment of a coherent personal narrative" (2000, 53). He argues that the pain and discomfort involved in obtaining a tattoo serves to heighten the individual's awareness of their own body, thereby enhancing their sense of embodied subjectivity. It is not uncommon for individuals to acquire tattoos to mark significant points in their lives, such as the beginning or end of a relationship or one's "coming of age." In this way, the body markings are a literal inscription of a person's biography onto their skin. They are seen as an act of "self-invention" in which individuals take control of their own bodies and mold them in accordance with their own desires.

However, this investment in the body as the only "authentic" grounding of self-identity is just as problematic as the arbitrary experimentation with "looks" engaged in by the postmodern "style-surfer." Just as the constant transmutations in appearance of the latter threaten to result in a total dissolution of the self, so, conversely, the attempt to permanently fix one's identity on the body fails to give due cognizance to the mutable nature of the self. Neither the infinitely malleable subject nor the fixed and unchanging self is a viable model for identity in contemporary society, which demands both flexibility as well as some sense of coherence.

A more adequate way to resist the reduction of the self to an incessant parade of empty masks, which do not convey anything about the wearer, is to recover the communicative function of dress. Rather than just being about the creation of a "look," the way one adorns oneself should reflect one's values and beliefs. The reduction of identity to appearance can only be avoided if appearance is recognized to be more than simply about the creation of an aesthetic "look," but refers to a self that is not constituted solely by it. While it is true that one's appearance contributes to the sense of who one is, the self is more than the masquerade. Identity and appearance, though interrelated, are not synonymous.

The recognition of the irreducibility of identity to appearance means that it is still meaningful to speak of sincerity and deception in appearances, contrary to the postmodern assumption that such a distinction is untenable since we are nothing but our outward appearance. Not all presentations of the self are equally "fake," as the contemporary notion of the self as masquerade presupposes, but some can be seen to more adequately express the values and beliefs of the wearer than others.

This is evident, for instance, in David Muggleton's analysis of contemporary subcultures, where he argues for the continued relevance of the concept of "authenticity" in relation to the assessment of styles of appearance in subcultures. As he points out (2004, 81–104), members of contemporary subcultures differentiate between those who just adopt the "look" without subscribing to the values of the subculture (and who are thereby judged to be "inauthentic") and those whose style of appearance reflects their values and beliefs. Style, in this latter situation, is not simply something that one "puts on" just for the sake of visual spectacle, but refers to something beyond itself—namely, the ideology of the wearer. In his study, Muggleton found that subcultural identity was constructed by the possession of certain attitudes and beliefs, not merely adopted by performing the requisite actions and dressing in the appropriate fashion. He goes on to point out that while subcultural identities are fluid and mobile, they are not as mutable as the postmodern model of the "style-surfer" suggests, since they are rooted in something deeper than one's outward appearance—namely, a belief in a certain set of values that orient one's actions.

Another example where one's outward appearance goes beyond merely the creation of a certain "look" is the employment of elements of traditional body adornment by members of ethnic or racial minorities as an assertion of their cultural identity in the face of Western hegemony. A case in point is the adoption of traditional African hairstyles such as cornrow plaits by Afro-Americans. As Kobena Mercer argues in his analysis of recent Afro-American hairstyles (1992, 247–63), black people's hair has historically been invested with pejorative connotations by Western culture. In order to counteract this negative stereotyping, black hairstyles amongst Afro-Americans have become an avenue through which to express pride in their cultural roots. While during the 1960s, the Afro look was adopted as a celebration of black identity because it exaggerated those ostensibly "natural" features of black hair which had been so maligned by Western culture, more recently, Afro-Americans have turned to traditional African hairstyles that are highly intricate and complex in nature and are reminiscent of the patternings of African cloth and the decorative designs of African ceramics, architecture, and embroidery. In doing so, they have demonstrated the richness of African culture, thereby challenging the Eurocentric assumption that Africans have no culture or civilization worthy of the name. Also, they have developed new "hybridized" styles, such as the curly perm of the 1980s which combine elements of African and Western hairstyling practices to produce a "neo-African" aesthetic, as Mercer terms it (1992, 257), attesting to the innovativeness of contemporary Afro-American culture that does not just rely on returning to the past or imitating the white Western aesthetic.

## Conclusion

What clearly emerges from the above discussion, then, are the fundamental limitations of the postmodern aestheticization of the self, where the fashioning of one's appearance is taken as an end in itself rather than as a vehicle for expressing one's values and beliefs. As long as one's identity continues to be defined primarily in aesthetic terms, all one is left with is a vapid experimentation with style for style's sake in which aesthetics substitutes for ethics. While the fashioning of one's appearance is an integral part of who one is—indeed, as Silverman suggests (1986, 145), it is one of the main ways through which the body is made "culturally visible"—nevertheless, it is not the only source of identity formation. The fact that it is an inevitable aspect of social interaction does not mean that we should accept, uncritically, the central role that it has come to play in postmodernity. For the focus on the aesthetic cult of the subject in contemporary culture results in a diminished conception of identity centered on the physical transformation of the self rather than on other forms of self-realization that could contribute to the betterment of society as well as an enrichment of the self.

It is in the light of this that the championing of the notion of the self as masquerade by recent theorists of fashion as an alternative to the functional dress advocated by feminists during the 1970s will be critically examined in the following chapter.

# 2

# Feminism and Fashion

Until the late 1980s, the predominant attitude of feminists toward fashion was a largely hostile one. Fashion was regarded primarily as an instrument of oppression in which women were turned into passive objects of the male gaze. Already in the latter half of the nineteenth century, feminists such as Amelia Bloomer, Elizabeth Cady Stanton, and Susan B. Anthony were criticizing female dress insofar as it hindered the physical mobility of women and was detrimental to their health. They regarded the highly ornate and impractical dress of women as an unnecessary and wasteful indulgence, symptomatic of the economic dependence of women on men. Somewhat later, in the 1940s, Simone de Beauvoir developed these arguments further and these formed the basis for the criticisms of female fashion in the 1970s and '80s by feminist theorists such as Una Stannard (1971), Nancy Baker (1984), Susan Brownmiller (1984), Robin Lakoff and Raquel Scherr (1984), and Rita Freedman (1986).

In order to signal their opposition to fashion, during the 1970s, feminists advocated more functional modes of dress, which eschewed adornment designed to enhance the sexual allure of the wearer.[1] Constricting items of dress such as bras, corsets, skirts, and high heels were replaced with jeans or dungarees teamed with T-shirts or loose shirts and flat shoes. Preference was given to "naturalness" over artifice, which meant the avoidance of makeup and the adoption of simple, short hairstyles that required a minimum of upkeep.

In the last couple of decades however, there has been a reevaluation of fashion by a number of theorists such as Elizabeth Wilson (1987 [1985]), Kaja Silverman (1986), Caroline Evans and Minna Thornton (1989), Iris Young (1994), Anne Hollander (1994), and most recently, Linda Scott (2005), who have sought to defend it as an avenue for self-expression and creativity. Questioning the assumption of earlier feminists that fashion is inherently oppressive of women, these theorists promote its emancipatory potential. In contrast to those who condemn fashion's ephemeral nature as symptomatic of an economy of waste based on planned obsolescence, these writers argue that the process of continually changing one's appearance is liberatory insofar as it serves to "denaturalize" the body, highlighting its status as an infinitely malleable cultural construction not fixed by biology.

From the perspective of these recent theorists, the rejection of fashion for its impracticality and irrationality represents a puritanical asceticism that fails to acknowledge the legitimacy of nonutilitarian needs such as those for beauty and sensuous pleasure. As they contend, dress has never been primarily functional, and it is this very freedom from practical necessity in which much of its appeal lies. In their view, those feminists who argue against fashion, in favor of more functional modes of dress, betray an unwitting alliance with Christian denunciations of fashion as too overtly erotic, as well as being complicit with the patriarchal devaluation of activities traditionally associated with women, such as the beautification of oneself. They argue that rather than share in this chauvinistic denigration of traditionally feminine pursuits, their value should be recognized and upheld.

However, while these theorists quite validly argue that the pleasures afforded by fashion should not be dismissed *tout court* as merely deceptive and manipulative of consumer desire, at the same time, as shall be argued here, the greatest concern today lies not in the failure to acknowledge its pleasures, but on the contrary, in the tendency to elevate fashion to the dominant principle in everyday life where the cultivation of one's physical appearance supplants all other sources of identity formation. Customarily, it has been women in particular who have been defined primarily in terms of their physical appearance, while other forms of self-realization have been devalued or neglected. But in contemporary culture, the importance of appearance in defining one's self is becoming more ubiquitous as men, as well as women, are increasingly being encouraged to become more image-conscious as manifested, for instance, in the burgeoning of fashion and lifestyle magazines for men.

While feminists have, until recently, been very circumspect about fashion, the same is not true of the general population, where fashion exercises a greater influence than ever before. Far from failing to appreciate the pleasures of fashion, then, the problem today is the elevation of fashion into a dominant principle of social life and interaction. Whereas the nonutilitarian nature of fashion may once have been subversive of the instrumental rationality of capitalism, in which productivity and self-denial were valued over instant gratification, now it is precisely the hedonistic experimentation with different styles of appearance that is the main legitimizing ideology of our age, as the consumption of commodities has come to assume more and more emphasis in the capitalist economy.

It is from this perspective that I shall examine the recent attempt to "rehabilitate" fashion from its derogation by earlier feminists. In order to set the context for my appraisal of these recent theories of fashion, it is necessary, firstly, to outline the feminist critique against which they have reacted.

## Fashion as Oppression

During the nineteenth century, when the first feminist critiques of fashion were developed, female dress was criticized for reinforcing the subservience of women to men because of its impractical and excessively ornate nature (Tickner, 1984). Amelia Bloomer, an American feminist in the 1850s, for instance, criticized the female dress of the day insofar as it hindered the physical mobility of women, reinforcing the confinement of women (at least those of the middle class) to a sedentary form of existence in the domestic sphere. Female dress, particularly the corset, was also criticized for being detrimental to the physical health of women. This contrasted with male dress, which, since the beginning of the nineteenth century, had become less elaborate and more functional in nature as the leisured life-style of the landed aristocracy gave way to the industrious bourgeois man of enterprise. Bloomer proposed a new form of dress for women that she saw as being more practical, comfortable, and hygienic—namely, panta-loons—to replace the many layers of heavy under-petticoats which were the fashion of the day.

Many of the elements of these early critiques of female fashion contin-ued to inform the writings of theorists later in the twentieth century, such as de Beauvoir, who, in *The second sex*, argued:

> The purpose of the fashions to which [woman] is enslaved is not to reveal her as an independent individual, but rather to offer her as prey to male desires; thus society is not seeking to further her projects but to thwart them. The skirt is less convenient than trousers, high heeled shoes impede walk-ing; the least practical of gowns and dress shoes, the most fragile of hats and stockings are the most elegant; the costume may disguise the body, deform it, or follow its curves; in any case it puts it on display. (1975 [1949], 543)

Hindered by inconvenient clothing, and by the rules of propriety, the bodies of women appeared to men as their property. This was further reinforced by makeup and jewelry, which served the purpose of transforming woman into an idol (1975 [1949], 189).

De Beauvoir also pointed out that elegance was bondage for women in that being well dressed required a great deal of money, time, and care, deflecting their energies away from other more worthy pursuits. While male identity was defined through projects of self-transcendence, for women, their main avenue of self-realization was through the cultivation of their appearance. Unable to exercise their creativity in other ways, women resorted to converting themselves into works of art, becoming self-absorbed in a narcissistic obsession with their appearance. Admired for their looks rather than for their achievements, women became passive objects for the male gaze.

Indicative of this was the fact that whereas male dress was generally not intended to attract attention, female attire was designed to enhance the sexual allure of the wearer, notwithstanding the requirement of a certain degree of modesty on the part of the "respectable" woman. As de Beauvoir comments: ". . . decency by no means consists in dressing with strict modesty. A woman who appeals too obviously to male desire is in bad taste; but one who seems to reject it is no more commendable . . . even in the most austere circles, the sexual aspect of woman will be emphasized . . ." (1975 [1949], 545–46).

The dependence of women on their looks as one of the primary sources of their self esteem left them totally at the mercy of the judgment of others, as de Beauvoir pointed out. Women only "came into being" through the admiring glances of others. Even where women asserted that they dressed for themselves, a consideration of how others saw them was always implied. The woman of fashion thus made herself into a thing in which she observed herself as others saw her. Given the inevitable deterioration of the body over time, the investment by women in their appearance was an extremely tenuous foundation on which to ground their sense of self worth since it was ultimately unsustainable. This accounted for why even extremely attractive women often remained unconvinced of their desirability, for they aimed at a permanent state of perfection that was not capable of realization.

In the 1970s and '80s, feminists such as Oakley (1981, 82–85), Brownmiller (1984), Baker (1984), Lakoff and Scherr (1984), and Freedman (1986) reiterated the oppressive nature of feminine ideals of beauty, which generated in women a permanent sense of dissatisfaction with their appearance, undermining their self-esteem. Concurring with the view of earlier critics, they argued that female dress, in contrast to male dress, was much more subject to the vagaries of fashion, each change signaling the eroticization of yet another part of the female body. For instance, while the advent of the mini-skirt in the 1960s enabled a greater freedom of movement, at the same time, it made women's legs a new focus of erotic interest (Freedman 1986, 90). Not only did these frequent changes in fashion construct the female body as a site of constantly shifting erogenous zones, but they also encouraged the female consumer to spend more and more on clothes in an effort to keep up to date. In this respect, women became yoked to the imperatives of the capitalist economy, which used the mechanism of built-in obsolescence as a way of increasing expenditure on consumer goods. Women's constant dissatisfaction with their looks was fertile ground for the fashion and cosmetics industry, which was able to trade on their never-ending pursuit of the beauty ideal (Oakley 1981, 82).

Feminists such as Orbach (1978), Chernin (1983), Baker (1984), and Coward (1984, 21–25, 39–46, 74–82), also drew attention to the new pressures brought to bear on women by the advent of body-shaping techniques such as plastic surgery, diet, and exercise. While female dress became less restrictive, this did not indicate that it had become more liberated since there were now more effective ways of molding the body in accordance with the ideals of feminine beauty. These new techniques for fashioning the female body operated in an insidious way. For, though women were now encouraged to participate in exercise and to eat wisely ostensibly to improve their health and fitness, the real *raison d'être* for these activities was to attain the body shape deemed desirable by a patriarchal society—a body shape which was becoming increasingly thinner. This new ideal, as Coward pointed out (1984, 39–46), was really that of the prepubescent female. What made such a figure attractive was that it symbolized a sexuality that was not yet aware of itself. The adolescent girl was someone who possessed erotic allure without, however, being in command of her sexual desires. The desirability of this ideal was reinforced by the use of young adolescent girls as fashion models, made up to look as though they were adults.

Decrying the oppressive nature of feminine norms of beauty, then, many feminists such as Brownmiller, Chernin, and Orbach argued for a return to the "natural" body, that is, for an acceptance of the way one was rather than seeking to mold one's body artificially in accordance with unrealistic aspirations.[2] More functional modes of dress that enhanced ease of movement and comfort, and deliberately eschewed those forms of adornment designed to promote the erotic appeal of the wearer, such as high heel shoes and cosmetics, were also advocated by members of the Women's Movement. In their place, feminists often adopted forms of dress considered "mannish," such as dungarees and boots.[3] The idea of "burning one's bra" became emblematic of the feminist attempt to dispense with the restricting yoke of female dress, which deformed the body into "unnatural" shapes in

order to conform to the prevailing ideals of female beauty. As Brownmiller
sums it up, she rejected skirts:

> [b]ecause I don't like this artificial gender distinction. Because I don't wish
> to start shaving my legs again. Because I don't want to return to the expense
> and aggravation of nylons . . . Because I'm at peace with the freedom and
> comfort of trousers. Because it costs less to wear nothing but pants. Because
> I remember how cold I used to feel in the winter wearing a short skirt and
> sheer stockings . . . Because I remember resenting the enormous amount of
> time I used to pour into superficial upkeep concerns, and because the nature
> of feminine dressing is superficial in essence . . . To care about feminine fash-
> ion, and do it well, is to be obsessively involved in inconsequential details on
> a serious basis. (1984, 81)

### The "Rehabilitation" of Fashion

However, since the mid-1980s, a number of theorists, such as Wilson
(1987; 1990a; 1990b), Silverman (1986), Evans and Thornton (1989),
Hollander(1994), and Scott (2005) have sought to "rehabilitate" fashion
as an avenue for self-expression and creativity rather than objectification.
In their view, feminists were misguided in their endeavor to step outside
of fashion by adopting an apparently more "natural" mode of dress that
eschewed artifice and was primarily functional in nature. As they argue,
this feminist dress code was based on the mistaken premise that there is
such a thing as a "natural" body which preexists culture, when in fact, the
body is always already encoded by culture. Hollander, for instance, in her
book *Seeing through clothes*, points to the impossibility of regarding the
body as unmediated by culture, as indicated by the fact that the way the
nude has been portrayed in art has been shaped by the prevailing notions
of fashionable dress. Rather than depicting the naked body "as it really is,"
artists have been unconsciously influenced by the ideals of beauty that were
manifest in the dress of the time. As Hollander writes:

> It is tempting to . . . subscribe to the notion of a universal, unadorned
> mankind that is universally naturally behaved when naked. But art proves
> that nakedness is not universally experienced and perceived any more than
> clothes are. At any time, the unadorned self has more kinship with its own
> usual *dressed* aspect than it has with any undressed human selves in other
> times and places, who have learned a different visual sense of the clothed
> body. It can be shown that the rendering of the nude in art usually derives
> from the current form in which the clothed figure is conceived. This correla-
> tion in turn demonstrates that both the perception and the self-perception

of nudity are dependent on a sense of clothing—and of clothing understood through the medium of a visual convention. (1993, xii and xiii)

Indeed, as Mascia-Lees and Sharpe point out, the very concept of a "natural" body is specific to Western society. They write that:

Often it is assumed that the unadorned, unmodified body is an unspoiled, pure surface on which culture works. This de-historicizes and de-contextualizes the body. It ignores the particular meaning that both the body and the specific modifications to which it is subjected have for the people being represented. It resolves all bodies into the Western notion of the body as prior to culture and thus, as natural. Contemporary theorizing . . . has contributed recently to exposing "the natural" as a Western cultural construct, calling into question the often taken for granted dichotomy between nature and culture . . . Understanding the body not as simple materiality but rather as constituted within language is intended to question traditional notions of the body as prior to or outside of culture. (1992, 3)

Once the social constitution of the body is acknowledged, then it is no longer tenable to uphold the naked body as being more "genuine" or "authentic" than the adorned body, and to see fashion as the repression of the "natural" body as earlier feminists tended to do, since both the naked and the clothed body are equally products of culture. Both are "artificial" in that they have been constituted by social conventions. A corollary of this is that the notion that certain modes of dress are more "natural" than others, and therefore, to be preferred can no longer be sustained. This is made quite clear by Wilson, who argues that:

the search for the "natural" in dress must . . . be a wild goose chase, for such a project tries to deny, or at least does not recognize that dress is no mere accommodation to the body as a biological entity, nor to geography or climate; nor does it merely link the two. It is a complex cultural form, as is the human conception of the body itself. (1987, 213)

She points out that the determination of what constitutes "functional" dress is by no means straightforward since what is considered a basic need in one culture may not be so in another. Thus, for example, while some cultures deem clothes to be an absolute necessity, other peoples living in the same climatic conditions have no need for clothes. The natives of Tierra del Fuego, for instance, did not wear clothes even though the climate was damp and chilly (Wilson 1987, 55). One cannot assume, then, that there is some universal, objectively given set of physiological needs in terms of which the rationality of particular forms of clothing can be assessed. It is too simplistic to assume, as many feminist critics of fashion have done, that there are certain universal criteria of comfort and practicability in dress, for what may be considered "functional" dress in one epoch or culture may not be so in another.

Scott argues, in a similar vein, that the notion of a "natural" mode of dress is unsustainable. As she points out, even with the so-called natural look promoted by feminists, a certain degree of artifice was required.[4] For instance, while elaborate hairstyles were avoided, feminists did not leave their hair unkempt, but still combed and cut it. Similarly, while they abstained from the use of makeup, they still washed their faces and engaged in other basic routines of body maintenance, such as brushing their teeth. Though these practices may seem "natural" to us, in fact, they are of relatively recent historical origin and reflect a culturally specific aesthetic. Scott suggests that, indeed, elaborate decoration of the body could be seen as more "natural" than the Western grooming practices described above, insofar as they are characteristic of almost all cultures. This leads her to assert that:

> From a cross-cultural perspective, the feminist notion of "natural" grooming is a perverse fiction. What is natural for human beings is artifice. Grooming, in fact, is part of the essence of being human, the mark of a creature who is inescapably social and inextricably enmeshed in the use of symbols. Our manner of self-presentation is central to both individual identity and group membership. (2005, 12)

For this reason, then, it is never possible simply to "opt out" of the discourse of fashion. Despite its claims to being outside of fashion, even the "natural look" championed by feminists during the 1970s itself became a fashion, as jeans, pullovers, and running shoes became popular not just amongst members of the women's movement, but were also taken up by the broader population.

The feminist critique of fashion has also been attacked by recent theorists for its puritanical denial of the legitimacy of the aesthetic and sensual pleasures derived from dress. As Wilson has argued, for instance (1987, 244), "to understand all 'uncomfortable' dress as merely one aspect of the oppression of women, is fatally to over-simplify," since dress is not, and never has been, primarily functional. As anthropologists are only too well aware, the reasons why people wear clothing and other forms of bodily adornment often have little to do with the functions of warmth and protection. The importance of the nonfunctional needs served by clothing is indicated by the fact that even those feminists who sought to adopt a practical mode of dress never entirely eliminated purely decorative elements. For example, while they wore masculine boots, they were sometimes painted in rainbow colors; they also often adorned themselves with rings and long, bright earrings made of feathers, beads, or metal, and colored their hair. Fashion, banished from clothing, reappeared surreptitiously in forms of adornment that were less obviously feminine or sexualized. Wilson also questions just how functional the feminist "uniform" of dungarees was, arguing that it was more for symbolic reasons—that is, the fact that they were traditionally regarded as male attire—rather than for their practicality, that they were worn.

In her view, the pointlessness of fashion is precisely what makes it valuable. As she writes, "It is in this marginalized area of the contingent, the decorative, the futile, that not simply a new aesthetic but a new cultural order may seed itself" (1987, 245). She contends that, in their one-sided emphasis on comfort and practicality, feminists have failed to acknowledge that as well as pragmatic needs, humans also have nonmaterial needs, such as the need for meaning, for understanding one's identity and relation to others, for beauty, and so on. In privileging the utilitarian over the aesthetic, feminists are complicitous with the technocratic rationality of the capitalism that values only that which has a practical utility.

The feminist rejection of the purely decorative in dress also betrays an unwitting alliance with puritanical, Christian denunciations of fashion. As both Wilson (1987, 209) and Scott (2005, 14) point out, many of the movements for dress reform in the nineteenth and early twentieth centuries were inspired by Victorian and Christian ideas of propriety. Indeed, prominent nineteenth-century feminists such as Susan B. Anthony and Elizabeth Cady Stanton had close affiliations with the Puritan community (Scott 2005, 40). These dress reform movements abhorred women's fashion insofar as it was seen to be too overtly erotic. In their view, the ornateness of women's fashion threatened to drag them into the stagnant waters of immorality. It was redolent of vanity, false values, social aspiration, and wastefulness. Equating moral purity with simplicity, Christian dress reformers advocated a plainer form of dress that was regarded as being more "natural," and hence "truer," than the elaborate artifice of the women's fashion of the day. Not only did they advocate this for Western women, but they sought to impose such dress codes on indigenous women in an attempt to "civilize" them. From this perspective then, as Wilson and Scott contend, the feminist rejection of the eroticizing nature of women's fashion, like that of the Christian dress reformers, is problematic insofar as it is predicated on a suppression of women's sexuality. The advocacy of plain, nonsensual modes of dress suggests that women can only be liberated if their sexuality is denied.

Scott believes that the feminist rejection of sensuality in dress is the outcome of the dominance of white, educated, middle class Protestant women within the Women's Movement who have imposed their views on the women of other classes and ethnic origins, for whom there is no such perception of sensual display as "immoral" (2005, 2–3, 13). By presenting their preferred mode of dress as "natural," feminists have made use of strategies similar to those in power who seek to legitimize their ideological position by "naturalizing" it. In their imposition of such a dress code, feminists, according to Scott, have failed to give due cognizance to the class, racial, and other differences between women.[5] Thus, for instance, at the same time that white, middle class women were rejecting eroticizing modes of appearance, during the 1970s, black women were embracing beautification as a strategy to further their political aims through the "Black is Beautiful" campaign, which sought to expand the definition of beauty beyond the white, Caucasian ideal (Scott 2005, 270). Similarly, lower class women's attitudes (particularly those who were housewives) toward beauty differed significantly from their middle class counterparts during the 1970s, as they were subjected to a more stringent disciplining of their sexuality at this time than were more educated women. In response to the sexual permissiveness of the 1960s, these women were taught by religious leaders that sexual pleasure was sinful and that the wearing of makeup and fashionable clothes was to be avoided. In this context, the plain, desexualized mode of dress of the feminist movement held little appeal for such women who saw it not as liberating, but as restrictive. At the same time, for nonacademic women who entered the workforce, dressing fashionably was one of the main ways in which they could achieve professional advancement (Scott 2005, 304–5).

Finally, recent theorists have criticized the feminist dismissal of fashion for partaking in the denigration of that which has traditionally been associated with the feminine. As they argue, activities such as taking care of one's appearance and of one's home have not been highly valued in patriarchal society because of their feminine associations. Insofar as feminists have also criticized such activities as trivial and superficial, they perpetuate this dismissal of all things feminine.

Hanson adumbrates further on this theme in her article "Dressing down dressing up: The philosophic fear of fashion" (1993). She argues that underpinning the hostility toward fashion is a fear of, or discomfort with, the body, which, in Western thought, has always been regarded as inferior to the mind. Underlying this hatred of the body is a wish to evade the acceptance of our mortality. Since fashion is intimately connected with the body, philosophers have thus been largely dismissive of it. As Hanson points out, philosophers can only appreciate the aesthetic when it is dissociated from the body. As a realm of disinterested pleasure, the aesthetic is granted a superior status to the merely physical pleasures of the senses.

Fashion, however, calls attention to the physicality of the body and to its ephemeral nature. While it may seek to disguise the changing, always ageing human body, in its very transitoriness, it actually ends up by underscoring the fact of mortality. Thus, whereas philosophers can appreciate the beauty of a work of art, attention to dress is scorned since it is inseparable from attention to the body.

Hanson argues that insofar as feminists share with philosophers their hostility toward fashion, they are unwittingly perpetuating this denigration of the body. This is particularly problematic for feminists since the body has traditionally been associated with the feminine, while the mind has been equated with the masculine. So, in being dismissive of the body and all that is associated with it, feminists are acquiescing to a patriarchal ideology that devalues all that which falls outside the sphere of the mind. As she writes:

> Philosophy's drive to get past what it takes to be the inessential has usually been linked with a denial or devaluation of what it has typically associated with the woman. Thus, even when traditional philosophy turns to aesthetics and for once, interest can focus unashamedly on appearances, an opportunity is still sought to disparage the body. A tradition that displays this sort of embarrassment about carnality may not be the most agreeable companion on the quest to reassert and revaluate women's lives and feminine experience. (1993, 235)

### Critical Appraisal of the "Rehabilitation" of Fashion

Having rejected the notion of "natural" or "functional" dress as a yardstick by which to assess the emancipatory potential of particular modes of dress, recent theorists of fashion such as Silverman, Wilson, and Young have proposed that the most liberatory form of dress is that which highlights the fact that the body is a cultural construction. Silverman, for instance (1986, 148), argues, contrary to earlier feminist critiques of fashion, that the constant transmutations of female dress, far from being oppressive of women, are potentially more disruptive both of gender and of the symbolic order than is the relatively static nature of male dress, which defines identity as fixed and stable rather than as fluid and mutable. According to Silverman, the fragmentation of female identity into a constantly changing plethora of guises, behind which there is no fixed self, represents a more "genuine" model of subjectivity than that of masculine identity, which continues to be premised on the centrality of the unified ego. She comments on the fact that female bodily adornment has been much more changeable than male attire over the last two centuries, making the female body far less stable and localized than its male counterpart. In her view, the construction of the female body as a site of constantly shifting erogenous zones, far from being problematic, is potentially subversive. As she writes:

> The endless transformations within female clothing construct female sexuality and subjectivity in ways that are at least potentially disruptive, both of gender and the symbolic order, which is predicated upon continuity and coherence. However, by freezing the male body into phallic rigidity, the uniform of orthodox male dress makes it a rock against which the waves of female fashion crash in vain. (1986, 148)

In particular, she champions "op shop" dressing, which involves the self-reflexive adoption of previous styles. What is salutary about this mode of dress, for her, is not simply that it acknowledges the "fake" nature of all styles, but that it highlights the fact that there is no true self behind the various guises that one adopts. One's identity is equated with the guises that one adopts. It is not the case that the self exists independently of the clothes that one wears. Rather, one is defined through one's mode of dress. As Silverman writes, "clothing not only draws the body so that it can be seen, but also maps out the shape of the ego" (1986, 149).

Likewise, Wilson argues for a mode of dress as masquerade, not in the sense of putting an ironic distance between the costume/uniform/camouflage and the wearer who sports it as a mask or disguise, but rather, as the form in which the body actually manifests itself. As she writes

> So far as women are concerned—and fashion is still primarily associated with women—contemporary fashions arguably have liberatory potential . . . For in "denaturalizing the wearer's specular identity" contemporary fashion refuses the dichotomy, nature/culture. Fashion in our epoch denaturalizes the body and thus divests itself of all essentialism. This must be good news for women, since essentialist ideologies have been oppressive to them. Fashion often plays with, and playfully transgresses, gender boundaries, inverting stereotypes and making us aware of the masquerade of femininity. (1990a, 233)

Young also praises fashion insofar as it offers women the invitation to play with identities. As she writes:

> One of the privileges of femininity in rationalized instrumental culture is an aesthetic freedom, the freedom to play with shape and color on the body, to don various styles and looks, and through them exhibit and imagine unreal possibilities . . . Such female imagination has liberating possibilities because it subverts, unsettles the order of respectable, functional rationality in a world where that rationality supports domination. (1994, 208–9)

The problem, however, is that a mode of dress that declares the constructed nature of identity is not sufficient to define it as liberatory. Indeed, in the present age, where self-identity has increasingly been defined in terms of one's physical appearance by the fashion and advertising industry, one could argue that modes of dress that promote the view of the self as a series of changing guises are conservative insofar as they leave unchallenged the reduction of self-identity to an image that is constructed by the commodities one buys. As Douglas Kellner points out in his analysis of Madonna, for instance, while her radical transmutations of appearance highlight the social constructedness of identity, fashion, and sexuality, at the same time,

> ... by constructing identity largely in terms of fashion and image, [she] plays into precisely the imperatives of the fashion and consumer industries that offer a "new you" and a solution to all of your problems by the purchase of products and services. By emphasizing image, she plays into the dynamics of the contemporary image culture that reduces art, politics, and the theatrics of everyday life to the play of image, downplaying the role of communication, commitment, solidarity and concern for others in the constitution of one's identity and personality. (1994, 178)

While Young promotes women's play with various guises as subversive of the instrumental rationality of capitalism, this form of rationality is no longer dominant. Now, it is precisely the hedonistic experimentation with different styles of appearance that is the main legitimizing ideology of our age, as the consumption of commodities has come to assume an ever-greater importance in the capitalist economy.[6] As Baudrillard (1981) has characterized it, capitalism has now entered a postindustrial phase in which the world of production has given way to the world of consumption and of the spectacle. Whereas the early phases of capitalism were governed by an instrumental rationality in which technical efficiency was the primary consideration, now, the main concern is with the styling of the appearance of commodities to seduce the consumer. The meaning of objects is no longer defined either in terms of their use value, their exchange value, or their symbolic value (that is, as symbolic of the relation between people as in gift exchange), but resides solely in their relation to other signs. As Baudrillard writes:

> ... an object is not an object of consumption unless it is released from its psychic determinations as *symbol*; from its functional determinations as *instrument*; from its commercial determinations as *product*; and is thus *liberated as a sign* to be recaptured by the formal logic of fashion. (1981, 67)

The modern individual is fashioned, and is more interested, in the authority of the sign than in the elements it represents. In contrast to earlier times, in which individuals were seen to have an identity apart from the goods they possessed, in the present era, one's identity is defined in terms of the image that one creates through one's consumption of goods, including the clothes one wears. Finkelstein concurs with this when she writes: "[I]n the modern era . . . we have fused together the capacity for conspicuous consumption with the presentation of personality" (1991, 5). She goes on to argue that:

> . . . the emphasis given to the presentation of the self in our daily social life, and the proliferation of goods, services and techniques aimed at allowing us to produce a distinctive identity, have the effect of deflecting attention away from a more valuable source of identity, namely, the historical precedents and the immediate politics of our circumstances. (1991, 190)

Although experimentation with various modes of dress can contribute to the subversion of traditional notions of gender identity, for instance, there is the very real danger in our present era where appearance has become the central means of defining one's identity, of losing sight of the fact that rebellion, through fashion, is not in itself sufficient to bring about social change. As Wilson herself acknowledges:

> . . . however we might want to get away from the puritanism of the left in order to celebrate fashion as a legitimate and highly aesthetic pleasure, there are still problems about defending it . . . This call to hedonism can represent a flight from more threatening problems; and the recognition of pleasure and beauty as important forces in our lives—which emphatically they are— . . . can easily degenerate into . . . an abdication of discrimination that is merely decadent. (1990b, 35–36)

In the postmodern era, rebellion has primarily taken the form of adopting a certain style—that is, of projecting a certain image—through the clothes one wears, rather than engaging with the economic and political structures that produce social inequality as evidenced by the various youth subcultures that first made their appearance in the postwar period. As Clarke, Hall, Jefferson, and Roberts write:

> [Subcultures] "solve," but in an imaginary way, problems which, at the concrete material level, remain unresolved. Thus the "Teddy Boy" expropriation of an upper class style of dress "covers" the gap between largely manual,

unskilled, near-lumpen real careers and life-chances, and the "all-dressed-up-and-nowhere-to-go" experience of Saturday evening. (1977, 47–48)

One must be careful, then, not to become so preoccupied with the experimentation with various guises that one loses sight of the fact that there is more to forging one's identity than changing appearances. While clothes are potent symbols, it is not sufficient to simply adopt a different appearance as a way of redefining oneself. To quote Finkelstein, once again:

> ... when a heightened or developed consciousness is sought through the cultivation of the body, then an era dawns in which only a partial understanding of collective social life can exist. In such a society, the continuity between the body politic and the private body has not been understood thoroughly enough to engender a sense of interest in those communal actions which are necessary for the progressive liberalization of a society. (1991, 190)

The task today, then, is not so much that of "denaturalizing" the body, since the fashion industry already does this, but rather, of challenging the reduction of self-identity to the image one constructs through the clothes one wears. While the affirmation of the legitimacy of the pleasures of fashion by recent theorists provides a useful antidote to the sensual impoverishment of the "natural look" championed by the feminist movement during the 1970s, it is hardly radical in the context of contemporary consumer society, where the concern with appearance has come to assume a greater importance than ever before. As Naomi Wolf points out (1991, 20–30), despite the growing professionalization of women, the importance of looks has not diminished, but has, in fact, increased, as evidenced for instance, by the fact that more and more professions into which women are entering are being reclassified as display professions.

As well as the increased emphasis on appearance for women, men are now becoming more image conscious—a process aided and abetted by the significant expansion in the promotion of men's fashion. Since the 1980s, there has been a concerted effort to market fashion items to men, as evidenced by the proliferation of fashion magazines for men, such as *GQ*, *Esquire*, and *Vogue for Men*, as well as various other health and lifestyle magazines that contain a significant number of advertisements for body care products, such as skin moisturizes and colognes. Once the exclusive domain of women, such products are now increasingly targeted to the male consumer. Accompanying this, there has been a dramatic increase in images of the male body in advertising over the last decade, as Gill et al.

point out (2005, 38–39), in which men are being presented in an analogous way to women as objects of spectacle.

Although, at first glance, it may seem that this is evidence of a growing equality between the sexes, at the same time, it exacerbates the overemphasis placed on appearance as a means of defining identity in contemporary culture—a culture where beauty matters more than ever before. Instead of women being judged less by their looks, now it is the case that men are increasingly being subjected to the same measure. Thus, for instance, men are now engaging more and more in activities such as bodybuilding, not in order to increase their strength and fitness, but in order to look good. Muscle development has become an aesthetic project disconnected from any functional imperatives (Dutton 1995, 369). As men have become more image conscious, so have the pathologies previously associated almost exclusively with women, such as eating disorders (Gill et al. 2005, 39). This indicates, then, that rather than affirming the pleasures of fashioning the body, the more pressing issue today is why so much importance is being placed on appearance than ever before, to the detriment of other forms of self-realization.

The other issue of concern, which is not adequately addressed simply by avowing the self-expressive potential of fashion, is a consideration of the conditions necessary for the genuine realization of these possibilities. Though Wilson voices caution as to the celebration of fashion as a problem-free liberating practice (2000, 122), the same cannot be said of a number of other recent fashion theorists. In their concern to rescue some specifically female pleasures in dress from their subsumption under the male gaze, there has been a tendency for several of these theorists to overlook the circumstances under which such pleasures can be realized in a nonexploitative manner.

Thus, for instance, while Silverman celebrates the constantly changing nature of women's fashions as a potentially liberating force that highlights the malleable nature of identity, under the current circumstances, such changeability is more likely to be an indication of the greater difficulty that women have in attaining a coherent sense of self in a society where they are frequently torn by conflicting demands and roles. This is borne out, for instance, by the study conducted by Alison Clarke and Daniel Miller (2002), who found that many women today face increasing anxiety about what to wear. Indeed, they suggest that this anxiety concerning fashion choices has become so ubiquitous that it is the normal condition for most women in contemporary culture. Even in instances where individual women are knowledgeable about fashion and style, they are often at a loss as to what is most appropriate for them to wear. This is ultimately due, they suggest, to women's greater uncertainty about their roles and relationships to people more generally. As they write of one of their subjects:

> Despite [her] immense confidence in knowing about style, such knowledge [did] not in and of itself tell her what she "like[d]," because to know what one likes is knowing what one wants to be in relation to others and how others will react to what you are doing, not merely a knowledge about what the possible range is. One can have a fine sense of the nuances of language without knowing what one wants to say (2002, 197).

In her positive appraisal of the changeable nature of women's fashions, Silverman thus overlooks the fact that while playing with one's appearance can be pleasurable, for many women today, it is a fraught process that can become a self-destructive obsession. Only in a context where one's self-esteem is not centrally dependent on one's looks can the experimentation with appearance be truly pleasurable. As long as the cultivation of one's appearance continues to be the main avenue for self-affirmation, it will remain a burdensome obligation for many rather than a genuine expression of self-creativity.

Similarly, Scott, in positively appraising the seductive appearance cultivated by single, working class women as an expression of their economic independence and rebellion against repressive sexual mores (2005, 171–78, 244–48), glosses over the fact that this was also one of the few means available to such women for social advancement. Denied access to power and status by legitimate means, they had to resort to using their looks as a means of furthering their aims. This was clearly the case, for instance, with many of the Hollywood stars who came from working class backgrounds, whose glamorous appearance served as a role model for other working class women yearning to escape their lowly origins. What Scott fails to recognize here is that under such conditions, the "play" with appearance can hardly be said to be empowering, even if it achieved the desired result of upward mobility and social recognition. As Lakoff and Scherr make clear in their book *Face value: The politics of beauty* (1984), the use of one's looks as a means of attaining status and power leaves women in a very tenuous position because attractiveness is ephemeral and ultimately unsustainable. While women's status is based on such flimsy foundations, it can easily be taken from them at any time. As they write: "The power of beauty is the power of the weak. It is a paradox, and a dangerous one for women. But women have been controlled and governed by the strength of that paradox, having no other options" (1984, 20).[7]

The neglect of the unequal social structures within which the cultivation of appearance takes place is particularly clear in Hollander's defense of fashion as an avenue for self-expression and creativity. In her book *Sex and suits* (1994), Hollander praises fashion for its openness to change and love of experimentation in comparison to the conservatism of traditional folk costume. Whereas clothing prior to the rise of fashion was based on preserving the sanctity of tradition and changed only incrementally, the motor of fashion is constant innovation and change in which the authority of the past is constantly under challenge. Fashion then, according to Hollander, far from being oppressive and stifling, actively encourages individual creativity and the subversion of convention. As she puts it:

> Western fashion offers a visual way out of the trap of tradition, the prison of unquestioning wisdom. Fashion allows clothing to create an image of skepticism, of comic possibility, of different powers and alternative thoughts, of manifold chances, of escape from fixed meanings and fixed roles. (1995, 19–20)

In her account of the experimental nature of fashion, she treats it as though it occurs in a social vacuum, conceiving of it primarily as a form of aesthetic play in which individuals experiment with a range of various "looks." For her, fashion is essentially a form of artistic expression that evolves according to its own formal logic, just as art in the modern era has. As she writes: "In speaking of dress, I am always concerned either with line and form or with sex and poetry, not with money and power. I'm working from the idea that sexuality and imagination are what originally produce the extraordinary formal imagery that can cause money and power to be reflected in clothes" (1994, 13). She continues that "[c]lothes show that visual form has its own capacity, independent of practical forces in the world, to satisfy people, perpetuate itself, and to make its own truth apart from linguistic reference and topical allusion . . . Fashion, like art, shows that visual satisfaction has its own remarkable laws, and that these are related to sexuality in its imaginative vein" (1994, 13).

Although it is true that changes in fashion cannot be explained simply as a reflex of social and political conditions that exist externally to it, nevertheless, at the same time, the forms that fashion takes are not purely aesthetic but inevitably carry a particular social and political significance, whether the designer or wearer is consciously aware of this or not. No "look" is politically neutral or "innocent." Thus, for instance, at the same time as the advent of shoulder pads in women's dress during the 1980s could, in part, be seen as the outcome of a purely aesthetic experimentation with past forms,[8] their social and political significance as the female appropriation of a symbol of male power cannot be ignored as a factor in their revival. Similarly, though the appeal of a silky blouse or slinky evening gown may lie primarily in the sensual and tactile pleasures they give to their wearers, they also carry other cultural connotations that go beyond their aesthetic qualities—connotations that can sometimes be directly at odds with the reasons why the wearer dons such garments.

Thus, while it is important to acknowledge that the pleasures that women experience from clothes cannot be explained simply through their vicarious identification with the male gaze, nevertheless, one should not lose sight of the impact that structural inequalities have on the way in which such pleasures are experienced. The enjoyment afforded by fashion cannot be considered independently of the social context within which it occurs. As much as one may wish to see fashion as a mode of aesthetic experimentation for its own sake, in which free rein is given to the imagination, ultimately, such experimentation cannot be insulated from the broader social environment of which it is a part. Though the meanings of fashion items are much less circumscribed than was the case with traditional modes of dress, nevertheless, they still have a social significance that goes beyond their aesthetic form.

## Conclusion

In conclusion then, while recent theorists of fashion have highlighted the deficiencies of the earlier feminist conception of "functional" dress, their championing of the notion of woman as artifice is equally as problematic in the current context where it has become one of the main promotional tools of contemporary consumer capitalism. While it is not a case of denying the pleasures of beauty in appearance or of eschewing sensuous display, as the earlier feminists proposed, neither is the mere celebration of the self as masquerade adequate. This is because it is convergent with our contemporary culture of the spectacle, where the cult of appearance is privileged over all other sources of identity formation. In their desire to rehabilitate the legitimacy of the aesthetic pleasures of dress, and to expose the one-sidedness of the utilitarian rationality of modernism, recent theorists of fashion have tended to lose sight of the equally limiting reduction of self-identity to appearance—a reduction that has been particularly damaging to women, but that is now increasingly affecting men.

Rather than simply affirming the enjoyment afforded by fashion, more crucial is the necessity to recognize the impediments that prevent the full realization of these pleasures in contemporary society. Although beauty practices can bring much delight, this can only be genuinely realized in a context where individuals are no longer judged primarily by their appearance, and where there are no longer marked inequalities in gender, race, and class. Beauty *per se* is not the problem, but the inequitable social structures that turn it into an instrument of oppression rather than of self-realization.

In the next chapter, the inadequacies of the cult of artifice advocated in recent fashion theory is further explored through an examination of the significance of cosmetic practices in postmodernity.

# 3

# Cosmetics and the Female Body

The wearing of cosmetics by women in Western culture has been subject to a diverse range of criticisms. One of the most frequently made
objections has been that cosmetics conceal the "true" self behind a "false"
mask. For many, the artifice of cosmetics has been regarded as a sign of
deception and inauthenticity in which the wearer masquerades as something she is not.

In more recent times, however, there has emerged a very different
paradigm for the appraisal of cosmetics. In this new approach, which is
informed by post-structuralist theory, the problem with cosmetics is not
that they mask a "true" self, but, on the contrary, that they are required to
accurately reflect a person's "inner" being. According to the proponents
of this view, such as Michel Thevoz (1984), Jean Baudrillard (1990b)
and Catherine Constable (2000), earlier critiques of cosmetics have been
based on a mistaken premise that there exists a "true" self, independent of
the masks one assumes when, in fact, the self is constituted by these very
masks. It makes no sense, then, to seek for an authentic self behind the
masquerade since the self is nothing but the masquerade. Thus, in contrast
to previous critics who proposed a return to the "natural" visage, these
more recent critics of cosmetics advocate a makeup that openly declares its
artificial nature, drawing attention to itself rather than seeking to simulate
a "natural" look.

However, as will be argued in this chapter, an overtly "artificial" cosmetic practice, which highlights the cultural constructedness of the body,
is not necessarily liberatory. While in the past there were instances where
 the wearing of highly visible makeup had emancipatory connotations,
such as during the 1920s, when it was adopted by the "modern" woman
who rejected a demure, domesticated femininity, in contemporary culture, where the radical "makeover" is actively promoted by the advertising

and fashion industries, it no longer carries the same radical message. The creation of an "artificial" look is no longer stigmatized in the way that it once was but has become increasingly acceptable, with celebrities such as Joan Collins, Kylie Minogue, and Madonna acting as role models. Now, the overt assertion of sexuality signaled by the wearing of visible makeup is a marketing strategy, enthusiastically adopted by advertisers rather than being the subject of social censure.

In this chapter, I shall begin with an outline of earlier appraisals of cosmetics before discussing the contrasting perspective of the post-structuralist critique. The limitations of the latter will then be discussed, demonstrating its unwitting complicity with contemporary ideologies of consumer capitalism.

### Early Critiques of Cosmetics

While the wearing of cosmetics has had a long history in Western culture, this has been accompanied by trenchant criticism of the practice. One of the main premises on which most critiques of Western cosmetic practice have been based is that it represents a defilement of the natural human form. This idea can be traced back to Classical antiquity. Because the human figure was taken as representative of divinity, all types of body marking were ruled out except those which served to perfect the natural human form. Natural beauty was seen to be indicative of moral virtue. In their cosmetic practice, the Greeks sought to distinguish between those cosmetics whose purpose was to preserve the body's natural state and keep the skin healthy, and those that were obviously artificial and intended primarily for display, such as rouge, eye makeup, lipstick, and so on. Only the former were acceptable since they were seen as enhancing, rather than defiling, nature, while the latter came to be associated with courtesans. As Ischomacus declared, for instance, "When I found [my wife] one day painted with rouge . . . I pointed out to her that she was being as dishonest in attempting to deceive me about her looks as I should be were I to deceive her about my property" (quoted in Corson 1981, 38).

This preference for "natural" over "artificial" beauty continued with the rise of Christianity. Under Christianity, humans were seen to be made in the image of God, and thus, anything which disfigured God's creation was regarded as anathema. Improving on nature through the "wicked" arts of false and dyed hair, makeup, and ornate clothes was seen to betray mistrust in the work of the Creator. In the words of one church father, Tertullianus: "Those things, then, are not the best by nature which are not from God, the Author of nature. They are understood to be from the devil, from the corruptor of nature" (quoted in Tseëlon, 1995, 35). Artificial beauty was condemned as vanity, as indicated by Jeremiah, who declared: "And you, O desolate one, what do you mean that you dress in scarlet, that you deck yourself with ornaments of gold, that you enlarge your eyes with paint? In vain you beautify yourself" (quoted in Synnott 1990, 64). The wearing of makeup by women was taken as evidence of their inherently duplicitous nature. Exemplifying this attitude was the medieval theologian Clement of Alexandria (c. AD 150–215), who declared: "For applying things unsuitable to the body, as if they were suitable, begets a practice of lying and a habit of falsehood" (quoted in Tseëlon 1995, 35). He forbade women to dye their hair, to pierce their ears, or to smear their faces "with the ensnaring devices of wily cunning" (quoted in Synnott 1990, 64). Cosmetics were also criticized for tempting men into sin, being used as a tool of seduction by women of easy virtue. As Jerome (AD 345–420) declared: "What have rouge and white lead to do on a Christian woman's face? . . . They are fires to influence young men, stimulants of lustful desire, plain evidence of an unchaste mind" (quoted in Synnott 1990, 65).

These sorts of criticisms of cosmetics have been reiterated throughout the history of Western culture, particularly from the seventeenth century onwards, when cosmetics first came into general use in England (see Corson, 1981). Thomas Tuke, for instance, in 1616, wrote *A treatise against painting and tincturing of men and women*, in which he exhorted women to keep a natural appearance rather than resorting to the deceptive practice of painting their faces. As he argued:

> [Woman] was not borne painted in this world . . . neither shall she ride painted in the next world, and I thinke she would be loth die painted, why then should she live painted . . . A painted face is a *superfluous* face. It were well if the world were well rid of all such superfluous creatures. (quoted in Corson 1981, 130)

Later, toward the end of the eighteenth century, a contributor to *The Gentleman's Magazine* condemned the wearing of rouge in similar terms. As he wrote

> For the single ladies who follow this practice there is some excuse . . . Husbands must be had, and if the young men of this age are so silly as to be allured by a little red paint, why red paint must be used; but for married women, mistresses of families, mothers, for these to be greedy of the gaze and admiration of the other sex is disgusting and betrays a frivolity of character unbecoming the dignity of a matron's situation. (quoted in Corson 1981, 265)

Others who criticized the wearing of cosmetics as a practice of deception include the nineteenth-century philosopher Arthur Schopenhauer, who declared:

> Nature has equipped . . . woman with the power of dissimulation as her means of attack and defense . . . to make use of it at every opportunity is as natural to her as it is for an animal to employ its means of defense whenever it is attacked . . . A completely truthful woman who does not practice dissimulation is perhaps an impossibility. (quoted in Tseëlon, 1995, 36)

The preference for unadorned nature underlying these critiques of cosmetics also found favor with the Romantics in the first half of the nineteenth century, for whom nature was superior to culture. Mindful of the destructive impact of modern industry and technology, the "natural" for the Romantics represented that which had escaped the corrupting influence of civilization. Hence, they eschewed those forms of appearance where the cult of artifice was evident in favor of a more "natural" look (Wilson 1987, 61, 108),

During the course of the twentieth century, the most trenchant critiques of cosmetics derived not from Christian theology, as was the case in earlier centuries, but from a feminist perspective. For feminist critics, what was objectionable about cosmetics was not that they defiled God's creation, but that they objectified women by turning them into spectacles for the male gaze. Where past critics had seen the wearing of cosmetics as indicative of an innate duplicity and vanity in women, feminists explained women's use of makeup with reference to the social pressures placed on women to conform to certain ideals of feminine beauty. Thus, for instance, Simone de Beauvoir (1975[1949], 189–91) saw makeup as a symbol of women's oppression and argued that the narcissistic preoccupation of many women with their appearance was a consequence of the lack of other opportunities for self-realization that ultimately impoverished, rather than enriched, them.

In the 1970s and '80s, other feminists, such as Stannard (1971), Lakoff and Scherr (1984), Brownmiller (1984), and Freedman (1986) developed this critique of beautification practices further, arguing that they were unnecessary, time-consuming, and expensive, and ultimately led to self-hatred and a feeling of inadequacy with the growing realization that the beauty ideal was unattainable. As Brownmiller commented, for instance: "Cosmetics have been seen historically as proof of feminine vanity, yet they are proof, if anything, of feminine insecurity, an abiding belief that the face underneath is insufficient unto itself"(1984, 158–59). Similarly, Freedman points to the gender-specific nature of cosmetic practices in contemporary Western society, arguing that women engage in such beautification rituals for fear of being stigmatized as "unfeminine" if they do not (1986, 47–52). Because an attractive appearance is considered more important for women than for men, women who refuse to use cosmetics to enhance their looks do so at their own peril.

While the feminist critique of cosmetics was based on very different premises from those of earlier critiques, it shared with the latter the assumption that the unadorned face was more "natural" and hence more "authentic" or "truthful" than the artificially made-up one. This is implicit, for instance, in de Beauvoir's critique of the made-up face for its denial of nature. As she argued (1975 [1949], 190–91), while woman, in beautifying herself, ostensibly seeks only to enhance her "natural" attributes, in actual fact, she denies nature by appearing ageless. The metamorphosis of woman into a changeless ideal through cosmetics serves as a defense against man's fear of his own mortality. It is for this reason that while "man wishes her to be carnal, her beauty like that of fruits and flowers . . . he would also have her smooth, hard, changeless as a pebble. The function of ornament is to make her share more intimately in nature and at the same time to remove her from the natural, it is to lend to palpitating life the rigor of artifice . . ." (de Beauvoir 1975 [1949, 190).

In a similar vein, both Stannard (1971) and Brownmiller (1984) have indicated their preference for the unadorned face on the grounds that it is more natural. "The modern cult of women's beauty," Stannard writes (1971, 123), "has nothing to do with what women naturally look like . . . For even the small percentage of women who fulfill the modern ideal of beauty are not allowed to be natural. They too are creatures of artifice." Likewise, Brownmiller indicates strongly her preference for "natural" over "artificial" beauty when she writes:

> . . . I think I am right to prefer my own authentic countenance and the authentic countenance of others—with breathing pores, a living map of human experience and admitted vulnerabilities—to the impersonal cosmetic mask of smooth polish and bright color. Makeup has been touted for centuries as basic feminine allure, but the allure is homogenized and distanced through the medium of routinely processed markings. (1984, 159)

### The Post-structuralist Critique of Cosmetics

In contrast to such views, Thevoz argues that the problem with Western cosmetics is not that they mask an "authentic" self, but on the contrary, that they are supposed to accurately reflect who a person "really" is. As he points out (1984, 72–74), Western cosmetics, in contrast with non-Western forms of body decoration, are premised on a belief in the unity and integrity of the ego in which there is assumed to be a concurrence between the inner and the outer self. The individual's physical appearance is taken to be a mirror of the soul, and an adequate cosmetic practice is thus seen to be one that provides an accurate reflection of a person's real identity. In Western culture, it is the face in particular that is regarded as central in revealing a person's "true" identity. Quoting Henri Michaux, Thevoz (1984, 25) writes that "[w]e lead an excessively facial life, meaning thereby that we invest in the physiognomy as the unified focus of our personalist psychology." [1]

Western makeup, then, is charged with the imperative of enhancing, rather than disguising, the features of the individual's face. In this respect, it provides a marked contrast to cosmetic practices of other cultures, where the facial features that distinguish one person from another are masked rather than heightened. Whereas Western makeup follows the contours of the facial features, emphasizing the eyes and the mouth in particular (these being the two aspects of a person's face which serve more than any other to distinguish one person from another), face painting in non-Western societies generally contravenes these features, masking the identity of the wearer.[2] As Andrew Strathern points out (1987) in his analysis of the face painting practices of the New Guinean highlanders, for instance, the purpose of these decorations was not to draw attention to the individual identity of the wearer, but to signify characteristics such as clan membership, fertility, sexual availability, strength, religious affiliation, status, and power—all characteristics that related to the collective nature of the social group rather than to the individual projection of "identity." Since the purpose of facial decoration was to symbolize the continuity of the tribe rather than the uniqueness of the individual, those who were too easily recognized through their face paint were regarded as not having decorated themselves well. [3]

In tribal cultures, the designs utilized in face and body painting were most frequently derived from the features of totem animals, with the aim being to embody the power and spirit of the totem animal whose features had been imitated. The totem spirit acted as an intermediary between man and nature, and its symbolic form, once painted on the body, acted as a "spiritual armor." Thus, far from being a statement about individual personality, as in Western cosmetics, the marked individual in tribal cultures submerged his/her identity into that of the totem animal whose characteristics s/he sought to assume. In stateless societies, as Thevoz argues:

... body painting, as a ritual means of establishing communication with the unlike beyond, is meant to make man unlike his usual self. It is meant to facilitate his initiatory, shamanic, possessional or other "journey," helping the officiant of the rite to become inhuman, to become animal, to become other ... The skin decoration is ... designed to dehumanize, depersonalize, disfigure, deface, transgress the natural form, to baffle identification. That is why ... it makes play with anti-natural elements such as straight lines, triangles, circles and all rigid, geometric figures which stand in conspicuous contrast with the mobility of facial features .... (1984, 34)

In its role as revelation of the self, Western cosmetic practice becomes entangled in a fundamental paradox, as Thevoz (1984, 72) points out. For while its aim is to enhance the "natural" features of the face, it achieves this by artificial means. It attempts to resolve this paradox by disavowing its artifice. Thus, when makeup is worn, it is normally applied in such a way as to appear inconspicuous. As Thevoz writes:

... like representational painting, make-up is tolerated only on the understanding that it shall fade away as such into its illusionistic function. When it breaks away from that function, it becomes indecent and reprehensible. A woman is expected to conceal her make-up behind her make-up if she wants to be respectable. (1984, 74)

Against this, Thevoz argues that Western cosmetic practice should openly declare its artificial nature rather than seeking to simulate nature. In this regard, he concurs with Charles Baudelaire's defense of the artifice of cosmetics (Thevoz 1984, 75). Baudelaire argued that because beauty is not a natural phenomenon, but a human construct:

face painting should not be used with the vulgar, unavowable object of imitating fair Nature and of entering into competition with youth ... Who would dare to assign to art the sterile function of imitating Nature? Maquillage has no need to hide itself or to shrink from being suspected; on the contrary, let it display itself, at least if it does so with frankness and honesty. (1978 [1863], 34)

Thevoz thus arrives at the opposite conclusion to that reached by earlier critics of cosmetics who preferred the supposedly "natural" (that is, unadorned) visage to the artifice of cosmetics. The sort of cosmetic practice that Thevoz envisages is one that deliberately seeks to contravene, rather than to imitate, the individual's facial features, thereby undermining the notion of the unified subject, central to Western thought. Rather than being judged in terms of how accurately it reveals the "inner" being of its wearer, makeup, according to him, should be assessed in terms of the degree to which it highlights the cultural construction of the body. A cosmetic practice that emphasizes its mask-like character serves, in his view, to highlight the fact that the self is the mask. Breaking free of the imperative of mimicking a self that supposedly exists behind the mask, the alternative cosmetic practice proposed by Thevoz undermines the essentialist notion of the self as something that exists apart from its inscription by culture. "The truth of the matter is that the Western adult is always made up already. To get at his true identity beneath the make-up is like peeling an onion to reach its kernel without knowing that it consists entirely of its layers of skin" (Thevoz 1984, 122).

Lingis (1983, 25) argues in a similar vein that the problem with Western makeup is that it is required to accurately represent the "inner" self. He indicates his preference for tribal body markings over Western cosmetic practice on the grounds that the former are unashamedly all surface.[4] In his view, tribal body markings such as tattooing and scarification are presignificatory, representing nothing other than themselves. Their effect is rendered directly through the physical experience of pain rather than interpreted intellectually through the decoding of signs, as occurs in Western cosmetic practice. As he writes, "the eye that looks at them does not read them; it winces, it senses the pain . . . The savage inscription is a working over the skin, all surface effects" (1983, 34). These inscriptions, he continues, "do not refer to intentions in an inner individual psychic depth, nor to meanings or concepts in some transcendent beyond . . . [They] are, for the most part, not representations" (37). By contrast, in the case of Western bodies:

> The surface is not laid out for itself; it is completely occupied by signs which simultaneously refract your gaze off into the street, into the horizon, into history where their signified referents are and open in upon the psychic depth where the intentions are being formed. (1983, 33)

Furthermore, whereas primitive body markings "decenter" the subject by extending, almost infinitely, the number of erogenous zones, through the multiplication of the number of orifices on the body surface, Western cosmetic practice reinforces the rigid fixity of the unified ego. In its requirement of a concurrence between outward appearance and "inner" self, it fails to recognize that there is no "essential" self beyond the masquerade, according to Lingis.

The embrace of overtly "artificial" cosmetics, advocated by Thevoz, to counter this "depth" model of subjectivity is epitomized by the portraits of

Andy Warhol.[5] Unlike the traditional practice of portraiture in which the physiognomy of the face is read as a reflection of the person's inner being, the faces in Warhol's portraits are all surface. Stripped of all those distinguishing features that are taken to be expressive of a person's character, Warhol's faces, marked only by impersonal cosmetic inscriptions, appear simply as masks, unanimated by any self lurking behind them. In Warhol's paintings, as Thevoz writes:

> The painted body . . . is not exactly the body represented by painting, since there is no longer any tangible reference system . . . It is the mirror body, the body which has let itself be vampirized so to speak by its normative image to the point of being volatilized in a pure mirage . . . What does he see of Elizabeth Taylor's face or Marilyn Monroe's? The make-up, the lipstick, the dyed hair—in short, a painted surface no different in nature from the painting itself. (1984, 113)

Likewise, Jean Baudrillard argues in his book *Seduction* that while philosophers have traditionally condemned cosmetics insofar as they operate within the realm of artifice and appearance, it is precisely this fact that constitutes their strength. He valorizes the feminine art of seduction through cosmetics insofar as it highlights the fact that there is nothing beyond the realm of appearances. As he writes:

> Our entire morality condemns the construction of the female as a sex object by the facial and bodily arts. The female is no longer denounced by God's judgment, but by the dictates of modern ideology, for prostituting her femininity in consumer culture, and subjecting her body to the reproduction of capital . . . In opposition to all these pious discourses, we must again praise the sex object; for it bears, in the sophistication of appearances, something of a challenge to the naive order of the world and sex; and it, and it alone, escapes the realm of production . . . and returns to that of seduction (1990a, 92).

In his view, women have generally been more adept than men at the game of appearances, and rather than criticizing women who wear makeup to enhance their erotic appeal, as feminists have done, they should recognize that women's real strength lies in their mastery of this realm. To quote him once again:

> Now woman is but appearance. And it is the feminine as appearance that thwarts masculine depth. Instead of rising up against such "insulting" counsel, women would do well to let themselves be seduced by its truth, for here lies

the secret of their strength, which they are in the process of losing by erecting a contrary, feminine depth. (1990a, 10)

Like Thevoz, he argues for a cosmetic practice that is not afraid to openly acknowledge its "artificial" nature, believing it to be "truer" than makeup that seeks to disavow its fakeness by simulating nature. As he says of the heavy makeup worn by the seductress:

Artifice does not alienate the subject, but mysteriously alters her ... Women are aware of this transformation when, in front of their mirrors, they must erase themselves in order to apply their makeup, and when, by applying their makeup, they make themselves into a pure appearance denuded of meaning. How can one mistake this "exceeding of nature" for a vulgar camouflaging of the truth? Only falsehoods can alienate the truth, but makeup is not false, or else ... it is falser than falsehood and so recovers a kind of superior innocence or transparency. (1990a, 94)

Other post-structuralist theorists who share Baudrillard's valorization of the "feminine" art of dissimulation include Mary Doane and Catherine Constable. Mary Doane, in her essay "Film and the masquerade: Theorizing the female spectator" (1990 [1982]), offers a defense of femininity as masquerade, drawing on Joan Rivière's essay, "Womanliness as masquerade" (1986 [1929]). In this essay, Rivière discusses the way in which women, particularly those who pose a threat to male authority through their participation in male dominated professions, often don makeup and dress in an ultra-feminine manner in order to avert anxiety and retribution feared from men (1986, 39).In this self-conscious assumption of the "mask" of femininity, femininity is revealed to be a masquerade—that is, as something that is put on for effect—rather than an essentialist biological category. For Doane, this is emancipatory insofar as it highlights the culturally constructed and hence mutable nature of femininity. As she writes:

The masquerade, in flaunting femininity, holds it at a distance. Womanliness is a mask which can be worn or removed. The masquerade's resistance to patriarchal positioning would therefore lie in its denial of the production of femininity as closeness, as presence-to-itself, as, precisely, imagistic. (1990 [1982], 49)

It is precisely through its exaggeration of the traditional signs of femininity, such as the wearing of highly visible makeup, that the masquerade reveals the artificial nature of gender constructions. In Doane's terms (1990 [1982], 49), "the masquerade doubles representation; it is constituted by a hyperbolization of the accoutrements of femininity" in which the woman produces herself as an excess of femininity. Through this process, she achieves a critical distance from herself and demonstrates the ease with which such cladding can be adopted or removed. In its defamiliarization of the category of femininity, the masquerade poses a challenge to patriarchal ideology.

Constable (2000), like Doane, champions the notion of "femininity as masquerade" as being disruptive of essentialist gender categories. She supports a cosmetic practice that foregrounds its "mask-like" character, seeing it as possessing a greater truthfulness than that which seeks to hide its artifice and simulate nature. While the "fake" character of cosmetics was one of the prime causes for their dismissal by earlier critics, Constable agrees with Baudrillard that it is the open acknowledgement of this feature that constitutes their "truth" (2000, 197). Drawing on Nietzsche, she describes the mask as "truthful illusion," that is, as an illusion that does not disguise its illusory status. She is critical of earlier feminists for their attempt to find a "true" face behind the "false" mask of makeup on the grounds that this presupposes the existence of a "natural" face beyond patriarchal representation when the face is always already constituted within culture. The mask, in Constable's view, does not cover up something else—it is all that exists. Thus, rather than seeking a position outside of culture, which is an impossibility, one should endeavor to disrupt its codes from within. That is, one should work with the mask itself rather than seeking something beyond it. As she puts it:

> The Nietzschean analysis of the mask as truthful illusion can . . . be seen to open up a more sophisticated way of analyzing glamorous images of women in film texts. Once the mask is not viewed as . . . merely indicative of the absence of the truth, it becomes a construct that can be mobilized in a variety of ways. This means that the mask can be seen to generate a wide variety of possible meanings rather than simply and reductively indicating its status as 'untruth' or the 'untruth of truth.' Furthermore, the analysis of the mask as truthful clearly has important implications for feminism in that it radically destabilizes the definition of glamour as objectification. This creates a space for thinking about the radical potential of the power to hold the gaze and the ways in which that power might be instantiated by a range of female icons (2000, 199).

While the focus of Doane's and Constable's analyses is on the glamorous Hollywood film stars of the past, such as Marlene Dietrich, there are other recent examples where highly visible makeup has been deployed in a more self-consciously ironic manner. One such example is the "lipstick" lesbian. Emerging in the late 1980s and early 1990s, the lipstick lesbian sought to disrupt the traditional association of the signs of femininity, such as makeup and high heels, with heterosexual desire, by appropriating them for herself. By taking on the "look" of heterosexual women, the aim was to break the assumed link between feminine appearance and the desire for male attention. The hyperfemininity of the lipstick lesbian was seen to be transgressive insofar as it undermined the heterosexual man's ability to distinguish the object of his desire—the heterosexual woman—from the lesbian, and in its suggestion that women could be attractive for other women rather than to solicit male desire. As well as disrupting stereotypes of the lesbian as "butch," it was also seen as having the potential to make heterosexual women question how their own appearance was read and how they viewed other women.[6]

Another example of the self-reflexive use of makeup as mask is the punk aesthetic. In describing this, Elizabeth Wilson writes:

> . . . with punk, women transgress norms of feminine beauty; when a young woman shaves her head and draws red lines round her eyes, the very notion of make-up and hairstyles as an enhancement of what "nature" has provided is gone and the body is treated more radically than ever before as an aspect of performance. (1990a, 216)

However, even in the case of the deliberately ironic use of makeup, it is questionable as to how radical a cosmetic practice that foregrounds its mask-like character is in contemporary culture, particularly with the example of the lipstick lesbian. Is it really the case that highly visible makeup, by dint of its overt artificiality, is inherently transgressive? Can it be assumed that such a cosmetic practice will be interpreted as a revelation of the culturally constructed nature of gender categories?

### Appraisal of the Post-structuralist Critique of Cosmetics

In their celebration of the artifice of cosmetics, what the above theorists fail to realize is that a mode of cosmetic practice, which openly parades its artificial nature, is not necessarily liberatory. To take the Rivière example cited by Doane in support of her claim for the radical nature of femininity as masquerade, this could more plausibly be seen as an instance where the use of overt makeup serves conservative rather than emancipatory purposes. For in this case, rather than demonstrating the culturally constructed nature of femininity, as is claimed by Doane, its purpose was to defuse the potential threat posed by the professional woman to male power. Far from disrupting patriarchal structures, it served to maintain them by reassuring men of the "femininity" of their female colleague. While the woman herself may have been conscious of the "put on" nature of her femininity, it is doubtful that it would have been interpreted in this way by others.[7]

In the context of contemporary Western culture, where visible cosmetics have become far more socially acceptable than they once were, as evidenced for example by the admiration accorded heavily made-up celebrities such as Kylie Minogue, Joan Collins, Princess Di, and the Spice Girls, the supposedly transgressive nature of such a practice is again highly questionable.

As Kathy Peiss points out (1996), the ideal of a cosmetic practice that simulates nature has increasingly become outdated. While in the nineteenth and early twentieth centuries, the woman who wore highly visible cosmetics was regarded as a figure of deception and of dubious moral reputation, by the 1930s, makeup had become integral to self-expression and the belief that identity was a purchasable style. An important factor in the greater acceptability of visible cosmetics was their use by stage actresses and film stars who, unlike the actresses of previous eras, were accorded a revered status. Such figures as Adah Mencken and the British Blondes brought to the American stage a new kind of actress who blurred the line between the performance of a theatrical role and the performance of her "real self." As Peiss writes:

> . . . the early twentieth century discourse on cosmetics, as articulated by producers and consumers of these commodities, shifted the burden of female identity from an essential, interior self to one formed in the marking and coloring of the face. Make-up contributed to the constitution of women's identity, no longer to its falsification. (1996, 330)

The move toward more overtly visible cosmetics gathered pace from the 1950s onwards (Corson 1981, 533). Thus, for instance, the use of eye makeup became much more widespread, with the proliferation of eye shadows, eyebrow pencils, mascara, and eyeliners in an ever growing range of different shades. Similarly, sales of lipsticks escalated dramatically, and again, the range of colors expanded exponentially.

During the '60s, the inclusion of glitter and glint into lipsticks and eye makeup further contributed to a less naturalistic look in cosmetics. Helena Rubinstein, for example, in 1967, introduced lipstick in three preciousmetal tones—Bronze Rage, Silver Rage, and Gold Rage—plus three shades with a hint of glint—Pink Rage, Orange Rage, and Flame Rage (Corson 1981, 572). False eyelashes and even rhinestones worn on the eyebrows also became popular.

By the 1970s, adventurousness in makeup hit a new peak, with no apparent restrictions on either color or design. "In London," as Corson writes, "models were using a variation of poster paint around the eyes and watercolors on the face, toning it with grey and mauve. One model painted rainbows around her eyes, reddened her lashes, and streaked her hair with green. *Vogue* featured a dark haired model with eyebrows bleached to a pale yellow" (1981, 586), To keep up with the color expansion, Revlon made frosted lipsticks (*Luminesque Lipfrosts*) in seventeen shades, including Apple Polish, Snowsilver Rose, Copper Mine, Iceblue Pink, String of Pearls, Salmon Ice, Ginger Glaze, and Mirrored Mauve (Corson 1981, 588). Mary Quant launched a whole range of colored crayons for the face to be applied over foundation and blended with the fingers, including colors such as dark blue, yellow and lilac for the eyes, brown and pink for the lips, and brown, red, and white for the cheeks, while the London firm Biba introduced purple nail varnish, mahogany lipstick, black face gloss, prune watercolors, yellow foundation, and a paint box containing six shades of powder, two watercolors, ten shades of face gloss, five brushes, and an applicator (Corson 1981, 591).

This trend has continued apace in the last couple of decades. Thus, for instance, in 1986, the book *Quant on makeup* was released, which quite explicitly promoted a cosmetic practice that emphasized its mask-like character and its arbitrary relation to the body.[8] In this book, femininity was presented as being composed of a set of various masks behind which there was no essential self. There was, for example, the Romantic Face, the Brief Encounter Face, the Sporty Face, the Spring Face, the Flapper Face, and so on. In each case, the makeup contravened the natural contours of the face so that the face became the mask. Indicative of the conception of makeup as "art," rather than as simulating nature, was the fact that a number of Quant's faces drew their inspiration from art movements such as the Art Deco Face and the Pop Party Face—a trend which is becoming more and more common in the fashion industry.

Today, advertisements for Max Factor cosmetics continue to promote this idea of makeup as "art," in which the artificial nature of the cosmetics is highlighted rather than disguised, and fashion designers such as Diana and Jazz parade a "look" that unashamedly announces its "unnaturalness" with its inclusion of indigo blue lipstick and bright blue eyeliner for eyes and eyebrows, punctuated by studs and rhinestones, for example (see image on cover)[9]. Thus, although there are still examples of cosmetics advertisements that promote a "natural" look, the marketing of highly visible cosmetics is more evident than ever before. Take, for example, a recent cosmetics advertisement for Estée Lauder that promotes a "pure color eyeshadow." The copy reads: "Multi colors. Multi finishes. Major impact. Make a statement with one dramatic shade, lash to brow. Or play with 30 colors and three finishes, matte to high pearl."[10]

In this context, then, the assumption made by theorists such as Thevoz, Baudrillard, Doane, and Constable that a cosmetic practice that highlights its artificiality is necessarily radical, appears highly problematic. Such a practice had more of a subversive edge in the 1910s and '20s when visible cosmetics had not yet gained wide acceptance. Peiss (1996, 320) draws attention to the fact that, during this period, some women, as they entered the public arena, deliberately adopted an "artificial" facial appearance in order to signal their rejection of traditional notions of femininity as demure and chaste. The use of cosmetics symbolized a sensuousness and hedonism at odds with the ascetic Protestant work ethic that was dominant in this period. "Such a feminization of the public sphere," as Rita Felski points out (1995, 90), "was clearly threatening to bourgeois man, whose psychic and social identity had been formed through an ethos of self-restraint and a repudiation of womanly feelings."[11]

Even in this context. however, the radicality of "artificial" cosmetics was limited. As Peiss herself acknowledges, at the same time as they disturbed traditional notions of femininity, cosmetics were also used to represent woman as a kind of merchandise or objectified spectacle. In this period, when dating and courtship increasingly occurred in a market context, physical appearance assumed a greater importance for women than ever before. "The popular ideology of romantic love," writes Peiss (1996, 326), ". . . promulgated notions of personal magnetism and fascination that, for women, merged with physical beauty." Likewise, Felski argues that the relative empowerment of women at this time

> went hand in hand with the emergence of new constraining influences on gendered identity. Not only did consumer culture subject women to norms of eroticized femininity that encouraged constant practices of self-surveillance but it provided a conduit through which heterogeneous forms of desire could often be deflected and channeled into the imperative to buy ever more commodities. Even as it exemplified the erosion of certain radical constraints upon desiring femininity, the culture of modernity also brought with it new, if less visible networks of social control" (1995, 90).

Whereas the wearing of visible cosmetics during the 1910s and '20s was seen as a daring assertion of women's sexuality, now it has become one of the main ways in which the sale of cosmetics is promoted. A case in point is Revlon's *Fire and Ice* advertising campaign.[12] First launched in 1952 and still in operation today, this campaign targeted the "modern" woman who sought amorous adventure. In its first incarnation, it chose a dark-haired model in a dress of silver sequins with a scarlet wrap in front of a glittering background. Accompanying the advertisement was a questionnaire designed to ascertain whether the consumer was "ready for Fire and Ice," which included questions such as "Have you ever danced with your shoes off?" and "Do you close your eyes when you're kissed?" The Revlon advertisement appealed to women's desire for sensuous pleasure, playing on their sexual fantasies. A more recent version from 1997 still makes use of a *femme fatale* type model clad in a slinky scarlet evening gown with long flowing locks and full red lips. Confronting the viewer with her piercing gaze and dominating pose, the viewer is again issued with a challenge: "Play with Fire, Skate on Thin Ice," suggestive of a woman who is not afraid to live dangerously and explore her sexual fantasies.[13] The advertising of Lancôme cosmetics operates with a similar trope of female sexuality. One of its latest products is an eye mascara called *Fatale*. The advertisement for this product, which features a close up of a woman's face with a sultry expression and a hypnotic gaze, declares that this mascara "[s]culpts lashes for exceptional volume, a femme fatale look to die for."

In light of this, the embrace of visible cosmetics by the lipstick lesbian has unwittingly played into the hands of the fashion and advertising industries. As Danae Clark (1991) notes, there is a growing degree of affiliation between contemporary sexual subcultures and the marketing strategies of a consumer society increasingly oriented toward style, performance, and overt sexuality. She warns that while the emergence of a high degree of fashion-consciousness within certain lesbian subcultures is regarded by its participants as an assertion of sexual and political freedom, it also converges with the fashion industry's desire to target that segment of the lesbian population that is becoming increasingly visible and affluent—namely those who are predominantly white, childless, middle class, and educated.[14] Underlining how easily the lipstick lesbian's experimentation with fashion can degenerate into a depoliticized style of consumption, Clark writes:

> Because style is a cultural construction, it is easily appropriated, reconstructed and divested of its original political or subcultural signification. Style as resistance becomes commodifiable as chic when it leaves the political realm and enters the fashion world . . . Resistant trends . . . become restyled as high-priced fashions. (1991, 193)

Experimentation with appearance is often also less threatening than direct challenges to the economic and political structures responsible for gender inequalities, as Craik points out:

Fashion and make-up have become key players in the body techniques of femininity where the conventions of display and gesture vie with other more essential techniques, in a politics of the body that transposes socio-political forms into bodily icons, where cosmetic magic is relied on over political resolution. (1989, 20)

David Bell et al. (1994) also question the supposed radicality of the lipstick lesbian. While the intention of those who adopt this style may be transgressive, it is doubtful as to whether it is interpreted this way by others who may well be unaware of the sexual orientation of those who assume this hyper-feminine look. As Bell et al. write:

The irony of heterosexual hegemony is that its very dominance means that many heterosexuals are ignorant of the changing homosexual landscape and have the arrogance not to think twice about the identities of "straight-acting" individuals. If lipstick lesbians are to achieve anything more than their own transgressive pleasure in secretly sending up the "hets," it requires a wider articulation of hyperfemininity as a political strategy. (1994, 42)

The lipstick lesbian, as they argue, presents more of a challenge to the androgynous style promoted by feminism in the 1970s and '80s than it does to mainstream heterosexual society.

A further problem with the post-structuralist appraisal of cosmetics lies with its criticism of Western makeup for reinforcing a unified notion of self, and its advocacy of an alternative cosmetic practice that dissolves this unity. In criticizing Western cosmetic practice in this way, what theorists such as Thevoz and Lingis overlook is that, while Western makeup ostensibly aims to enhance the self, it actually undermines it to the extent that it is governed by standardized beauty ideals. As Marilyn Strathern (1979, 242) points out, Western beauty rituals are based on an impossible conundrum in which makeup enhances our facial features while simultaneously detracting from "our uniqueness." Though apparently highlighting the special qualities of the individual, makeup actually makes people appear more the same insofar as it employs stereotyped conventions that are laid out in the numerous beauty features in women's magazines and in beauty manuals.[15] Bartky elaborates on this point arguing that

. . . [i]n the language of fashion magazines and cosmetic ads, making-up is typically portrayed as an aesthetic activity in which a woman can express her individuality. In reality, while cosmetic styles change every decade or so, and while some variation in makeup is permitted depending on the occasion, making-up the face is, in fact, a highly stylized activity that gives little rein to self-expression. Painting the face is not like painting a picture; at best, it might be described as painting the same picture over and over again with minor variations. Little latitude is permitted in what is considered appropriate makeup for the office and for most social occasions; indeed, the woman who uses cosmetics in a genuinely novel and imaginative way is liable to be seen not as an artist but as an eccentric. (1988, 70)

From this point of view, what is wrong with traditional beauty rituals is not that they reinforce a unified sense of self, but on the contrary, that they depersonalize individuals while ostensibly enhancing their uniqueness.[16] As Finkelstein writes:

The idea of self may occupy a central place in our everyday practices, but this is no assurance of its substantiality. On the contrary, the new, fashioned self appears more like a concatenation of disparate elements than it does a coherent manner of living in and understanding the world. (1991, 171)

Thus, the celebration of the dissolution of the self into a myriad of impersonal guises or masks by theorists such as Thevoz, Baudrillard, et al. represents not a radical alternative to current cosmetic practice, but rather, a realization of its worst features. In advocating a cosmetic practice that highlights, rather than disguises, the decentering of the ego, what such theorists fail to realize is that, far from being liberatory, the dissolving of ego boundaries in contemporary society is symptomatic of the increasing difficulty that individuals have, in a globalized and commodified economy, to shape the course of their lives in a significant way.

As Pauline Johnson argues, the performative notion of self advocated by a number of post-structuralist theorists represents a retreat by individuals from the task of forging, for themselves, a meaningful way of life through an active engagement with the circumstances in which they find themselves. In its place is substituted an agnostic play with various guises in which individuals adopt a disengaged attitude toward all social conventions. Concerned only to dramatize the purely artificial character of all cultural constructions of identity, the postmodern self resiles from adjudicating between them as more or less adequate interpretations of the diverse and unequal situations in which individuals find themselves. To quote Johnson, implicit in the performative notion of self is the image of

...an individual endowed with the capacity and the will to turn her back on "the finite world of mundane existence." So totalizing is the dissatisfaction of this individual with the impositions of the world, it can be symbolized only

in a public display of her refusal to seek public recognition for her own interpretations of her specific needs, experiences and aspirations. (1994, 63)

The conception of the self as a myriad of changing masks turns life into
a work of art in a manner reminiscent of aesthetes such as Oscar Wilde and
Baudelaire from the nineteenth century, for whom the cultivation of style
became their guiding rationale. Aesthetic criteria come to supplant ethical
ones in the conduct of one's life so that the basis of decision-making is no
longer "Is this a good thing to do?" but "Does it look good?" This aestheticization of life, as Johnson (1994, 124) points out, "does not presuppose
the normativity of any particular kind of social subjectivity but encourages
only an attitude of playful experimentation toward all those culturally produced effects which represent both the limit and the potential of the modern self." She continues that "the standpoint of an 'aesthetics of existence'
obscures from us the fact that we do, constantly, make, at least implicit,
judgments on the character of a desirable and worthwhile life and that we
need to be as aware as possible of the character and the implications of the
criteria we use in making such judgments" (1994, 126).[17]

Finally, the various defenses of femininity as masquerade, which have
been offered by theorists such as Doane and Constable, are problematic
insofar as they efface the desperation of many women who undergo constant transmutations of their appearance. While some women may delight
in the possibilities opened up by a parodic play with body image, for many
others, the preoccupation with appearance becomes a compulsive obsession. Susan Bordo (1993b, 247) quotes the example of the plastic surgery
addict, for instance, who returns for operation after operation in perpetual
quest of the elusive goal of the "perfect" face and body.

Likewise, the anorexic, in submitting her body to extreme regimes of
dieting and exercise, does so out of a desperate sense to experience a feeling
of control that she otherwise lacks. As Anthony Giddens argues:

Anorexia should . . . be understood in terms of the plurality of options which
late modernity makes available—against the backdrop of the continuing
exclusion of women from full participation in the universe of social activity
which generates those options. Women today have the nominal opportunity
to allow a whole variety of possibilities and chances: yet, in a masculinist
culture, many of these avenues remain effectively foreclosed. (1991, 106)

While these may be extreme cases, they serve to highlight the fact that
women's preoccupation with their appearance is often symptomatic of
their relative disempowerment in other areas of their lives. In this light, the
constant experiments with appearance in which many women engage, far

from being a cause for celebration, can be seen, in many cases, as serving as a compensatory mechanism for the lack of options open to them in the other areas of social life.

What these cases also reveal is that the apparently greater freedom that women have in comparison with men to experiment with various modes of self-presentation is premised on a very restrictive conception of female identity as being constituted primarily in terms of physical appearance rather than in terms of women's actual achievements. As Celia Lury argues (1996, 152–55), women's play with appearances is always constrained by the fact that their identities are defined more in terms of how others (particularly men) view them than is the case with men, whose concept of self is less reliant on the opinions and expectations of others. Women's play with self-identity occurs under very different conditions than is the case with men. To quote Lury:

> Men and women do not have the same relation to the performance of their personal identities, in paid work, at home or in leisure activities . . . [W]omen, on the whole, do not have the same capacity to claim ownership of the identities they perform as men. This [is] . . . a consequence of the relative lack of control that women have in relation to the definition of their own self identity, which is typically set in relation to masculine demands and expectations . . . [W]omen's relationship to personal identity is therefore not only or not best described as reflexivity, strategic experimentation or the calculated decontrol that Featherstone describes as typical of the new middle classes, but as an enforced decontrol, in which women's claims to self-possession are often on shaky ground. (1996, 242)

In contrast to the reflexive engagement characteristic of middle class males, the feminine practice of masquerade,

> . . . is a relation of imitation, adopted as a strategy of resistance in situations in which women do not have the power directly to refuse the terms of their address by the male gaze, but may sidestep its force by turning it to their own ends. In this sense, it is not exclusionary but compensatory. It is also not a relation of self-possession but of displacement, in which the subjects and objects of consumer culture are confused. (Lury 1996, 148)

Women's apparent freedom to experiment with their appearance, and the supposedly liberating effects of this activity, then, need to be regarded with more circumspection than has been the case with many post-structuralist theorists. While in some circumstances, it may provide opportunities to challenge the strictures of traditional gender boundaries and expectations, in many cases, it serves only to reinforce the centrality of the

importance of physical appearance for women in our culture. This is something that Hilary Radner (1989) loses sight of in her defense of the pleasures of making up. Challenging the assumption that the primary purpose
of makeup is to attract male attention, Radner argues that it is the pleasures
gained from the process of making up which are often more significant
to women than the final result. However, though it may well be the case
that the making up process is pleasurable for some women, this practice
cannot be divorced from how the final result—the made-up face—will be
perceived by others. What needs to be recognized is that the decision as
to whether to wear makeup or not, and the type of maquillage adopted,
is not just a purely aesthetic one. Different modes of facial presentation
carry different social and cultural meanings, whether one acknowledges
this or not. It is important, then, to take cognizance of this rather than just
seeing the process of making up as a "game" where one experiments with
different looks.

## Conclusion

As has emerged from the above discussion, the determination of whether
a particular cosmetic practice is liberatory or not depends on the context
within which it occurs. In some circumstances, such as during the 1910s
and '20s, the adoption of an openly artificial look may well have been challenging to traditional notions of a demure and domesticated femininity,
just as it would be in Moslem countries today, where women are forbidden to wear makeup and even to show their faces in public, for fear of
inflaming the passions of men.[18] However, in the context of contemporary
Western societies, where such a look is actively promoted by the fashion
and advertising industries, it no longer carries the radical significance that
it once had. Contrary to the claims of recent proponents of the notion
of femininity as masquerade, one cannot assume that a cosmetic practice
that openly declares its artificiality is inherently subversive. Indeed, it could
be argued that in today's society, where the marketing of cosmetics has
become big business, the eschewal of makeup is the more radical stance,
not because it represents a supposedly more "natural" or "authentic" look,
but because it indicates a resistance to the total commodification of the
body. While the unmade up face is just as much a cultural construction as
one that is made up, the refusal of cosmetics poses a challenge to the idea
of the self as a marketable commodity. In the present circumstances, the
mask-like visage championed by a number of post-structuralist theorists
represents not an emancipatory vision, but on the contrary, is complicit
with the increasing commodification of the self in which individuals find

it more and more difficult to make sense of their lives except in terms of the goods they consume.

This increasing commodification of the body is evident not just in the proliferation of cosmetics products that are being more intensely marketed than ever before, but also in the growing popularity of cosmetic surgery, which is the focus of the following chapter. In this chapter, the more sympathetic attitude toward cosmetic surgery, evident in the writings of theorists such as Kathy Davis, as well as the use of it as a tool of subversion by the performance artist Orlan, is criticized for its failure to challenge this conversion of the body into a commodity that is forever in need of constant "improvement."

# 4

# Cosmetic Surgery and the Eclipse of Identity

Within feminist theory, cosmetic surgery has been viewed largely as an oppressive technology that colonizes women's bodies in a quite literal way, directly intervening in the body to mold it in accordance with the prevalent ideals of feminine beauty. Those women who undergo cosmetic surgery for purely aesthetic reasons are regarded as victims of a patriarchal ideology in which the self-esteem of women is primarily dependent on their physical appearance. The burgeoning in the use of cosmetic surgery by women is seen to be symptomatic of the permanent sense of dissatisfaction that most women have with their physical appearance as a result of being relentlessly bombarded with images of perfection by the mass media. As such, the predominant response to such a technology by feminists has been one of rejection.[1]

However, in a number of recent writings, there has been a discernible shift in attitude among some feminists toward the practice of cosmetic surgery. Kathy Davis, in her book *Reshaping the female body: The dilemma of cosmetic surgery* (1995), offers a guarded "defense" of the practice as a strategy that enables women to exercise a degree of control over their lives in circumstances where there are very few other opportunities for self-realization. Contrary to those feminists who condemn the practice of cosmetic surgery as irredeemably oppressive, Davis claims that those women who opt for cosmetic surgery are not blindly submitting to the dictates of patriarchal ideology, but are actively engaging with it, knowledgeable of its drawbacks as well as its benefits. While they are aware of its problematic aspects, they nevertheless see these as being outweighed by the enhanced sense of self-esteem and power that eventuates. She believes, then, that under certain circumstances, the decision to undergo cosmetic surgery can actually be an act of empowerment rather than of oppression.

Others go even further than Davis in advocating the redeployment of cosmetic surgery for feminist purposes. Both Kathryn Morgan (1991, 44–47) and Anne Balsamo (1996, 78–79), for instance, although highly critical of the mainstream employment of cosmetic surgery, consider the possibility of its use as a tool by women seeking to subvert the dominant patriarchal ideals of feminine beauty. According to Balsamo, while cosmetic surgery has been applied in such a way as to produce bodies that are very traditionally gendered, there is also the potential for it to be used "as a vehicle for staging cultural identities." In her view, the surgical refashioning of the body opens up the possibility of highlighting the artificial or culturally constructed nature of beauty, undermining neoromantic conceptions of the body as "natural." Although cosmetic surgery, as it is currently practiced, presents the surgically altered body as "natural" by disguising all traces of its intervention, Balsamo envisages a surgical practice that openly acknowledges, rather than disavows, its role in the reconstruction of the body.

Similarly, Morgan argues that cosmetic surgery can be employed in a subversive way by demonstrating the artifactual nature of the body. She proposes the use of cosmetic surgery to produce what the culture constitutes as "ugly" so as to destabilize the "beautiful" and expose its technologically and culturally constitutive origin and its political consequences. She also sees cosmetic surgery as having a liberatory potential insofar as it can be used to destabilize notions of the subject as fixed and immutable. Following Judith Butler (1990a), she regards the disruption of stable bodily contours as an important precondition for the undermining of repressive gender constructs. While such proposals may seem far-fetched, they have been realized in practice by the French performance artist Orlan, who has undergone a series of operations to modify her face and body in ways that contravene established norms of feminine beauty.

The concern of this chapter is to critically appraise this "rehabilitation" of cosmetic surgery within recent feminist theory and practice, and to question whether it does in fact provide a viable means for destabilizing patriarchal ideals of feminine appearance. I shall begin my discussion with a consideration of Davis's (1995) guarded "defense" of cosmetic surgery, before examining the more radical proposals of Balsamo, Morgan, and Orlan.

### Cosmetic Surgery is not an Act of Empowerment

Davis argues in her book, *Reshaping the female body: The dilemma of cosmetic surgery* (1995), that it is far too simplistic to regard cosmetic surgery as a pernicious horror inflicted by the medical system upon women's bodies, and to treat those women who undergo it as nothing more than misguided or deluded victims (1995, 56–67, 159–81). In her view, such a conception of the practice of cosmetic surgery is problematic for a number of reasons. Firstly, it fails to take into account women's active and lived relation to their bodies, treating them rather as disembodied robots who passively submit to the patriarchal ideals of feminine beauty in an unthinking and uncritical way. However, her interviews with women who elected to have cosmetic surgery revealed that they were reasonably well informed about the risks involved and were also aware of the moral dilemmas to which such a practice gives rise. Most were highly critical of the cult of feminine beauty within contemporary Western society and of the role that cosmetic surgery had played in reinforcing such an emphasis on physical attractiveness, and saw themselves as undergoing cosmetic surgery not in order to conform with patriarchal ideals of beauty, but rather to refashion their bodies so that they were more in accord with how they saw themselves. Those women who elected to have cosmetic surgery did so because they felt a profound sense of estrangement from their bodies, and for them, the operation enabled the achievement of a more embodied sense of self where the psychic and physical self were more integrated with each other. According to Davis:

> Cosmetic surgery was presented as part of a woman's struggle to feel at home in her body—a subject with a body rather than just a body. Paradoxically, cosmetic surgery enabled these women to become embodied subjects rather than objectified bodies. (1995, 161)

On the whole, the women who underwent cosmetic surgery were skeptical of it as a general remedy for women's dissatisfaction with their appearance, regarding it rather as the lesser of two evils in their own particular circumstances where other options for dealing with their problems were not available.

Davis goes on to point out that these women did not undergo such surgery at the behest of their husbands or their male surgeons. Indeed, in most cases, the women's decision to have cosmetic surgery met with strong opposition from their male partners. Far from being an act of submission to outside pressures, then, the women saw their decision to have cosmetic surgery as an act of self assertion—as one of the few occasions when they exercised some control over their own destiny. Many reported experiencing a feeling of elation after undergoing such surgery—an experience radically at odds with the conception of cosmetic surgery recipients as passive victims. Even when the results of the surgery did not come up to expectations and, in some cases, produced serious side effects and disfigurement, the women did not express regret at their decision to have cosmetic surgery, but saw it as an act of self-empowerment undertaken with knowledge of the risks involved.

Davis argues, then, that rather than seeing these women as blindly following the dictates of patriarchal ideology, it would be more accurate to regard them as actively negotiating with the practice of cosmetic surgery in ways that are beneficial to them. Against the total condemnation of cosmetic surgery by other feminists, she contends that the practice has legitimacy under certain circumstances. As she writes:

> Cosmetic surgery is not about beauty but about identity. For a woman who feels trapped in a body which does not fit her sense of who she is, cosmetic surgery becomes a way to renegotiate identity through her body. Cosmetic surgery is about exercising power under conditions which are not of one's own making. In a context of limited possibilities for action, cosmetic surgery can be a way for an individual woman to give shape to her life by reshaping her body. (1995, 163)

Rather than adopting an attitude of moralistic condemnation toward recipients of cosmetic surgery, then, Davis urges a reevaluation of the practice of cosmetic surgery that is more respectful of the reasons given by the recipients themselves for undertaking it. In her view, cosmetic surgery should not be seen simply as yet another instance of the subjugation of women, but as a more contradictory phenomenon than this—both "symptom of oppression and act of empowerment all in one," as she puts it (1997, 169).

Davis's qualified defense of the practice of cosmetic surgery, however, is problematic in a number of respects. First, in her concern to grant at least a partial legitimacy to cosmetic surgery as a means of overcoming women's problems of identity, Davis tends to lose sight of the fact that such a "solution" leaves unaddressed the causes for women's dissatisfaction with their bodies in the first place. Although Davis is not unaware of the social structures of gender inequality that give rise to women's sense of estrangement from their bodies, these are bracketed out of consideration in her analysis of the reasons why women undergo cosmetic surgery. Consequently, she individualizes the problem of women's self-identity, focusing on how particular women cope with this dilemma within the parameters of the given system, without considering how the parameters themselves can be challenged or undermined. Indeed, she tends to be dismissive of strategies that seek to challenge the systemic and structural causes for women's experience of disembodiment as being utopian and for failing to address, in any immediate way, the problems confronted by individual women. As she writes:

> While feminist visions of a surgery-free future are comforting, they can also close our eyes to the less dramatic instances of resistance, compliance, or discursive penetration which are part and parcel of any social practice. Our alternatives become nothing more than utopian—leaving us little to say of relevance concerning women's lived relationships to their bodies. (1995, 180)

Against this however, it needs to be pointed out that while cosmetic surgery may appear to offer some sort of short term "remedy" for women's problems of self-estrangement, it can actually hinder the progress toward any lasting solutions by deflecting attention away from the underlying causes for women's dissatisfaction with their bodies. As long as women can find solace in surgical solutions to their problems of self-identity, there is the very real possibility that they will be less inclined to tackle the social and cultural factors responsible for the experience of alienation from their bodies in the first place. The limitation of cosmetic surgery is that it offers a technological solution to a social problem. As Sander Gilman points out (1999, 19), with the development of cosmetic surgery at the end of the nineteenth century, the Enlightenment belief in the ability of individuals to transform themselves, which had originally been articulated as a social and political task, came to be redefined in biological and medical terms. This had the effect of shifting the locus of change from the transformation of social structures to transforming the body itself. To quote him:

> The political "unhappiness" of class and poverty, which led to the storming of the Bastille, came to be experienced as the "unhappiness" found within the body . . . In the former, it was revolutionary change that would cure the body; in the latter, it was the cure of the individual by which the unhappiness would be resolved. (1999, 19)

From this perspective, then, far from providing instances of piecemeal resistance to the dominant ideology, the practice of cosmetic surgery can actually be seen to reinforce it by providing women with a solution to their problems of self-identity that does not necessitate any challenge to the social and political parameters of the beauty system itself. Thus, while individual women themselves may not see their resort to cosmetic surgery as a submission to patriarchal ideology, but as an act of self-empowerment, it is a conservative practice insofar as it leaves unaddressed the underlying causes for women's poor body image. The decision to have cosmetic surgery is an individualistic "solution" that does nothing to tackle the broader social problem as to why women should feel dissatisfaction with their appearance in the first place. While one can understand how, under certain circumstances, plastic surgery may appear to be the most rational solution for a woman, it is important not to lose sight of the limitations of this solution and also to consider ways of tackling the social and cultural factors that are responsible for women's estrangement from their bodies, rather than treating them as unchangeable givens.

In pointing to the ultimately conservative effects of cosmetic surgery, the intention is not to be dismissive of the reasons why individual women undergo it. Rather, it is to make clear the disjuncture between the individual and social consequences of such a practice. What may be a solution for a particular individual in certain circumstances may not be so at the social level insofar as it still leaves intact the structures of gender inequality that present women with few options but to have plastic surgery. The criticism of the practice of cosmetic surgery, then, is not directed at the individual women who undergo it, but rather at the social and cultural system that engenders in women a state of permanent dissatisfaction with their physical appearance. The point is not to morally condemn those women who choose to have cosmetic surgery, but rather, to expose the inequities of a society that necessitates such a practice in the first place.

The source of Davis' neglect of the structural/systemic factors underlying women's dissatisfaction with their bodies is her concern to give due weight to the agency of individuals—a concern that she shares with a number of recent post-structuralist theorists who have found unsatisfactory the previous models of power as monolithic and oppressive. However, while she is correct to point out the inadequacies of a conception of human subjects as totally passive victims, she tends to overstate the degree to which individuals are able to actively intervene in the system and construct meanings that are counter to those of the dominant ideology. While individuals certainly do reinterpret cultural practices in ways that are at odds with their dominant meanings, the fact remains that some meanings continue to have predominance over others because not everyone has equal access to, or control over, the resources needed to realize their interpretations.

Susan Bordo makes a similar point in the introduction to her book *Unbearable weight* (1993c). Critical of the tendency by a number of recent post-structuralist theorists to overemphasize the degree of creative agency exercised by individuals, she points out that while it is too simplistic to regard individuals as cultural "dopes," nevertheless, there are still significant constraints on the degree to which individuals can subvert the dominant ideology. As she writes:

. . . the fact that cultural resistance is continual does not mean it is on an equal footing with forms that are culturally entrenched . . . [I]n contemporary Western constructions of beauty there are dominant, strongly "normalizing" (racial and gendered) forms to contend with. To struggle effectively against the coerciveness of those forms it is first necessary to recognize that they *have* dominance, and not to efface such recognition through a facile and abstract celebration of "heterogeneity," "difference," "subversive reading," and so forth. (1993c, 29)

She continues:

Some forms of postmodern feminism . . . are distressingly at one with the culture in celebrating the creative agency of individuals and denying systemic pattern. It seems to me that feminist theory has taken a very strange turn indeed when plastic surgery can be described, as it has been by Kathy Davis, as "*first and foremost* . . . about taking one's life into one's own hands." (1993c, 31)[2]

Thus, while women who undergo cosmetic surgery may seek to have changes that do not conform with patriarchally and racially defined norms of feminine beauty, nevertheless, the degree of control which they have in defining the nature of the facial or bodily modifications they desire is limited. Ultimately, they are in the hands of surgeons whose training has been based on a white, Western ideal of beauty. As Balsamo points out (1996, 58–63), even though they work with faces that are individually distinct, surgeons use the codified measurements that are laid out in their training manuals as guidelines for determining treatment goals, and they attempt to bring the distinctive face in alignment with artistic ideals of symmetry and proportion. These ideals, as Balsamo shows, are based on a white, Western aesthetic of feminine beauty. In this regard, she cites (1996, 59) the volume *Proportions of the aesthetic face* published by the American Academy of Facial Plastic and Reconstructive Surgery and widely used by plastic surgeons. The purpose of this book, according to its authors, is to document, objectively, the guidelines for facial symmetry and proportion. In actual fact, however, the "ideal face" depicted throughout this book is of a white woman whose face is perfectly symmetrical in line and profile. The only illustration of a male face is contained in the glossary. Furthermore, while the authors acknowledge that "bone structure is different in all racial identities" and that "surgeons must acknowledge that racial qualities are appreciated differently in various cultures," in the end, they argue that "the facial form [should be] able to confer harmony and aesthetic appeal regardless of race"(quoted in Balsamo 1996, 60). Implicitly, then, the authors suggest that non-white faces can be evaluated in terms of ideal proportions determined by the measurement of Caucasian faces. This point is reinforced by Gilman, who, in his book *Making the body beautiful* (1999), develops, at great length, the racial assumptions behind Western ideals of beauty. It is not surprising, then, that it is rare for cosmetic operations to depart radically from white, Western ideals of feminine beauty, even where the patients themselves desire an appearance that does not conform with such conventions.[3]

Morgan points out the paradox of women's use of cosmetic surgery as a means for escaping the constraints of the "given." As she argues (1991, 38), while women seek to gain independence through this process, the net result is an increasing dependence on male assessment and on the services of all those experts they initially bought to render them independent. Likewise, Gilman observes: "When we turn to the physician, we demonstrate our autonomy and abdicate it simultaneously" (1999, 334).

Another paradox arising out of the practice of cosmetic surgery that Davis overlooks is that while it ostensibly enables women to feel an embodied sense of self, at the same time, it is premised on the very alienation from the body it is supposed to overcome. For what makes possible such a practice in the first place is a separation of the mind from the body, in which the body is seen as something that can be manipulated at will. As Balsamo (1996, 56–57) points out, plastic surgery is premised on a distanciation from the body, which is viewed as an object that can be fragmented into isolated parts, capable of transformation. Davis herself acknowledges this in her account of particular case studies where the recipients compartmentalized their bodies into segments, some of which they regarded as satisfactory, while others were in need of remedy. As she writes, with each woman she interviewed:

> hated body parts were dissociated from the rest of her body as objects—"those things," "mountains of fat," "sagging knockers." They were described as pieces of flesh which had been imposed upon her—inanimate and yet acting against her. They became something which each woman wanted to, literally, cut out of her life. (1995, 74)

And the sense of self-embodiment apparently achieved after cosmetic surgery was also subsequently qualified by some recipients, for example, Diana, of whom Davis writes: "Cosmetic surgery may have transformed her into 'just a nice face,' but she retains the emptiness and sense that she will never be 'completely one' with herself." (1995, 108). It appears, then, that the notion of cosmetic surgery as an act of self-empowerment needs to be treated with more circumspection than does Davis, despite all the qualifications she makes to her defense of this practice.

While Davis provides a guarded support for the practice of cosmetic surgery as a way for individual women to alleviate the suffering endured from their experience of alienation from their bodies, she stops short of advocating its redeployment as a political weapon to challenge dominant ideals of feminine beauty.[4] However, a number of feminists have, in recent times, canvassed such a possibility, including Morgan, Balsamo, and Orlan. It is to these that I now turn.

## Cosmetic Surgery is not a Tool of Political Critique

Though Morgan and Balsamo are highly critical of cosmetic surgery as it is currently practiced, they see a potential for its redeployment for feminist purposes. For both Morgan and Balsamo, the revolutionary potential of cosmetic surgery lies in its capacity to highlight the fact that the body is a cultural construct rather than a natural entity that is fixed and immutable. They see it as a tool that can be used to deconstruct the notion of a unified and unchanging self, replacing it with a performative conception of the self as being in a constant state of transmutation.

Influential for both Morgan and Balsamo have been the ideas of Donna Haraway, particularly her championing of the figure of the cyborg—half human and half machine—as the new model for a liberated conception of the self (1991, 149–81). Traditionally, in Western culture, the body has been regarded as a biological given whose organic integrity is inviolable. It has been associated with the innate, the immutable, or the God-given. However, the advent of new biotechnologies such as IVF, genetic engineering, and cosmetic surgery, which provide us with an unprecedented capacity to intervene in and refashion our bodies, has radically changed our conception of the body as an unalterable fact of nature. Rather than being seen as determined by nature, the body is increasingly coming to be regarded as a social and cultural construct, capable of radical transformation. Against those who seek to preserve the integrity of the body from the encroachment of technology, Haraway argues that such interventions can be productive of fruitful new conjunctions that disrupt the rigid oppositions between human/machine, nature/culture, male/female, and so on—dualisms that have been "systemic to the logics and practices of domination of women, people of color, nature, workers and animals" (1991, 177). While there are some feminists who decry the technological intervention into women's bodies,[5] Haraway believes that women should embrace these technologies and learn to use them for their own ends. If they refuse to do so, they run the risk of reiterating the traditional patriarchal binarism that aligns women with nature and opposes them to culture. As Haraway writes:

> From one perspective, a cyborg world is about the final appropriation of women's bodies in a masculinist orgy of war. From another, a cyborg world might be about lived social and bodily realities in which people are not afraid of their joint kinship with animals and machines, not afraid of permanently partial identities and contradictory standpoints. The political struggle is to see from both perspectives at once because each reveals both dominations and possibilities unimaginable from the other vantage point. (1991, 154)

In opposition to the idea of organic holism, then, Haraway argues for a notion of the body as a hybrid entity whose contours are permeable and constantly mutating as it enters into new linkages with the nonorganic. Rather than treating technology as the enemy, it should be regarded as an aspect of our embodiment. She sees such a conception as underpinning a new understanding of the self as fluid and open to constant change, rather than as fixed and immutable, and goes so far as to entertain the possibility of a post-gender world where gender distinctions will be transcended.[6]

Balsamo and Morgan both believe that cosmetic surgery could be one means by which the organic unity of the subject could be destabilized. Already in contemporary society, as Balsamo notes, the body and technology are conjoined in a literal sense—machines assume organic functions and the body is materially redesigned through the application of newly developed technologies. She writes that:

> the "natural" body has been dramatically refashioned through the application of new technologies of corporeality. By the end of the 1980s the idea of the merger of the biological with the technological has infiltrated the imagination of Western culture where the "technological human" has become a familiar figuration of the subject of postmodernity ... This merger relies on a reconceptualization of the human body as a "techno-body," a boundary figure belonging simultaneously to at least two previously incompatible systems of meaning—the "organic/natural" and the "technological/cultural." (1996, 5)

With the widespread technological refashioning of the "natural" human body, she suggests that there is a potential for gender boundaries to be blurred or reconstructed. While she acknowledges that, at present, biotechnologies such as cosmetic surgery are employed to vigilantly guard gender boundaries and to present them as natural rather than as culturally constructed, nevertheless, they offer the possibility for radically redefining who we are (1996, 78–79). Instead of effacing its intervention in the reconstruction of bodies, as it currently does in an endeavor to create a "natural" look, cosmetic surgery could be employed in such a way as to emphasize the artificiality of beauty and to disrupt the present cultural coding of the female body as "natural." It offers the possibility of new forms of embodiment that defy the natural givenness of physical gender identity. The surgically refashioned face and body need not necessarily be the mark of an oppressed subjectivity, according to Balsamo, but could be used as a way of challenging patriarchal conceptions of beauty as exemplified by the anti-aesthetic of cyberpunk (where body piercing and other forms of prosthesis are employed) and grunge fashion.

Like Balsamo, Morgan considers that cosmetic surgery could be a useful means for unmasking the dominant ideals of feminine beauty as cultural artifacts rather than as natural properties of the female body (1991, 44–47). She sees it as having the potential to destabilize the naturalized categories of masculinity and femininity by highlighting the fact that gender is a performance rather than a biologically determined given. Employed in a parodic way, the techniques and procedures of cosmetic surgery could be used to magnify the role that technology plays in the construction of femininity. One way in which this could be achieved would be through the use of surgical techniques to produce what is normally perceived as ugly (for example, sagging breasts and wrinkles), thereby upsetting the cultural constraints upon women to comply with the norms of beauty and throwing into question what is traditionally considered as beautiful. In reply to the objection that having oneself surgically "disfigured" as a political statement seems rather extreme, Morgan argues that:

> . . . if we cringe from contemplating this alternative, this may, in fact, testify . . . to the hold that the beauty imperative has on our imagination and our bodies. If we recoil from this lived alteration of the contours of our bodies and regard it as "mutilation," then so, too, ought we to shirk from contemplation of the cosmetic surgeons who de-skin and alter the contours of women's bodies so that we become more and more like athletic or emaciated (depending on what's in vogue) mannequins with large breasts in the shop windows of modern patriarchal culture. In what sense are these not equivalent mutilations? (1991, 46)

As more women gain knowledge of the techniques of cosmetic surgery, so it becomes possible for them to usurp men's control over these technologies and undermine the power dynamic that makes women dependent on male expertise.

While Balsamo and Morgan have canvassed the possibility of the feminist redeployment of cosmetic surgery in theory, the French performance artist Orlan has sought to do this in practice. In 1990, she embarked on a project, *The ultimate masterpiece: The reincarnation of Saint Orlan*, involving a number of cosmetic surgery operations designed to transform her face in ways which destabilized male-defined notions of idealized female beauty.[7] In an endeavor to convert plastic surgery from an instrument of domination into a means for reinventing her own body and creating her own self-portrait, Orlan produced her own blueprints for the surgeons to follow.[8] She also refused a general anesthetic so that she could stage-manage the actual operations themselves, transforming what is normally a medical procedure carried out behind closed doors into a theatrical performance that featured the reading of psychoanalytic and literary texts, interactive communication with an often international audience via fax and live satellite telecast, music, dance, and outlandish costumes often designed by famous couturiers.

Her blueprints consisted of computer composites, combining her own facial features with those derived from five famous Renaissance and post-Renaissance images of women: the chin of Sandro Botticelli's Venus in *The birth of Venus* (ca. 1480); the nose of François Gérard's Psyche in *First kiss of Eros and Psyche* (ca. 1820); the eyes of Diana in the anonymous school-of-Fontainebleau sculpture *Diane chasseresse*; the mouth of Gustav Moreau's Europa in *Abduction of Europa* (ca. 1876), and the brow of Leonardo Da Vinci's Mona Lisa (ca. 1503–1505). These representations were chosen not just for their physical attributes, but also for their mythological or historical importance. Thus, Diana was selected because she was a goddess who refused to submit to the gods and men; Europa, because she looked to another continent and embraced an unknown future; the Mona Lisa, because of her androgyny; Venus, because of her association with fertility and creativity; and Psyche, because of her desire for love and spiritual beauty.

While these five works have traditionally been regarded as icons of feminine beauty, Orlan sought to transform their original significance through her appropriation and recontextualization of their facial features. Thus, whereas mainstream cosmetic surgery tends to erase the distinctive features of individual faces in an endeavor to make them conform to a prototypical image of the ideal, Orlan's composite face emphasizes what is unique and idiosyncratic to each face. By combining distinctive elements from each face, she seeks to disturb the notion of the perfected, the fixed, and the standardized, producing a result that is at odds with conventional ideals of beauty. As Moss puts it:

> [Orlan] (re)imagines an image under different circumstances from the artist's originary impulse and reappropriates and dissimulates constituents of

the ideal face feature by feature. She undoes her face in an alternate visioning and estranges, makes strange, each master's imagistic accretions—memory, fantasy, fetish, story and the rhetoric of woman and beauty. (1999, 1–2)

Her disruption of conventional ideals of feminine beauty is even more apparent in her seventh, eighth, and ninth operations—known as her *Omnipresence* series—which involved implants into the upper cheeks and the sides of the forehead to give the impression of budding horns.

An important element of Orlan's project is the making public of the actual operation and its immediate aftermath. As well as televising the surgical process itself, Orlan has produced a series of postoperative photographs revealing all the bruising and wounds from her surgery and also a series of "reliquaries," consisting in "souvenirs" from her operations, such as blood-stained gauze, bits of her bone, and fat removed through liposuction. Her purpose here is to confront all those taboos that surround the violation of the integrity of the body in Western culture.

What is particularly disturbing about her work is that the main site of this violation is her face, which, in Western culture, is taken as emblematic of our self-identity. As Deleuze and Guattari argue (1988, 167–91), only in the West do we operate with a conception of the face as the seat and expression of a unique subjectivity. In our culture, the face is deemed the most precious characteristic of human identity and therefore enjoys a privileged status to the rest of the body. It becomes the site of signification and subjectification. To quote them:

> *Certain assemblages of power (pouvoir) require the production of a face*, others do not. If we consider primitive societies, we see that there is very little that operates through the face: their semiotic is nonsignifying, nonsubjective, essentially collective, polyvocal and corporeal, playing on very diverse forms and substances. (1988, 175; emphasis in original)

They continue: "Paintings, tattoos, or marks on the skin embrace the multidimensionality of bodies. Even masks ensure the head's belonging to the body, rather than making it a face" (1988, 176). By contrast, in the West, bodies are subject to what they call a process of "faciality," whereby they are constituted as unique subjects endowed with psychic interiority through the imposition of the concept of the "face" upon them.

The operations undergone by Orlan, where the face is literally peeled away from the body, radically unsettles this identification of self with body, as Hirschhorn argues (1996, 128–29). This is reinforced by the text that she reads at the beginning of each of her operations—an excerpt from Eugénie Lemoine-Luccioni's book *The Dress*:

Skin is deceiving . . . in life, one only has one's skin . . . there is a bad exchange in human relations because one never is what one has . . . I have the skin of a crocodile but I am a poodle, the skin of a black person but I am a white, the skin of a woman, but I am a man; I never have the skin of what I am. There is no exception to the rule because I am never what I have. (quoted in Moss 1999, 10)

Furthermore, the constant reconfigurations of her face to incorporate a pastiche of elements derived from other faces highlight the socially constructed nature of the face and undermine any notion of identity as stable and unified.[9] As Moss comments *a propos* of Orlan's practice:

Through her transgression of facial boundaries Orlan confronts each spectator's understandings and psychical investment in the face as a site for the imaging of self. Orlan's disruptive practice negates the social inscriptions of power that accept or deny the non-conforming face. Her face is a nonface, multiple, shifting and hybridized from different visions and competing imaginings. (1999, 3)

The totally artificial and fluctuating nature of Orlan's face is reinforced by her adoption of the name "Orlan," which, as Moss points out, "evokes allusions to the synthetic—the material Orlon, to masquerade—the French cosmetic brand Orlane, to gender fluidity—the Maid of Orléans (Joan of Arc) and Virginia Woolf's Orlando, and the malleability of gold—*d'or*" (1999, 2). Far from denoting a particular identity, her name connotes its infinite malleability.

As with Balsamo and Morgan, then, the employment of cosmetic surgery by Orlan is seen by many interpreters of her work as subversive insofar as it "denaturalizes" the body and destabilizes the fixity of identity. Such a defense of cosmetic surgery presents a marked contrast to that of Davis. Whereas for Davis, the value of cosmetic surgery lay in its ability to enable some women to achieve a sense of self-embodiment, for Balsamo, Morgan, and Orlan, its value lies precisely in its disarticulation of the unity of the self.[10] The question still remains, however, as to whether such a redeployment of cosmetic surgery is as emancipatory as it purports to be.

One of the main problems arising out of the conceptualization of cosmetic surgery as an instrument enabling "the staging of cultural identities" is that it fails to give due weight to the materiality of the body. This is somewhat of a paradox, given the criticisms that postmodern theorists have made of mainstream philosophy and social theory for its neglect of the body. While the body has moved center stage in postmodern theory, its existence as a natural/physical entity has been all but totally erased by its conceptualization as a social and cultural construct. In rejecting the notion of the body as a biological given determined by nature, postmodern theorists have swung to the other extreme in regarding the body as almost infinitely malleable. Thus, for instance, Orlan goes so far as to say that with the advent of technologies such as cosmetic surgery, which enable the radical refashioning of the body, the natural body is obsolete (Hirschhorn 1996, 120). She describes her body as "a sack or costume to be shed" (Rose 1993, 86), declaring that her work "is a struggle against: the innate, the inexorable, the programmed, Nature, DNA (which is our direct rival as . . . artists of representation) and God!" (cited in Goodall, 152). In doing so, she uncritically accepts the idea that technology can transcend all bodily limits and tends to downplay the fact that we are defined by certain inescapable biological constraints and processes such as ageing and dying, which, although culturally mediated, cannot be eliminated. While Jane Goodall (1999, 152) defends Orlan's declaration of the obsolescence of the body as a radical undermining of the patriarchal identification of women with their bodies, I would argue that it partakes of another patriarchal myth— namely, that of the transcendence of nature through technology.[11]

Likewise, Haraway's notion of the cyborg, in which the natural and the artificial are indistinguishable, encourages a view of the transcendence of the natural body by technology. As she writes: "Any objects or persons can be reasonably thought of in terms of disassembly and reassembly; no 'natural' architectures constrain system design"(1991, 162). Contrary to Balsamo's claim (1996, 33–4) that Haraway's notion of the cyborg reasserts the materiality of the body insofar as it does not treat the body simply as a discursive construct, as some versions of postmodern theory do, I would argue that it perpetuates the dematerialization of the body in its treatment of it as not subject to any material limits. Rather than overcoming the dichotomy between the human and the machine, what has occurred with the figure of the cyborg is a reduction of the human to the machine, where the body is treated as a nonsentient thing that can be manipulated in the same way as inorganic matter. Symptomatic of this is the replacement of organic by mechanical metaphors in post-structuralist discussions of the body, particularly in the writings of Deleuze and Guattari, who speak of bodies as "assemblages," "desiring machines," and so on. As they write:

> There is no such thing as either man or nature now, only a process that produces the one within the other and couples the machines together. Producing-machines, desiring-machines everywhere, schizophrenic machines, all of species life: the self and the non-self, outside and inside, no longer have any meaning whatsoever. (1983, 2)

Thus, despite the great preoccupation with the body in postmodern theory, there is, at the same time, a profound estrangement from it. This is made quite explicit by Orlan, who regards her body as mere matter that can be manipulated at will. As she herself says, she has always felt distanced from her body, and consequently is somewhat indifferent to the image produced by her body (Hirschhorn 1996, 122). In contrast to Julie Clarke (1999, 188), who interprets Orlan's operations as a reinstatement of the corporeality of the body in an age where the electronic imaging and coding of the body has all but displaced "real" flesh and blood, I see Orlan's work as perpetuating this postmodern alienation from the body. For, while Orlan alters her body in a directly physical way (rather than simply through virtual manipulation), her practice in no way undermines the belief that the body is almost infinitely malleable.[12]

Likewise, Balsamo, though apparently more circumspect than Orlan as regards the technological transcendence of the "natural" body (1996, 2, 77–78), proposes that cosmetic surgery be thought of as "fashion surgery" (78)—a suggestion that implies that it is just as easy to surgically transform the body as it is to change the clothes one wears.

As a result of this neglect of the materiality of the body, there is a tendency to discount the risks and suffering involved in the practice of cosmetic surgery. As Morgan comments, for instance, "although submitting to the procedures of cosmetic surgery involves pain, risks, undesirable side effects . . . it is also fairly clear that, most of the time, the pain and risks are relatively short-term" (1991, 50).[13] Similarly, Orlan is quite nonchalant about the pain she endures, claiming that the audience experiences more pain watching her undergoing surgery than she does.[14] In contrast to the Christian conception of pain as the path to redemption, Orlan adamantly rejects suffering as a necessary part of her project, declaring "Carnal Art judges the famous 'you will give birth in pain' to be anachronistic and ridiculous [. . .] now we have epidurals and multiple anesthetics as well as analgesics, long live morphine! Down with pain!" (quoted in Ince 2000, 63). However, as Davis points out, Orlan's denial of pain

> is belied by the post-operative faces of the artist—proceeding from swollen and discolored to, several months later, pale and scarred. Whether a woman has her wrinkles smoothed out surgically or carved in has little effect on the pain she feels during the surgery. Such models, therefore, presuppose a nonsentient female body—a body which feels no pain. (1997, 178)

While O'Bryan (2005, 21) defends Orlan's disavowal of the pain and discomfort involved in undergoing such procedures on the grounds that it enables her to distance herself from accusations of masochism and associations with the figure of the sick/mentally ill woman, at the same time, it perpetuates the disassociation of the mind from the body characteristic of Western patriarchal ideology in which the body is subordinated to the intellect.

Another problem arising from the promotion of the surgical restyling of the body by Balsamo, Morgan, and Orlan is that they overlook the extent to which this is complicit with the commodification of the body within contemporary consumer culture. As Finkelstein has pointed out, with the increasing availability of surgical and other techniques for altering appearance, the body has come to be treated as a commodity in constant need of upgrading. In her words: "It is as if the body were a utensil—a car, a refrigerator, a house—which can be continuously upgraded and modified in accord with new interests and greater resources" (1991, 87). Similarly, Bordo points out the resemblance between the post-structuralist conception of the body as infinitely transformable and the cosmetic surgery industry's advocacy of the idea of the body as something that can be sculpted at will. Writes Bordo:

> Gradually and surely, a technology that was first aimed at the replacement of malfunctioning parts has generated an industry and an ideology fuelled by fantasies of rearranging, transforming and correcting; an ideology of limitless improvement and change, defying the historicity, the mortality and indeed, the very materiality of the body. In place of that materiality we now have what I will call the cultural plastic . . . This disdain for material limits and the concomitant intoxication with freedom, changes and self determination are enacted not only on the level of the contemporary technology of the body but in a wide range of contexts including much contemporary discourse on the body, both popular and academic (1993b, 245–46).

Contrary to Goodall's claim (1999, 157) that the idea that one can remake one's own body according to one's own will is deeply heretical, such a belief is now widely endorsed and promoted by the fashion industry. While once it posed a fundamental challenge to Christianity's belief in the inviolability of the divinely created human form, such a conviction no longer has wide currency.

Even though Balsamo, Morgan, and Orlan envisage a different mode of self transformation from that currently practiced by the cosmetic surgery industry, nevertheless, they still remain within the same terms insofar as they treat the body as an instrument to be continuously modified through technological means. Indeed, Morgan suggests the establishment of "Beautiful Body Boutique" franchises to advertise and market a range of services and products for body modification that parody those currently offered by the cosmetic surgery industry, such as freeze-dried fat cells for fat implantation and transplant (1991, 46). While her intention here is subversive of the mainstream cosmetic industry, nevertheless, it still participates in the commodification of the body. Likewise, the convergence between Orlan's attitude toward the body and that of the fashion industry is indicated by the fact that her practices of body modification are starting to be emulated by some in the fashion world.[15] In the process, she, like Morgan and Balsamo, leaves unexamined the question as to why it is that the body has become so significant to our self-identity and the consequences of this.

One of the paradoxes to emerge from the growing investment in the body as a source of identity is that as our capacity to refashion our bodies increases with the advances in surgical procedures and other biotechnologies, our sense of who we are becomes less and less certain. As Shilling writes:

> We now have the means to exert an unprecedented degree of control over our bodies, yet we are also living in an age which has thrown into doubt our certainty of what our bodies are and how we should control them. The basic dynamic working behind this paradox can be traced to the reflexivity of modernity: the greater the knowledge we gain about our bodies and how to control them, the more is our certainty undermined about what the body is and how it should be controlled. (1994, 183)

While science has provided us with the means by which to transform our bodies, it is unable to give us any guidance as to how these means should be employed. To quote Shilling once again: "As science facilitates greater degrees of intervention into the body, it destabilizes our knowledge of what bodies are and runs ahead of our ability to make moral judgments about how far science should be allowed to reconstruct the body" (1994, 4).

That is why, for many, the surgical refashioning of their bodies becomes a never-ending process as they engage in an impossible search for an identity that is forever beyond reach. Even in the case of a more critically engaged application of cosmetic surgery, as advocated by Orlan and others, the process becomes an infinite one of deconstruction of existing cultural identities without any clearly defined alternatives. Orlan has already undergone many operations and has left open the option of undergoing more in the future.[16] The continual transformations of identity promoted by Orlan, Balsamo, and Morgan can be seen as a way of avoiding the issue of who we are rather than as offering a solution to it. Their refusal to embody any positioned subjectivity at all simply defers, indefinitely, the necessity of confronting the question of self-definition. As such, it can be seen as a symptom of, rather than an answer to, the dilemmas to which biotechnologies such as cosmetic surgery have given rise. While a conception of the self as fixed and unchanging is stultifying, the advocacy of a constantly mutating self is equally as disabling, for without a sense of continuity, it is impossible to act effectively in the world.[17] As Flax points out, the decentering of the subject is not wholly positive, since it can lead to a dislocation from history and a sense of political and intellectual vertigo and paralysis (1991, 218–19). As a therapist, Flax is very much aware of the terror that literally decentered selves endure as well as the limitations of the fragmented and heterogeneous subjectivity of post-structuralist theory as a principle for human action.

The irony of the postmodern attack on subjectivity is that it is occurring during an era when women are beginning to experience themselves as "self-determining" subjects for the first time. As Nancy Hartsock writes:

> Why is it, just at the moment in Western history when previously silenced populations have begun to speak for themselves and on behalf of their subjectivities, that the concept of the subject and the possibility of discovering/creating a liberating "truth" become suspect? . . . The postmodern suspicion of the subject effectively prohibits the exploration of (a repressed) subjectivity by and on behalf of women. (quoted in Di Stefano,1990, 75)

Paradoxically, it is only those who already have a secure sense of their own identity who can afford to entertain the possibility of its dissolution. In the words of Nancy Miller (quoted in Modleski 1991, 22), "only those who have it can play with not having it." As Morgan herself acknowledges:

> Women who are increasingly immobilized bodily through physical weakness, passivity, withdrawal and domestic sequestration in situations of hysteria, agoraphobia and anorexia cannot possibly engage in radical gender performatives of an active public sort or in other acts by which the feminist subject is robustly constituted. In contrast, healthy women who have a feminist understanding of cosmetic surgery are in a situation to deploy cosmetic surgery in the name of its feminist potential for parody and protest. (1991, 45)

This point is reiterated by Davis, who comments that

> the visions presented by both Orlan and Morgan involve women who are clearly unaffected by the crippling constraints of femininity. They are not dissatisfied with their appearance as most women are; nor indeed do they seem to care what happens to their bodies at all. (1997, 179)

Finally, a further problem with the advocacy of cosmetic surgery as a political weapon is that it effaces the social inequalities within which such body transformations occur. As Bordo (1993b, 247) points out, the surgical refashioning of the body is not an option that is equally available to everyone, but requires considerable economic means. As such, it is a rather "aristocratic" form of revolt that can only be engaged in by those who have the freedom from economic need to be able to contemplate and realize different forms of embodiment. Likewise, Felski argues that economic privilege serves as a fundamental prerequisite for the self-conscious experimentation with different forms of body appearance. As she writes, "The cultivation of a self consciously aestheticized personality presumes a certain distance from the realm of immediate need; not everyone can live life as a work of art" (1995, 201).

## Conclusion

As can be seen from the above then, the "rehabilitation" of cosmetic surgery within recent feminist theory and practice is somewhat problematic. In the case of Davis, her guarded "defense" of cosmetic surgery leaves unchallenged the social structures of inequality responsible for women's dissatisfaction with their bodies. Her conception of cosmetic surgery as a "solution" in certain circumstances is premised on the acceptance of the parameters of the given system as unalterable. While Balsamo, Morgan, and Orlan envisage a more radical deployment of cosmetic surgery, which contravenes the conventions governing its present application, nevertheless, they, too, continue to operate within its terms in certain respects. In particular, they share with the cosmetic surgery industry its instrumentalization of the body as mere matter that is almost infinitely transformable.

In making such criticisms, I am not speaking from the point of view of a nostalgic Romanticism that argues for the preservation of the organic integrity of the body, but simply sounding a cautionary note for the uncritical embracement of the cyborg as an emblem of a liberated humanity. While the notion of the organic/natural body "untainted" by technology is untenable, so, too, is the notion of the cyborg where the distinction between the human and the machine is effaced. At the same time as the simple refusal of all technological interventions in the body is both unrealistic and undesirable, one should not lose sight of the dangers in placing too much faith in the surgical refashioning of the body.

In the following chapter, the attention shifts to another form of body modification—namely, that of tattooing. Tattooing, because of its nature as a permanent inscription on the body, has become an increasingly popular means by which to secure one's identity in contrast to the ephemeral nature of fashion. However, despite its apparent opposition to fashion, tattoos are becoming more and more prevalent in the advertising of men's fashion items. It is the paradoxical nature of the tattoo's relation to fashion in postmodern culture that is the subject of the ensuing chapter.

# 5

# Body Art and Men's Fashion

Tattoos, because of their relatively permanent nature, have been seen by many as being antithetical to fashion, whose governing imperative is that of constant change. As David Curry (1993, 80) states, tattooing "can never be a true fashion . . . because tattoos cannot be put on and left off by the season." Ted Polhemus concurs, arguing that "any permanent body decoration like a tattoo is as anti-fashion as it is possible to get— literally making change difficult if not impossible" (1994, 13). Reinforcing the apparent antithesis of tattoos to fashion is the fact that while they were once employed primarily to indicate one's affiliation with a group, they are now more frequently adopted as individualized statements of personal identity. Thus, rather than relying on standardized "flash" motifs, today's tattoo wearers are more likely to choose customized designs as a way of signaling their "uniqueness" and lack of conformity. As Susan Benson writes, ". . . central to a lot of contemporary tattoo and piercing talk is the idea of *individuation*; of the tattoo . . . as a 'declaration of me-ness'" (2000, 245).

However, despite their apparent incompatibility with fashion, tattoos are increasingly being promoted and used as fashion items, as evidenced by their growing prevalence in advertising and on the catwalk, as well as their adoption by celebrities in the sports and entertainment worlds. Jean-Paul Gaultier, Calvin Klein, Hugo Boss, and Katherine Hamnett, for instance, have all recently utilized tattoos in their advertising campaigns.

In this chapter, I am interested in exploring this paradox, focusing in particular on men's fashion. It will be argued that despite their physically permanent nature, tattoos have become popular icons in men's fashion advertising because of their semiotic multivalency. Whereas once, tattoos were employed as unambiguous affirmations of masculinity, now their relation to traditional notions of masculinity has become much more equivocal as increasing numbers of women and nonheterosexual men have adopted them. It is this very ambiguity that has led to their growing popularity within the men's fashion industry, which seeks symbols that can be made to mean different things to different segments of the male market.

As a number of writers have noted (for example, Wernick 1991, 48–66; Mort 1996, 45–73, and Nixon 1992), one of the main features of the promotion of men's fashion since the 1980s has been the expansion and diversification of its markets. Whereas in the past, the main target was the white, middle class, heterosexual male, the market has increasingly recognized the economic potential of gay male consumers, who tend to have a greater interest in style and fashion than their heterosexual counterparts. In order to appeal to this new market without alienating heterosexual men, one of the strategies adopted by the men's fashion industry has been the creation of advertisements where signs are employed as relatively "free-floating" signifiers, capable of being invested with a multiplicity of meanings depending on the audience who is responding to them. Tattoos are particularly appropriate in this regard since their meanings over the last few decades have been very labile, ranging from affirmations of traditional masculinity, on the one hand (particularly within the military and biker communities), to subversions of it, on the other (as has occurred within gay subcultures, for instance).

Furthermore, the function of tattoos as markers of individual identity, far from militating against their use by the fashion industry, is the very feature that commends them to it. Precisely because tattooing is seen as a badge of individual identity, it lends itself to advertisers who seek to market mass-produced, standardized items under the guise of them being individual statements. This is enhanced by the tattoo's association with the transgressive, which carries suggestions of rebellion and nonconformity—of standing out from the crowd.

## Tattoos as Anti-fashion?

It is commonly assumed that the permanent nature of tattoos makes them inherently antithetical to fashion, which is premised on the idea of constant change. Unlike other items of body adornment, such as clothing or jewelry, which can be easily adopted or removed without permanently altering the body in accordance with the whims of fashion, tattoos mark the body in an indelible and largely irreversible way. As a number of commentators have argued, such as Lentini (1999), Benson (2000) and Salecl (2001), it is this feature that accounts for their growing popularity in contemporary culture, where individuals are increasingly uncertain about their sense of who they are. In an era where the logic of fashion has permeated most aspects of social life, individuals are confronted by a constantly transforming world where "everything solid melts into air."[1] In response to this experience of constantly shifting parameters, individuals seek to stabilize their sense of identity through fixing it permanently on their skin. The physical body is taken as the ground on which individuals can anchor their identity in an otherwise completely mutable world where nothing remains the same. As Lentini argues, for instance:

> . . . many members of Generation X face social insecurity in respect to future job prospects, financial security and domestic situations. They have witnessed rapid transformations of world events challenging or de-centering fixed notions of identity such as class and nation . . . Given this scenario, tattooing becomes an act of exerting self-control in an atmosphere where the individual has very little control over his or her daily affairs. (1999, 45)

In contrast to the evanescence of fashion, the material physicality of the body seems to provide a more solid grounding for identity. It appears to be more "real" and substantial than the ephemeral world of advertising images. As Renate Salecl writes:

> Making a cut in the body does not mean that the subject is merely playing with his or her identity; by irreversibly marking the body, the subject also protests against the ideology that makes everything changeable. The body thus appears as the ultimate point of the subject's identity. Since the subject does not want simply to play with the imaginary simulacra presented by the dominant fashion ideologies, he or she tries to find in the body the site of the real. (2001, 32)

Arthur and Marilouise Kroker suggest that this desire to ground one's identity in the apparent certainty of the physical body is heightened by the growing sense of its obsolescence as more and more of the body's functions are replaced by technological devices. As they write:

> In technological society, the body has achieved a purely *rhetorical* existence: its reality is that of refuse expelled as surplus-matter, no longer necessary for the autonomous functioning of the technoscape . . . [W]hy the concern over the body today if not to emphasize the fact that the (natural) body in the postmodern condition has *already* disappeared, and what we experience as the body is only a fantastic simulacra of body rhetorics? (1987, 22)

This sense of the obsolescence of the body has become particularly acute in recent times with the growing ubiquity of the virtual world of cyberspace. In such a context, invocations of the corporeality of the body represent a last ditch attempt to rescue the "real" from its absorption into the realm of simulation, where the original referents have fallen out of sight. Baudrillard, in a somewhat hyperbolic fashion, writes of the body in postmodern culture as having been assimilated to the general condition of "hyperreality," which represents a panic attempt to simulate a sense of the "real" in the wake of its disappearance (1984, 128). However, this desperate assertion of the real is but a hollow façade, masking the decorporealization of the body in contemporary cyberculture.

Baudrillard describes the body in cyberspace as a "pure screen." Plugged into an infinitely expanding network of communications, the body loses a sense of itself as bounded and separate. No longer a site for the interiority of the individual, the body becomes "a switching centre for all the networks of influence" (1984, 133). This "culture of telecontact" is based on a contradiction, for at the same time as it places everyone in instant contact with everyone else, it alienates people from themselves and from each other, since this contact is achieved not through direct physical interaction but by remote control through digitized information networks. As a consequence of this disembodied form of communication, or "skinless propinquity," as Steven Connor refers to it, we lose a sense of our presence in the here and now, and our capacity for direct sensory experience is undermined. Connor describes such a world in the following manner:

> [E]verything can touch everything else at a distance . . . Everything takes place at a remove from the actual individual sensorium, but this general mediation produces an overwhelming sense of the intolerable immediacy and proximity of everything, in which nothing is in fact sufficiently apart from the self or from any other thing to allow it either to exist, in the Heideggerian sense of "standing clear" or "standing out" against some background, or to communicate, in the sense of a making common of what is separate. (2001, 42)

In a similar manner to the Krokers and Baudrillard, Connor interprets our contemporary obsession with the corporeality of the body as a desperate bid to recapture the "real" and reactivate the senses. He sees the current-day practices of body marking, such as tattooing, branding, and piercing, as attempts to reassert the "reality" of the body as a living presence. Whereas in the Christian tradition, the mortification of the body was intended as a means of transcending the physical body in order to attain spiritual redemption, contemporary forms of mortification, on the contrary, aim to "transfix the body in its presence." "Disfiguring the skin is a way of keeping it visible," as Connor puts it (2001, 50).

However, such attempts to permanently fix one's identity in one's body
are ultimately doomed to failure since the meaning of tattoos is changeable. While the tattoo itself, as a material signifier, may remain unchanged,
that which it signifies is mutable, and the various meanings that may be
attributed to it are not within the control of the wearer, but are subject to
the changing vagaries of fashion. This is particularly the case in contemporary culture, where tattoos have become multivalent symbols invested with
a plethora of different meanings. As we shall see in the following section,
the meanings of tattoos during the twentieth century ranged from affirmations of patriarchal masculinity, on the one hand, to subversions of it, on
the other, and it is this feature that has recommended itself to advertisers who seek semiotically rich symbols that are capable of appealing to a
diverse market.

Similarly, the individualistic nature of contemporary tattoos, far from
being a hindrance to their incorporation by the fashion industry, has facili-
tated it. Whereas once they were employed primarily as symbols of membership of a particular subcultural group, such as bikers, a military unit, or
prison gang, now tattoos are seen as highly personalized signs of identity.
This is emphasized by Benson, who argues that, today, ". . . tattooing and
piercing are read explicitly as statements of the self. No longer is tattooing
accounted for as drunken impulse or forcible subjection: tattoos, like pierc-
ings, are to be 'chosen' after much deliberation" (2000, 244). The individual
who acquires tattoos today sees this most frequently as an act of self-assertion rather than as a capitulation to the trends of fashion or as indicative of
conformity with a social group. Indicative of this is the fact that, increasingly, individuals prefer customized designs to the standardized "flash"
tattoos that were once the norm. Nowadays, individuals tend to be much
more particular about the design and placement of tattoos, often choosing
or creating designs that best complement the particular features of their
own bodies. In this way, the tattoo acts as "a statement of ownership over
the flesh" (quoted in Benson 2000, 251). Benson goes on to suggest that it
is within this framework that the significance of the pain undergone in the
acquisition of tattoos needs to be understood. As she writes: "Pain, like the
tattoo itself, is something that cannot be appropriated; it is yours alone; it
stands outside the system of signification and exchange that threatens the
autonomy of the self. And . . . like the flesh itself, pain is conceived of as
really 'real'; it speaks its own truth" (2000, 151).[2]

However, while the highly personal nature of many contemporary
tattoos may seem to militate against the idea of them as fashion items, I
would argue that it is precisely because of their role as badges of individual
identity that they have become popular in the promotion of men's fashion
and body care products, where advertisers seek to market mass produced,

standardized items under the guise of them being individual statements. One of the main marketing strategies today consists in persuading the customer that in buying a particular product, they are not conforming to a fashion trend but are exercising their individual discernment and judgment. This is aided and abetted by the construction of a distinctive company identity through the use of eye-catching logos. It is not so much the product, but the brand name, that is marketed, the aim being for consumers to associate themselves with the distinctiveness of a particular brand. As Naomi Klein points out (1999, 3–8, 15–26), since the 1980s, the primary focus of corporations has shifted from the marketing of products to the construction of an image or brand name, where what is being sold is an "identity" or "lifestyle" rather than a product. Instead of manufacturing commodities that they then advertise, many of the best known companies today buy products and "brand" them. As the market has become flooded with uniform, mass-produced goods that are virtually indistinguishable from each other, competitive branding has become the primary means by which to establish product differentiation. In this context, logos have come to assume an increasingly important role in serving to counteract the anonymity of mass-produced goods.

In the marketing of men's fashion, an increasing number of advertisements seek to associate the tattoo as a mark of the uniqueness of the wearer, with the distinctiveness of the company logo. The suggestion here is that the brand name, like the tattoo, serves to distinguish the individual as someone who stands out from the crowd. The association of tattoos with the transgressive and the marginalized also enhances their role as individual statements. Previously associated with stigmatized groups, they are seen by those who wear them as badges of nonconformity. In this way, tattoos, like company logos, become a useful means for the marketing of "individuality" in an era where clothing is becoming increasingly homogenized through the globalization of production.

Tattoos then, because of their semiotic multivalency and their role as signifiers of individual identity, have become popular icons in the promotion of men's fashion, despite their apparently anti-fashion status. Before examining the ways in which they have been employed in advertisements for men's fashion in recent times, the various meanings with which they have been invested will be discussed, focusing in particular on the changing conceptions of masculinity that they have come to represent.

## Tattoos and Masculinity

Until the 1970s, the wearing of tattoos was a predominantly masculine practice, especially prevalent amongst the military, prisoner, and biker communities. There were significant differences between the tattoos acquired by each of these groups. In particular, military tattoos were often patriotic in nature, whereas biker tattoos tended to express more antisocial themes (DeMello 2000, 68). In each case, however, their adoption of tattoos was predicated on an affirmation of a patriarchal conception of masculinity as an antidote to the disempowerment they experienced in many aspects of their lives.

As a number of commentators have argued (for example, Lentini 1999, 40–41 and Benson 2000, 238–39), tattoos have frequently been acquired by individuals in situations where they no longer feel in control of their own destinies. These could be situations where they are subject to intense regimes of discipline and surveillance, such as the military and amongst prisoners, or situations of economic and social insecurity, as experienced by disaffected working class youth. In these circumstances, self-chosen tattoos have been seen as a defiant assertion of control over at least one aspect of one's life—namely, one's body. As American tattoo artist and tattoo historian Don Ed Hardy states:

> A tattoo is a confirmation. You put it on yourself with the knowledge that *this body is yours to have and enjoy while you're there . . .* That's why tattooing is such a big thing in prison; it's an expression of freedom—one of the *only* expressions of freedom there. They can lock you down, control everything *but* "I've got my mind, I can tattoo my body—alter it as an act of *personal* will." (quoted in Lentini 1999, 41)

Tattooing, however, as it has occurred within the military, prisoner, and biker communities, has not just been an act of self-assertion, but more specifically, an affirmation of a particular type of masculine identity. As Coe et al. (1993, 199) have argued, tattoos, in these contexts, serve to forge and reinforce male alliances, identifying individuals as members of a cohesive group with a shared set of values. This is indicated by the fact that males who are members of the same group tend to acquire similar, if not identical, design motifs that utilize similar colors and are placed on the same parts of the body. Not only does the tattoo serve as a badge of male identity, but the process of its acquisition also contributes to the sense of male bonding, as men in the same platoon or gang often acquire their tattoos at the same time. The actual process of tattooing thus serves as a type of initiation rite in which individual men have the sense of being inducted into a particular community. The stoic endurance of pain is integral to this experience, being seen as a proof of one's manhood.

Paradoxically, while the acquisition of tattoos has been seen as an affront to bourgeois values, challenging Judeo-Christian beliefs about the sanctity of the body and its inviolability, at the same time, the sense of masculinity that such tattoos affirm is a very conservative one based on patriarchal values. As Lentini points out:

> Although those who become tattooed certainly challenge the conventional Eurocentric constructions of the body, demonstrating individual agency and self-empowerment, many of the spirits and images associated with tattoos are reactionary, reflecting violence and misogyny . . . Tattoos often reflect and reinforce the values of the hegemonic form of masculinity . . . that values courage, inner direction, aggression, autonomy, technological mastery, group solidarity, adventure, physical and mental toughness, the subordination of women to men and the dominance of heterosexuality over homosexuality. (1999, 41–42)

This is clearly revealed in the type of iconography that predominates in tattoos among the biker, prisoner, and military groups. As DeMello (2000, 62) has observed, the most popular designs amongst servicemen have been patriotic motifs such as flags or eagles, naval emblems such as ships and anchors, sea themes (mermaids, dolphins, and whales), and "girlie tattoos" (nude women, hula dancers, harem girls, sailor girls, cowgirls, and geisha girls). The girls have traditionally been patterned after stereotypical female icons, such as the Gibson girl or the Mandarin girl from the movie *The world of Suzie Wong*. Many of these tattoos have been of barebreasted women or women in sexually subservient poses. Classic biker tattoos include Harley Davidson motorcycles and emblems, V-twin engines, club logos, marijuana leaves, swastikas, knives, skulls, aggressive animals, and antisocial slogans.

This symbolism of a virile masculinity has been reinforced by the style and placement of these tattoos. Usually, they use bold lines and are placed in prominent areas of the body where they can be easily seen. In the military, the primary areas to get tattooed have been the back, chest (and/or stomach), biceps, forearms (front, side, and back), and both sides of the calves, while the more obscure areas such as the thighs, sides of the body, and under the arms are usually ignored.[3] Biker tattoos are also located on easily visible areas of the body, again highlighting their role as a public assertion of machismo. They tend to be on the arms, back, chest, hands, and head (very few on the legs, as bikers wear jeans when riding).

The conception of masculinity represented by these tattoos is not only one that subjugates the feminine and the nonheterosexual, but also expunges the "primitive." The practice of wearing tattoos in the West first became popular among sailors during the eighteenth and nineteenth centuries as a result of their contact with tribal cultures, where tattooing was a long-standing tradition. During the first half of the twentieth century, however, tribal motifs all but disappeared from Western tattoos (DeMello 2000, 49–53). In their place, a new "homegrown" tradition of iconography, using mostly symbols derived from Western culture, developed amongst the largely working class clientele who adopted them. During this time, the only non-European cultures to exercise a significant influence over Western tattooing were the Chinese and Japanese traditions, with motifs such as dragons, Chinese characters, and tigers being the most popular. Thus, what could have been a symbol of cultural exchange ended up as a sign of a defensive and bounded masculinity that disavowed its connections with "savage" cultures.

Therefore, while tattooing in the first half of the twentieth century grew out of a need to reclaim a sense of control over one's destiny in situations where one's life was subjected to external disciplinary regimes, such as those of the military or prison, it was based on a patriarchal conception of masculinity that suppressed the feminine, the nonheterosexual, and the primitive. At the same time as tattoos provided a protective carapace for those who embraced them, it also sealed them off from communication with other marginalized or disempowered groups.

During the 1970s, however, this hypermasculine symbolism of tattoos began to be undermined with the growing popularity of tattoos amongst gay men, women, and the middle class. Within the context of gay subcultures, tattoos, far from affirming phallocentric masculinity, were deployed as a means of subverting it. More particularly, tattoos were adopted as a way of liberating "repressed" urges and reclaiming the sensual self. Because of their physical, visceral nature, they were seen as a vehicle for heightening awareness of the sensuality of the body's surfaces. As such, they represented an antidote to Western culture's longstanding subordination of the body to the mind. While women in Western culture have traditionally been associated with the body, masculine identity has been predicated on a privileging of the rational and cognitive over the sensuous. This has served to perpetuate the subordination of women to men, and it has also resulted in the alienation of men from their physical selves.

This bodily estrangement has been reinforced by male dress since the beginning of the nineteenth century, as Polhemus points out (2000, 44). While female dress has frequently been designed to enhance and draw attention to the physicality of the body, male dress, on the contrary, has tended to deemphasize the body, as exemplified by the advent of the suit, which has been the white, middle class man's "uniform" for the last two hundred years. With the adoption of the suit, there was a shift away from the sensual display of the body, which had characterized the more decorative modes of male dress of earlier centuries, to a more austere and functional sartorial code which signaled rationality and sobriety—a process that dress theorist Flugel termed the "great masculine renunciation" (1930, 110). In emphasizing the cerebral over the bodily, this mode of dress was taken to be indicative of the assumed superiority of the masculine over the feminine and the primitive. With reference to the latter, Polhemus writes: "European colonists literally embodied their presumed superiority in their 'rational' and 'civilized' appearance, in contrast to the 'primitive' body decorations and 'absurd' frivolity of non-European male styles" (2000, 46). In the process, however, men lost touch with the physicality of their own bodies. The resurgence of popularity in tattoos during the 1970s, then, can be seen as a desire by men to reconnect with their physical selves (Polhemus 2000, 47–48).

In contrast with the earlier tattoo tradition associated with the military, prisoners, and biker groups, which disavowed any connection with the "primitive," many of the new tattoo enthusiasts saw themselves as "modern primitives" (a term coined by Fakir Musafar—one of the movement's spokespersons), embracing an art form that had been regarded in the West as a sign of barbarism. This identification with the "primitive" manifested itself in the adoption of tribal motifs from tattoo traditions such as those of Samoa, Hawaii, Native America, and Micronesia. For adherents of this movement, "primitive" cultures offered an alternative to the repressions of modern Western civilization insofar as they were seen to celebrate, rather than suppress, the sensuality of the body. Fakir Musafar writes:

> [W]e're all suffering from a lot of repressive conditioning which you can't undo in just a *mental* way. Most of it has to do with sexuality and sexual energy. If you get into any practices of other cultures you're bound to be involved with a lot of sexuality in other states and guises that aren't even acknowledged as being in *existence* in this culture. (quoted in Vale and Juno 1989, 14–15)

Such ideas have received more theoretical elaboration in the writings of Alphonso Lingis (1983). He interprets "primitive" body markings as a challenge to Oedipal sexuality that is centered on the phallus. In his view, practices such as tattooing and scarification, which involve directly cutting into or perforating the skin, serve to eroticize the whole surface of the body. As such, these marks are not signs of an interior self or identity, but rather, serve to decenter the ego through the release of polymorphous, libidinous urges. Rather than conveying meaning, he sees such marks as points of "sensation," which operate primarily on a visceral rather than a semiotic level. He writes:

> These cicatrizations, these scarifications, these perforations, these incisions on the bodies of savages—they hurt. The eye that looks at them does not read them; it winces, it senses the pain. They are points of high tension; intensities zigzag across them, releasing themselves, dying away orgasmically, into a tingling pleasure . . . The savage inscription is a working over the skin, all surface effects. This cutting in orifices and raising tumescences does not . . . multiply ever more subtle signs for the psychic depth where personal intentions would be being formed; it extends the erotogenic surface. (1983, 33–34)

This is underlined by the abstract, geometric nature of "primitive" body markings. In contrast with the representational or pictographic nature of Western and Japanese tattooing, tribal markings, according to Lingis, are not a system of signs pointing to a meaning beyond themselves that needs to be deciphered, but rather, operate directly on the senses, circumventing interpretation. To quote him, once more:

> What we have, then, is a spacing, a distributive system of marks. They form not representations and not signifying chains, but figures, figures of intensive points, whose law of systematic distribution is lateral and immanent, horizontal and not transverse. (1983, 37)

Such a view of tattooing was seen as liberating for gay men, who embraced it as a visible way of expressing non-normative desires, pleasures, and identities. Taking a practice that had hitherto been used to exclude them, they now converted it into a public display of the body's potential for a non-phallocentric eroticism. In contrast with the earlier tattoo tradition, which had sought to fix masculine identity, they destabilized it, highlighting the indeterminacy of a sexuality that refused to be regulated by Oedipal imperatives. As Victoria Pitts explains:

> Queer marks,[4] by inscribing the body with badges celebrating prohibited pleasures and identities, underscore the contested nature of embodiment and sexuality. They fix queer identity literally onto the body as a gesture of rebellion. This fixing . . . does not necessarily reiterate an essentialism in which same-sex desire is naturalized as an innate identity, nor does it aim for

an assimilated gay identity. Rather, queer body marks rely on provocation as a symbolic resource for *un*fixing *heteronormative* inscription. (2003, 114)

At the same time, however, as this practice of body marking sought to subvert patriarchal constructions of masculinity through a reconnection with tribal cultures, its conception of the "primitive" was still very much inflected by Western colonialist assumptions. In particular, insofar as it viewed "primitive" body markings as being a manifestation of a pre-Oedipal eroticism, unfettered by the constraints of "civilization," it reproduced imperialist assumptions about the hypersexuality of "primitive" peoples. Although it regarded this in a positive, rather than a negative, light, it failed to recognize that this is very much a Western projection onto tribal cultures, which bears little relation to how native peoples themselves conceive of the practices of body marking. Most commonly, indigenous peoples regard practices of body marking primarily as a means of induction of members of the tribal group into socially prescribed roles rather than as a vehicle for eroticizing the body.[5] Thus, while a gesture was made toward the acknowledgement of the value of tribal cultures, to a large extent, it was based on a Eurocentric construction of the "primitive."[6] Pitts makes a similar point when she writes that:

> The modern primitivism underlying these narratives [of queer body marking] reflects a strategy of traitorous identity, but also echoes historical imaginaries of the eroticized "primitive" body that are the legacy of colonial racism. Primitivism and homosexuality were linked by colonialism long before the rise of modern primitivism. Both were used in essentialist and contagion discourses that affirmed the white, European, heterosexual body as pure and healthy, while imagining the bodies of Others as physically and morally polluted by hypersexuality. Ironically this new use of symbols of Otherness by white queers affirms not only gay body modifiers' outsiderness, but also the privileged position they *share* with all white Westerners and the dominant culture to define cultural and ethnic others. (2003, 116–17)

As emerges clearly from the above discussion, then, the relationship of tattoos to masculinity in Western culture during the course of the twentieth century has been a highly contested affair. On the one hand, they have been used as emblems of a patriarchal, heterosexual masculinity that has been predicated on a disavowal of the feminine and the primitive, while, on the other hand, they have become an expression of a non-phallocentric sexuality which seeks to reconnect with the primitive, though in a rather problematic way. It is this very contradictory nature of the relationship between tattoos and masculinity that accounts for their growing prevalence within advertisements for men's fashion and body care products.

## Tattoos in Men's Fashion Advertising

Before the 1980s, tattoos were rarely included in advertising images, and when they were, they served primarily as symbols of a "red-blooded" masculinity. A good example of this is the Marlboro cigarette ad campaign of the 1950s. In 1956, the makers of Marlboro, whose sales were beginning to sag, set out to change the image of the typical Marlboro smoker. Up until this time, Marlboro cigarettes had been known as a woman's cigarette. In an effort to create a new market amongst men, the revamped advertising campaign featured virile men sporting military tattoos on the backs of their hands. As Bordo describes it: "The original Marlboro Man . . . was bulky . . . and tattooed, his body a kind of visual masculine hyperbole . . . The Marlboro Man's excessive virility, in the eyes of the heterosexual admen who created him, was precisely what assured the consumer of his heterosexuality" (1999a, 153–54). Significantly, the tattoos that were chosen for the advertisements were derived from the military, whose patriotic themes made them more socially acceptable than those worn by prisoners and bikers. The advertisements immediately struck a chord, prompting hundreds of letters from men wanting to pose as a Marlboro Man.

Since the beginning of the 1980s, tattoos in advertisements, particularly those promoting men's fashion and body care products, have not only become more prevalent, but also increasingly complex in their meanings, inviting a range of possible interpretations depending on the nature of the viewing audience. While there are still advertisements that use tattoos in the traditional way, to affirm patriarchal constructions of masculinity,[7] more often, they are deployed in ways that connote a diversity of masculinities and/or play ironically with conventional conceptions of masculinity.

This reflects the imperative of advertisers to expand and diversify the male market for fashion and body care products. Whereas prior to the 1980s, the market for men's fashions was comparatively small and primarily addressed the relatively mature, white, Protestant, middle class, heterosexual male consumer, during the 1980s, there was a concerted effort to target a wider male constituency.[8] While in the past, the main commodities that were marketed to men were items such as cars, alcohol, certain brands of cigarettes, mechanical tools, life insurance, and so on, over the last two decades an increasing array of fashion and body care products, and accessories from jewelry to bath oil, deodorants, and hair dye have been promoted to male consumers.

This has partly been in response to the growing involvement of men in consumption activities previously regarded as the province of women only. As more women have entered the workforce and have become financially independent, men have increasingly come to rely on other attributes, such as physical beauty, to attract a mate. It is also in recognition of the potentially lucrative gay market. As the stigma associated with homosexuality has lessened, advertisers have increasingly sought to incorporate this group of male consumers into its marketing strategies, cognizant of the fact that single gay men without family responsibilities tend to have higher disposable incomes than their heterosexual counterparts, and also often take a greater interest in their personal appearance.

In their promotion of fashion and style to male consumers, advertisers have faced two main challenges: firstly, how to persuade heterosexual men to take a greater interest in this traditionally "feminine" arena while allaying their fears of emasculation, and secondly, how to address the new, lucrative market amongst homosexual men without alienating the heterosexual male consumer. In order to meet these challenges, a new type of advertising has been developed that uses polysemic symbols capable of expressing a range of different conceptions of masculinity. In these advertisements, the trappings of masculinity are presented as relatively "free-floating" signifiers, inviting the audience to see masculinity as a cultural artifact rather than as a biological given. As Nixon describes it, this genre of advertising: "place[s] stress on the unfixed nature of identities: mixing different bits and pieces in the self-conscious assemblage of a look. The overall tone [is] one of irony, ambiguity and self-conscious play with identity" (1992, 162).

As such, they are decidedly "camp" in sensibility, in Susan Sontag's sense of the term (1966, 275–92). "Camp," as she defines it, is the love of artifice and exaggeration in which style is privileged over content and where things are not what they seem to be. "Camp," according to her, "sees everything in quotation marks. It's not a lamp but a 'lamp'; not a woman but a 'woman.' To perceive Camp in objects and persons is to understand Being-as-Playing-a-Role. It is the farthest extension, in sensibility, of the metaphor of life as theatre" (1966, 280). Camp is playful rather than serious, employing duplicitous gestures that are susceptible of a double interpretation. It requires a certain detachment, and for this reason, has a preference for things of the past from which we have become distanced with the passage of time.

Such a strategy of theatrical impersonation has become popular amongst gay men since the 1980s. As Shaun Cole argues (2000), in reaction against the stereotype of the effeminate gay man, during the 1980s, a "macho" look, which played with the traditional signifiers of masculinity, became popular in the homosexual community. Known as the "clone" look, this self-conscious assumption of a hypermasculine style—which employed many of the clichéd symbols of the butch male, such as worn jeans, leather jackets, T-shirts, and lace-up work boots—parodied conventional notions of masculinity by exaggerating them. In adopting this look, gay men could appear to be like "real" men while, at the same time, challenging traditional assumptions about what constituted masculinity. They wore their garments in a self-consciously tight manner to enhance their physical attractiveness, thereby infusing them with a new meaning of eroticism and overt sexuality. This masculinization of homosexuality and emphasis on overtly masculine images and physiques that was first ushered in by the clone look continues today in other forms, and has become one of the primary modes of self-presentation for gay men today, as Cole points out.[9]

One of the many symbols of masculinity that has lent itself to such parodic play has been the tattoo. Because of the extremely diverse range of connotations they have acquired over the last few decades, this has made them equally appealing to "straight" and gay men, though for very different reasons. While for heterosexual men, they can serve as traditional signifiers of masculinity, confirming their sense of manliness despite their participation in the "feminine" domain of appearance, for gay men, they appear rather as ironic subversions of this very concept of manhood. This is exemplified by a series of advertisements that were produced during the 1990s to promote Calvin Klein jeans, and also by the advertising campaign for Jean-Paul Gaultier's perfume "Le Male," launched in 1995.

As far as the campaign for Jean Paul Gaultier's perfume "Le Male" is concerned, while it quite explicitly sets out to target the male consumer (as indicated by the name of the perfume and also by the shape of the perfume bottle, which takes the form of a male torso), it does not seek to present masculinity as a fixed and unitary construction. On the contrary, it plays with the traditional signifiers of masculinity.

The central icon of this campaign is that of the tattooed sailor.[10] Traditionally, the tattoos worn by sailors were seen as signifiers of a life of daring and adventure, free from the normal constraints of society. In these advertisements, these associations are invoked, insofar as they "dare" the heterosexual male consumer to buy a product traditionally associated with women. Rather than "feminizing" him, the suggestion is that of being "man" enough to take on the challenge. This is particularly the case with one of the advertisements that shows two sailors arm-wrestling each other. Prominently on display are their well-muscled upper bodies and arms, emblazoned with tattoos—all conventional symbols of masculinity.

Though perhaps not as overt, a similar sense of bravado is suggested in another advertisement in which a single sailor gazes nonchalantly out of the picture with arms crossed in a casual, but confident, manner. Once again, the tattoos are prominently displayed, this time on the muscular upper body and arms, conveying an air of self-assurance and defiance. In both cases, the tattoos are old style ones of the sort originally worn by sailors and "rough" working class men.

At the same time, however, there is a strong element of parody in these images of a seemingly confident masculinity, suggesting another interpretation of the sailor icon—namely, that of object of male desire.[11] For instance, in the first advertisement, the rugged masculinity of the two sailors is undermined by the obvious staginess of their poses, which bear all the hallmarks of being carefully choreographed for the camera. Their smooth, airbrushed faces, which carry a hint of makeup, also serve to undercut their apparent virility. From this perspective, the snarling tiger tattoo on the bicep of the sailor on the left appears as a comic exaggeration of masculinity, while the heart shaped tattoo emblazoned on the arm of the other sailor hints at something other than heterosexual love.

In the second advertisement, the supposed masculinity of the sailor is undermined by the placement of the tattoos appearing on his chest and upper arms, which are arranged in such a way that they resemble decorative lacework.[12] The exposure of his decorated upper body and the slight tilt of his head also "feminizes" him, making him into an erotic object of display. In this context, the tattoo on his upper arm showing the embrace of a heterosexual couple appears as a fake and sentimentalized icon of a bygone era, at odds with the type of desire he is arousing.

A similar game of double entendre is evident in a number of advertisements for Calvin Klein jeans that feature young, tattooed men, three of which I shall focus on here.[13] In these advertisements, the association of jeans with tattooed men serves, at one level, to remind us of the original significance of jeans as working men's garb, designed to be tough and durable. The tattoos, which are prominently displayed on the men's upper arms, are reminiscent of the style of working class tattoos, featuring motifs such as semi-naked women and fearsome monsters. This symbolism of a tough and rugged masculinity is further reinforced in two instances by the nature of the setting within which the model is placed—in one case, an industrialized landscape with power pylons in the background, and in the other, a bodybuilding studio. Further indications of a tough masculinity are the well-muscled bodies of the models and the occasional scar, suggestive of a rough lifestyle.

At the same time, however, there are other elements in these advertisements that contradict these bold assertions of masculinity. Firstly, the poses of the male models are reminiscent of those of the reclining female nude, and in each case, the upper body is naked and prominently on display. Furthermore, the gazes of the models are either self-absorbed or sultry, rather than confrontational. This has the effect of converting these models into objects of desire, though for whom is indeterminate. In these examples, then, the men appear to be offering themselves to the audience for its delectation rather than exerting authority over it. This presents a marked contrast with traditional advertisements for men's fashion in the past, where the model was usually presented in a more active pose. The eroticization of the male bodies in these advertisements is further underlined in one case where the model is reclining on a bed with rumpled sheets. Viewed in this light, their tattoos, rather than symbolizing a traditional, working class masculinity, serve to sensualize their bodies. A hint of makeup (eye shadow and lipstick), in one instance, reinforces this reading of body art as aesthetic enhancement.

While these advertisements involve a play with traditional signifiers of masculinity, making use of old style, working class men's tattoos, other advertisements reference the newer style of "neotribal" tattoos that have been custom designed. The appeal here is to the man who does not adhere to convention but demonstrates his "coolness" by not wearing a standardized "flash" tattoo. Two examples of this are an advertisement for Pepe jeans and another for Jean-Paul Gaultier fashions, both of which appeared in 1995.

In the advertisement for Pepe jeans, what is depicted is not the product itself, but the back view of the head of a male model, which has been shaved to reveal a distinctive custom designed tattoo incorporating tribal and Oriental references, and heavily pierced ears.[14] This image is accompanied by prominent text that reads "Always carry your ID," followed by the brand name—"Pepe jeans, London." While we normally recognize a person by their facial features, here, it is the distinctive nature of the tattoo that serves as a mark of individual identity. The suggestion here is that just as the tattoo serves to distinguish the individual as someone who stands apart from the crowd, so, too, do Pepe jeans. The association of the product logo with the tattoo serves to confer on both, the connotations of individual distinctiveness and nonconformity. This is underlined by the fact that the logo takes the form of personalized handwritten script rather than standardized typography. The transgressive connotations of the tattoo are also exploited in this advertisement through the placement of a notice warning children to beware of suspicious looking characters next to the picture of the tattooed model. This juxtaposition implies that the tattooed model could be such a person of which children should be wary.

In the advertisement for Jean-Paul Gaultier, there is, once again, a close association between the tattoo and the brand name logo.[15] Even more overtly than with the advertisement for Pepe jeans, it is the brand-name that is being marketed rather than a particular product. What is placed center stage is the designer label rather than the items that carry this label. The tattoos here, which are of neotribal design, feature prominently on the shaved head and the front of the neck of the male model on the left. As his face is partially obscured by discs carrying the logo "JPG Paris," the implication is that it is the tattoos and the designer label, rather than the features of his face, that signal his individual identity. This advertisement is designed to appeal to the "new" man, that is, the man who no longer identifies with old-fashioned patriarchal conceptions of masculinity, but sees himself as "enlightened." Whether gay or heterosexual, he sees himself as a nonconformist who rejects an overtly butch form of masculinity. This is implied by the refined artistry of the tattoos that suggests a man of discernment and taste—the sort of man who can appreciate the sophistication of the Jean-Paul Gaultier label. At the same time, there is a hint of the transgressive suggested by the boldness of the tattoos, which are highly visible. The message here seems to be that the fashions of Jean-Paul Gaultier are not for the fainthearted but for the man who is prepared to take risks—to explore new forms of masculinity that transcend the bounds of the traditional patriarchal male.

## Conclusion

These examples, then, clearly demonstrate how tattoos have been employed as polysemic signifiers in recent advertising for men's fashion and personal care products. The fact that tattoos have come to represent a number of different conceptions of masculinity makes them popular emblems in the contemporary fashion industry, which is constantly searching for symbols that can be equally appealing to a range of different male markets. Though the physically permanent nature of tattoos may seem to militate against their use as fashion icons, their semiotic multivalency has led to their widespread employment in the marketing of men's style. While tattoos are often used by individuals in a bid to fix their identity by permanently imprinting it onto their skin, it is their very unfixity of meaning that has led to their appropriation by the fashion and advertising industries. Thus, paradoxically, at the same time as tattoos are increasingly being seen as markers of individual, rather than group, identity, their deployment as fashion items is becoming more and more common. Indeed, it is precisely because they have become so individualized that they appeal to advertisers who are seeking to counter the anonymity of mass-produced items through the personalizing of the brand name. Such is the ubiquity of fashion in contemporary culture that even those forms of body adornment most resistant to change, such as tattoos, have not escaped its influence.

The growing prevalence of tattooing in mainstream fashion indicates the increased importance placed on ornament in the molding of one's appearance in postmodernity. Whereas during the period of modernism, ornament was largely eschewed in favor of a pared back minimalism in all areas of design, there has since been a renewal of interest in ornament. This is the subject of the following chapter, where the "rehabilitation" of ornament is considered, particularly in relation to women's dress and the "feminine" more generally. It is argued that while the recognition of the legitimacy of ornament is to be welcomed, the way in which it has been employed in postmodern fashion threatens to drain it of meaning, robbing it of its communicative potential.

# 6

# Ornament and the Feminine

During the period of modernism, ornament was much maligned as inessential, superficial, deceptive, and irrational. Thanks to the doctrine of functionalism, which was the central platform of modernist design philosophy, all that did not contribute to or enhance the practical utility of an object was regarded as an unnecessary excrescence. Coupled with the denigration of ornament was its association with the feminine. As a number of theorists, such as Norma Broude (1982), Naomi Schor (1987), Penny Sparke (1995), and Wendy Steiner (2001) have pointed out, ornament was considered an intrinsically feminine domain. Thus, the devaluation of ornament meant, at the same time, a dismissal of the feminine as inferior.

Since the beginning of the 1980s, however, there has been a "rehabilitation" of ornament by a number of feminist theorists, such as Norma Broude (1982), Naomi Schor (1987), Kim Sawchuk (1987), Caroline Evans and Minna Thornton (1989), Penny Sparke (1995), and Wendy Steiner (2001). The very features of ornament so bemoaned by the modernists—namely, its lack of function, its sensuousness, and its irrationality—now have become the qualities most appreciated by many of its recent defenders. In their eyes, ornament represents an antidote to the puritanical asceticism of modernism. Ornament, with its freedom from practical necessity, invokes the pleasures of the senses, disrupting the dominance of the instrumental rationality of modern society, which submits everything to a calculating logic. In contrast with the restraint and austerity of modernism, the recent defenders of ornament champion it for its emphasis on the sensuous over the rational and the pleasurable over the serious. Its seductive qualities are now lauded, rather than maligned as deceptive and superficial, and the uninhibited deployment of ornament is celebrated as a way of bringing to the fore the "repressed underside" of modernism, overturning its derogation of the feminine.

However, while these recent feminist defenses of ornament have quite rightly problematized the denigration of the feminine implicit in modernist functionalism, they still remain bound within its parameters insofar as they uncritically accept its conception of ornament as decorative embellishment, devoid of meaning. The only respect in which they differ from modernism is in giving ornament and its features a positive, rather than a negative, valuation, while leaving the definition of ornament intact. Consequently, their defense of ornament as a reassertion of the legitimacy of the feminine ultimately perpetuates, rather than undermines, stereotypical associations of the feminine with the sensuous, the superficial, and the irrational.

A more thoroughgoing challenge would question the way in which ornament was defined during the period of modernism, and in particular, the oppositions on which it was predicated—namely, those between the superfluous and the essential; surface and depth; purposelessness and functionality; the sensuous and the rational. As will be argued, the modernist definition of ornament is highly reductionistic insofar as it denies its role as a carrier of meaning. To conceive of ornament as being concerned simply with surface effects, lacking in substance, is to "short change" its richness and value as a communicative medium. Insofar as recent feminist champions of ornament defend the value of the "inessential" over the essential, surface over depth, the sensuous over the rational, and excess over restraint, they merely reverse the terms of these modernist dichotomies rather than transcending them.

### The Denigration of the Feminine in the Modernist Conception of Ornament

While, as Ernst Gombrich points out (1980, 19–23), there has been a long-standing association of ornament with the feminine, during the period of modernism, the derogatory connotations of such an association became more pronounced than ever before. With the advent of modernism, particularly within the field of design, ornament came to be dismissed wholesale as superficial embellishment. Ornament, for the modernists, was maligned as that which was impractical, irrational, and superfluous, being clearly distinguished from, and opposed to, the realm of the functional, the essential, and the rational, which was coded as masculine.

This was in contrast to previous eras, where there was no clear distinction between the "merely" ornamental elements of an object and those aspects that related to its function. Rather, the two were intimately connected with each other. Thus, for instance, as Massimo Carboni points out (1991, 109), the elaborate ornamental stitching used by some Native American peoples in their animal hide clothes were functional insofar as they held the garment together, at the same time as being decorative. Far from being a superfluous embellishment that was "tacked on" *a posteriori*, ornament was considered integral to the proper functioning of the object it adorned.

Furthermore, this "function" was not just considered in practical terms, but also in terms of its role as a communicator of meaning. Ornament was regarded as an indispensable element insofar as it made comprehensible or rendered culturally "legible" that which it embellished. Indeed, it could be said that ornament brought things into being in the sense that it was only once things had been ornamented that they became culturally meaningful. As such, it was not an optional extra which could be added on later, but was necessary for the completion of the object. Robert Nelson puts it succinctly when he writes that: "Ornament [was] not a device for soaking up meaningless space but an artifice for claiming space as meaningful" (Nelson, 1993, 5). This applied not just to artifacts but to the human body as well. As Claude Lévi-Strauss points out, with reference to face painting in American Indian culture, it was through decoration that the face was brought into existence by giving it human and spiritual meaning.[1] "Decoration is conceived for the face, but the face itself exists only through decoration" (quoted in Carboni 1991, 110).

Ornament, then, served to present the things or beings that it adorned as culturally significant. It fulfilled the need for identification, indicating what an artifact was, how it should be used, and for what purpose it was intended. As such, it embodied social rituals or ways of behaving. In giving "sense" to the objects or persons that it decorated, ornament served to contextualize them in time and space, providing information about their historical and geographical location. As Hans-Georg Gadamer writes:

> The nature of decoration consists in performing [a] two-sided mediation; namely to draw the attention of the viewer to itself, to satisfy his taste, and then to redirect it away from itself to the greater whole of the context of life which it accompanies. (Gadamer 1975, 140)

Rather than being an end in itself, ornament fulfilled its role when it pointed beyond itself to that which it was not. As such, it needed to be conspicuous enough to be noticed. But, at the same time, it also needed to direct the viewer's attention away from itself to the broader context in which it was located, rather than become the central focus.

Thus, at the same time that ornament constituted objects as culturally meaningful, ornament itself only had meaning in relation to that which it decorated. Ornament was only ornament when it was seen to have a necessary connection with the object that it adorned. To quote Gadamer, once more:

> Ornament or decoration is determined by its relation to what it decorates, by what carries it. It does not possess an aesthetic import of its own which only afterwards acquires a limiting condition by its relation to what it is decorating. Even Kant, who endorsed this opinion, admits in his famous judgment on tattooing that ornament is only ornament when it suits its wearer . . . Ornament is not primarily something by itself that is then applied to something else but belongs to the self-presentation of its wearer. (Gadamer 1975, 141)

As well as serving to contextualize objects, ornament often also had an important symbolic role, imparting to objects meanings that went beyond their immediate time, place, or purpose. This is made clearly evident by Sylvia Kleinert (1992) in her discussion of the significance of decoration in aboriginal cultures. She highlights the ethnocentrism of anthropologists in the early part of the twentieth century who assumed that the decorations on everyday items of use such as boomerangs, spears, shields, and so on, were merely aesthetic embellishments devoid of meaning. In doing so, they failed to recognize that the apparently "abstract," geometric designs that adorned these items were an important means by which the values and beliefs of the culture were transmitted, and as such, integral to their function.

Finally, ornament was a marker of social value, endowing objects with dignity, as in the decoration of sacred items for use in church ritual, such as papal robes and altarpieces, for instance. Indeed, as Nelson points out, in its original meaning, to "ornament" something meant to honor it, to give it an elevated status, to make it something special. It was thus not so much an aesthetic but a moral concept that involved the imbuing of an object not just with physical beauty, but virtue. Ornament was "a metaphor for good things, for things appropriate and seemly and, above all, valuable in a social sense" (Nelson 1993, 10).

Even during periods when there was a preference for the plainer, more austere style of Classicism, it was still acknowledged that ornament had a role to play in rendering "comprehensible" and endowing value to that which it adorned. Rather than rejecting ornament in a wholesale manner, premodernist critiques of ornament generally distinguished between legitimate and illegitimate uses of it, granting that, when employed appropriately, it had an important communicative function to play.

The modernist dismissal of ornament had its roots in the latter half of the nineteenth century, when a number of designers and architects, such as John Ruskin, Augustus W. Pugin, Charles Eastlake, and John Pollard Seddon voiced their concerns about the gratuitous use of ornament for gaudy effects that disguised the underlying structure and materials out of which the object was composed. Much of their criticism was provoked by what they saw as the arbitrary ransacking of historical styles from the past, where decorative elements from a wide range of epochs were juxtaposed in a haphazard manner, unrelated to the meaning and function of the buildings or artifacts to which they were applied. As Seddon argued, for instance:

> The modern idea of ornament consists in . . . simply cramming a certain amount of carved work upon the face of a building without reference to its meaning or propriety, the only aim being to attract the eye of the spectator by the general richness of the effects it produces, and to excite his astonishment at the wealth which can afford so lavish a display. (quoted in Jensen and Conway 1982, 6)

Significantly, where ornament was used for no other purpose than for showy display, it was often quite explicitly associated with the feminine—an association that was strengthened during the modernist period, when all ornament came to be seen as meaningless embellishment. Frequently, women came under criticism by nineteenth-century design reformers for their "lack of taste" in the decoration of their domestic interiors (Forty 1992, 105–13; Sparke 1995, chap. 3; and Saisselin 1985, 66–74). The collection of *objets d'art* by women and their amateur creative efforts were bracketed together as manifestations of their lack of aesthetic knowledge and skill. The eclectic accumulation of bric-a-brac, where stylistically diverse objects from various epochs were brought together in an arbitrary way, was seen, by the writers of domestic manuals at the time, as a feminine weakness, and was unfavorably compared with the more manly enterprise of collecting works of art, which was seen to be a sign of education and culture. Women, it was believed, collected artifacts in accordance with the whims of fashion, viewing them simply as items of decoration without any deeper intellectual purpose, while the collection of art by men was informed by a carefully thought through philosophy and purpose. As a painter with a trained eye in Paul Bourget's novel *Blue duchess* remarked of Parisian interiors in the mid-nineteenth century, for example:

> How not detest the impressions made by these furnishings and furniture which taste of pillaging and the junk shop; for nothing is in its place: tapestries of the eighteenth century alternate with paintings of the sixteenth,

furniture of the Louis XV period with a bishop's seat, modern draw curtain with antique material on a *chaise longue*, the back of an armchair or some cushion or divan! (quoted in Saisselin 1985, 68)

The middle class housewife was also castigated for her preoccupation with surface effects, rather than with substance. For example, as Eastlake commented in his book, *Hints on household taste*:

> The lace trimmings and edgings used for "anti-macassars" and similar articles of household use are often open to objection on account of the flimsiness and extravagance of their design. It is a great pity that ladies who devote much of their time to the execution of the wretched patterns sold at "fancy-work shops" do not exercise a little more discrimination in their choice. (Eastlake 1971 [1872], 98–99)

Elsewhere, he attributes the duplicitous use of decoration to the ineptitude of female taste as evidenced in the following quote:

> . . . the so-called "ornamental" leather-work which a few years ago was in vogue with young ladies, who used it for the construction of brackets, baskets, picture-frames, etc was—like potichomanie, diaphenie, and other modern drawing-room pursuits—utterly opposed to sound principles of taste. Pieces of leather cut into the shape of leaves and flowers, glued together and varnished, represent at best but a wretched parody of the carver's art. The characteristic beauty of oriental china and of painted windows can never be even suggested by bits of colored paper gummed to the surface of glass. Such work as this may be the rage for a few seasons, but sooner or later must fall, as it deserves to fall, into universal Contempt. (Eastlake 1971 [1872], 191–92)

This abhorrence of the excessiveness of ornament applied not just to architecture and interior design, but also to dress. Thus, for instance, Mary Haweis, a prominent advocate of dress reform in the late nineteenth century, deplored ostentatious ornament as a sign of moral degeneracy. As she declared in her book *The art of dress*, published in 1879: "A simple garb usually springs from simple manners while a complex social state and a lowered *morale* [my emphasis] fly to furbelows and 'intemperance in ornament.'" She continued that "[c]oarse vulgar curves, unmeaning lumps, superabundant ornament . . . are to be avoided . . ." (quoted in Newton 1974, 56), and expressed her admiration for the simplicity of the garb of the ancient Athenians, who had given up "an extravagance of dress and an excess of personal ornament which, in the first flush of a newly discovered luxury, had been adopted by some of the richer classes"(quoted in Newton

1974, 58). In her book *The art of beauty*, she again criticized what she called "Imbecile Ornament," declaring that "[p]robably nothing that is not useful is in any high sense beautiful" (quoted in Newton 1974, 75). For her, the ideal form of dress was one that followed the natural lines of the female body. She also expressed a preference for muted, subtle colors rather than ones that appealed to the public's vulgar craving for gaudiness (Newton 1974, 73–74).

In a similar vein, the Reverend J. P. Faunthorpe, in his 1879 book *Household science: Readings in necessary knowledge for girls and young women*, warned that it was not desirable to "adopt any of the ugly head-coverings so fashionable at the time," and that plain and serviceable shoes were preferable to the "showy and fashionable" ones available in the shops. While a small degree of bodily display was permitted in the form of a bunch of artificial flowers attached to a simple straw hat, the reader was cautioned to "be very particular to secure the best possible imitations of the real flowers, for gaudy distortions of nature are most offensive to persons of refined taste" (quoted in Sparke 1995, 81).

This critique of ornament became even more pronounced with the advent of modernism in the early twentieth century, where all forms of ornament were regarded as extravagant frippery devoid of meaning. In the view of the modernist designers, good design was that in which the functionality of the object was uppermost, function being defined primarily in terms of "practical utility." The famous aphorism "form follows function" encapsulated the modernist idea that, in the designing of objects for everyday use, function should be given priority over form. All that which detracted from, or was superfluous to, the efficient functioning of the object was to be avoided. This included ornament and decoration that were regarded by modernist designers as unnecessary luxuries, wasteful of labor, time, and money. Purity, universality, simplicity, geometry, and standardization were linked, in modernist rhetoric, in their ability to transcend the ephemeral and confront the essence. Originating within a context dominated by a faith in modern science and technology, modernist design was premised on a desire to rationalize everything from domestic interiors to the aesthetics of everyday items.

Nowhere was this attitude more clearly expressed than in the writings of Adolf Loos, one of the foremost modernist designers in the first decades of the twentieth century. In an essay entitled "Ornament and Crime," which he wrote in 1908, he declared that the abolition of ornament was as necessary a social discipline as toilet training. In his view, the decorative urge was a sign of infantile, libidinal impulses that needed to be suppressed for civilization to progress. As he wrote:

It is possible to estimate a country's culture by the amount of scrawling on lavatory walls. In children this is a natural phenomenon: their first artistic expression is scribbling erotic symbols on walls. But what is natural for a Papuan and a child is degenerate for modern man. I have discovered the following truth and present it to the world: *cultural evolution is equivalent to the removal of ornament from articles in daily use.* (Loos 1966 [1908], 226–27)

Furthermore, he regarded ornament as a wasteful luxury, costly both in economic terms and in terms of human labor, pointing out that:

the lack of ornament means shorter working hours and consequently higher wages. Chinese carvers work sixteen hours, American workers eight. If I pay as much for a smooth box as for a decorated one, the difference in labor time belongs to the worker. And if there were no ornament at all . . . a man would have to work only four hours instead of eight, for half the work done at present is still for ornamentation. Ornament is wasted labor and hence wasted health. (Loos, 1966 [1908], 229)

In his dismissal of ornament as an irrational, costly, and wasteful extravagance, Loos associated it with the feminine, as Schor points out (1987, 51–53). According to him, the love of decorative effects was particularly characteristic of women, and was indicative of erotic impulses uncurbed by civilizing influences. This was exemplified by women's attire, which was much more ornamented and impractical than was men's dress. Thus, in his article on "Ladies' Fashion," he wrote that

[t]he clothing of the woman is distinguished externally from that of the man by the preference for the ornamental and colorful effects and by the long skirt that covers the legs completely. These two factors demonstrate to us that woman has fallen behind sharply in her development in recent centuries. No period of culture has known as great differences as our own between the clothing of the free man and the free woman. In earlier eras, men also wore clothing that was colorful and richly adorned and whose hem reached the floor. Happily, the grandiose development in which our culture has taken part this century has overcome ornament. (Loos 1982 [1902], 102)

The reason for the lack of progress toward a more rational form of dress for women lay in the fact that they remained economically subservient to men, and so still depended on their appearance to attract, and then keep, a husband. Whereas men gained a sense of their own identity through their activities in the public arena, women were defined primarily by their appearance. To quote Loos, once more:

That which is noble in a woman knows only one desire: that she hold on to her place by the side of the big, strong man. At present this desire can only be fulfilled if the woman wins the love of the man ... Thus the woman is forced to appeal to the man's sensuality through her clothing, to appeal unconsciously to his sickly sensuality for which only the culture of the times can be blamed. The vicissitudes of women's fashion are dictated only by changes in sensuality. (1982 [1902], 103)

These views were echoed by social theorist Thorstein Veblen, writing at about the same time as Loos. In his book, *The theory of the leisure class*, Veblen criticized the highly decorative and impractical dress of women of his day whose primary function was to symbolize the wealth and status of their husbands. Whereas prior to the nineteenth century, the dress of both men and women of the upper classes had been extremely ornate, symbolizing the fact that they did not have to work for a living, in the nineteenth century, ornate dress became the sole preserve of middle class women, their male counterparts adopting much more austere forms of dress. The reason for this lay in the fact that whereas previously, women had participated actively in the economic life of the household, once the place of work became physically separated from the place of domicile, they were no longer required to engage in any form of labor, including domestic labor, which was generally carried out by servants. The fact that middle class women did not have to work for a living was seen as indicative of the wealth and status of their husbands and was made visible by the extravagant clothes that they wore. As Veblen wrote:

It has in the course of economic development become the office of the woman to consume vicariously for the head of the household; and her apparel is contrived with this object in view. It has come about that obviously productive labor is in a peculiar degree derogatory to respectable women, and therefore special pains should be taken in the construction of women's dress, to impress upon the beholder the fact ... that the wearer does not and cannot habitually engage in useful work. Propriety requires respectable women to abstain more consistently from useful effort and to make more of a show of leisure than men of the same social classes ... By virtue of its descent from a patriarchal past, our social system makes it the woman's function in an especial degree to put in evidence her household's ability to pay. ... (1970 [1899], 126)

Furthermore, the fact that women consented to wearing these clothes was symptomatic of their subservience to their husbands or fathers, since women's clothing was far more uncomfortable and incapacitating than the dress for men. As Veblen wrote:

Wherever wasteful expenditure and the show of abstention from effort is . . . carried to the extent of showing obvious discomfort or voluntarily induced physical disability, there the immediate inference is that the individual in question does not perform this wasteful expenditure and undergo this disability for her own personal gain in pecuniary repute, but in behalf of someone else to whom she stands in a relation of economic dependence; a relation which in the last analysis must . . . reduce itself to a relation of servitude . . . The high heel, the skirt, the impracticable bonnet, the corset, and the general disregard of the wearer's comfort which is an obvious feature of all civilized women's apparel, are so many items of evidence to the effect that in the modern civilized scheme of life the woman is still, in theory, the economic dependent of the man—that, perhaps in a highly idealized sense, she still is the man's chattel. (1970 [1899], 127)

While Loos and Veblen explained women's ornamental and impractical dress as a consequence of their economically subservient position, others regarded it as symptomatic of the superficial, irrational, and frivolous nature of women. Thus, for example, Karl Scheffler, a German critic and writer on the decorative arts at the beginning of the twentieth century, wrote that women could not understand "pure form" because they thought too amorphously (Anger 1996, 136). While women had a talent for the decorative and the ornamental, excelling at such activities as table setting, makeup, and house decoration, they were, in Scheffler's view, unable to appreciate abstract form as could men, whose minds were more ordered and rational.

Likewise, Le Corbusier was quite scathing of the supposedly "feminine" taste for the decorative. His strongest condemnation was for the shop-girl, whose love of flowery, peasantstyle dresses epitomized her lack of taste (Sparke 1995, 111). She was equally indiscriminate in her attraction to the highly decorated items sold in department stores. As he wrote:

Today decorative objects flood the shelves of the Department Stores; they sell cheaply to *shop-girls* [my emphasis]. If they sell cheaply, it is because they are badly made and because decoration hides faults in their manufacture and the poor quality of their materials: decoration is disguise. It pays the manufacturer to employ a decorator to disguise the faults in his products, to conceal the poor quality of their materials and to distract the eye from their blemishes by offering it the spiced morsels of glowing gold-plate and strident symphonies. Trash is always abundantly decorated; the luxury object is well made, neat and clean, pure and healthy, and its bareness reveals the quality of its manufacture. (Le Corbusier, 1987 [1925], 87)

Le Corbusier abhorred all that the middle class Victorian home had stood for, especially its emphasis on the decorative, proposing instead that a house was essentially a "machine for living" whose primary purpose was to provide a shelter against the elements and against intruders. The reduction to these basic functional requirements of existence served to standardize the needs of the user and to eliminate space for display. No naturalistic ornament and no decorative application of color or line were permitted in modernist architecture and design. Both implied a denial of function, purity, and the essential universality of the object. While specific room functions continued to exist, the equipment within these spaces was to become less indicative of social ritual and more utilitarian in nature.

In the area of fashion design, these ideas manifested themselves in the work of Coco Chanel, whose concern was to create simpler, more practical clothes for working women who sought comfort instead of artifice. As Bonnie English points out:

> She was the first haute couture designer to consider the functional aspects of dress, rationally deconstructing women's dress through cut, fabric and simplicity of design. Her work deliberately disrupted and overturned social class indicators in so far as it discarded the dominant concept of conspicuous consumption as a means of achieving status. (2007, 32)

Against the exclusivity of the one-off designs of other *haute couture* designers, Chanel introduced designs that could be mass produced and that used relatively inexpensive materials, such as jersey. Their simplicity and lack of decoration also enhanced their affordability as well as their practicality. This was epitomized by her famous range of black dresses, whose pared back minimalism was compared to the standardized design of Henry Ford's Model T car. Chanel insisted that elements such as pockets, buttons, and buttonholes should be treated as functional and not just as decorative appendages. While she did not eschew decoration altogether (for instance, she often added jewelry to her ensembles), nevertheless, simplicity and practicality were her primary considerations, as indicated by her strong preference for pure lines and plain colors. In her endeavor to develop a simple, rational style for women, she drew inspiration from elements of male dress, such as blazers, men's woolen sweaters, reefer jackets, cuffed shirts, and tailored clothes in thick woolen tweed. She also accelerated the adoption of trousers by women, designing loose sailor-style trousers, known as "yachting pants," for leisurewear, for instance.

While at the time, this was seen as liberating for women, recent theorists such as Evans and Thornton suggest that it betrayed "a cultural rejection of the feminine in favor of an exclusively masculine model of power" (1991, 58). Sparke (1995, 101, 108), and Schor (1987, 50–55) argue similarly that although the rationale behind the pared back minimalism of the modernists was to democratize design and break down class distinctions, it unwittingly served, at the same time, to suppress the feminine. In their view, modernism's dismissal of ornament as superfluous, irrational excess, betrayed a contempt for the feminine, which was closely associated with ornament. Thus gender hierarchies were reinforced and accentuated.

## The Feminist Rehabilitation of Ornament

Since the 1980s, in reaction to this denigration of the feminine within modernist design, a number of feminist theorists such as Broude (1982), Schor (1987), Evans and Thornton (1989), and Sawchuk (1987) have argued for a "rehabilitation" of ornament. In contrast with the modernist derision of ornament as "useless" and "superficial," many of the recent defenders of ornament praise it for precisely these qualities. As Jensen and Conway point out:

> At the heart of the Ornamental movement is an awakening of the long-suppressed decorative impulse and a desire to re-assert the legitimate pleasures that flow from that impulse. Ornamentalism is characterized by a fascination with the surface of things as opposed to their essence; elaboration as opposed to simplicity; borrowing as opposed to originating; sensory stimulation as opposed to intellectual discipline. Sometimes it attempts to fool the eye, favoring humor and illusion over the honest expression of structure and function upon which Modernism had so long insisted . . . The universal appeal of ornament is precisely its "uselessness" in the strict functionalist sense of that word. Because ornament is not there to hold things up or to make things work, it is not bound by all the utilitarian constraints that threaten at times, to suffocate us. Ornament is essentially free: free to move the eye, to intrigue the mind, to rest the soul; free simply to delight us. (1982, 2–3)

This attitude is exemplified by Broude's article, "Miriam Schapiro and 'Femmage': Reflections on the Conflict Between Decoration and Abstraction in Twentieth Century Art" (1982), where she defends ornament as purely visual display without any deeper meaning. Broude criticizes the way in which modernist artists sought to distance their employment of abstract forms from any association with the decorative, by imbuing them with significant content. Thus, for instance, while Kandinsky's early experiments with abstraction were clearly influenced by the decorative crafts, he was at pains to distinguish his works from the latter by claiming that his forms were not meaningless patterns designed merely to please the senses but carried a more profound spiritual significance.[2] As he wrote:

> If we begin at once to break the bonds that bind us to nature and to devote ourselves purely to combinations of pure color and independent form, we shall produce works which are mere geometric decoration, resembling something like a necktie or a carpet. Beauty of form and color is no sufficient aim by itself . . . The nerve vibrations are there (as we feel when confronted by applied art), but they get no further than the nerves because the corresponding vibrations of the spirit which they call forth are weak. (quoted in Broude 1982, 317)

Underlying Kandinsky's concern to distance himself from the decorative crafts, as Broude argues, was his desire to maintain the high art status of his work. Only by imbuing his nonrepresentational forms with meaning could he ensure that his work would not descend to the realm of the more lowly regarded crafts.

Similarly, while the decorative crafts (particularly Islamic art, the arts and crafts movement, and art nouveau) had an important influence on Matisse's work, their impact was largely disguised through his employment of the traditional high art methods and materials of oil paint on canvas. Even his paper cutouts merely imitated the look, but not the materials or methods, of the crafts. Though Matisse was not as concerned as Kandinsky that his work might be seen as decorative, critics such as Clement Greenberg again sought to clearly differentiate his employment of abstract form from "mere" decoration.[3] Writing about his paper cutouts for instance, Greenberg argued that despite the fact that they were originally designed primarily to have a decorative function, they were "more truly pictorial than decorative" (quoted in Broude 1982, 320).

Broude goes on to contrast this modernist disavowal of the decorative with the active espousal of it by the feminist artist Miriam Schapiro. Unlike artists such as Matisse and Kandinsky, Schapiro highlights, rather than effaces, the materials and methods of the decorative crafts in her works, which take the form of collages composed of pieces of fabric. Drawing on traditional craft techniques such as sewing, piecing, hooking, quilting, and appliquéing, which have been practiced by women for centuries, she refers to her collages as "femmages" to emphasize the "feminine" derivation of these processes.[4] In employing the techniques and materials of the "female" crafts in her art practice, her aim is to challenge the denigration of the feminine implicit in the hierarchical art/craft distinction.

While in her elevation of the decorative, Schapiro could be said to be investing it with a social and political content, for Broude, the principle value of her work lies in its celebration of the decorative as valuable in its own right, that is, as a purely sensuous play of form without any deeper meaning. Broude here criticizes those who seek to rehabilitate ornament by investing it with meaning, arguing that such a strategy "masculinizes" it by privileging intellectual content over sensuous form. As she writes with reference to recent exhibitions of "decorative" artists:

> [They] have been grouped together and distinguished . . . on the grounds that they all display an ability to invest the decorative with significant content . . . What is involved here, one feels, is a strange contradiction in terms. For [it] merely engages us once again in the fruitless . . . exercise of attempting to elevate the "decorative" . . . by endowing it with . . . arcane meanings. By so doing, of course, it continues to deny to the decorative the right to exist as art on its own terms. (Broude 1982, 326–27)

What Broude fails to realize here, however, is that in defending ornament as a purely sensuous form devoid of meaning, she herself is perpetuating the very stereotypes and hierarchies she seeks to undermine. While ornament continues to be treated merely as visual display, the defense of it as a form of feminine culture does little to undermine stereotypical notions of femininity as irrational, superficial, and sensuous, rather than intellectual. It is only if the oppositions between ornament versus meaning, surface versus depth, and the sensuous versus the rational are dismantled that these stereotypes can be overcome. Furthermore, in her defense of ornament as sensuous embellishment, Broude perpetuates the reductionistic conception of it that prevailed during the period of modernism, where it was denuded of its communicative functions.

A similar failure to transcend modernism's reductionistic notion of ornament can be seen in Schor's defense of it. While she seeks to go beyond the hierarchical oppositions between the general and the particular, mass and detail, the essential and the superfluous, masculine and feminine, her defense of ornament ultimately remains trapped within these parameters. This clearly emerges in her discussion of Roland Barthes' rehabilitation of the "detail" (1987, 79–97). Schor largely accepts Barthes' conception of the "detail," which bears a striking resemblance to the modernist definition of ornament, but without its negative valuation.

The Barthesian "detail," as outlined by Schor, refers to that which is incidental or accidental to the meaning of the whole. Thus, for example, in
realist literary texts, there exist "useless," totally parasitic details that contribute neither to the advancing of the plot nor to enhancing our knowledge
of the characters and their physical surroundings. While traditional modes
of literary criticism seek to integrate all details, no matter how apparently
aberrant, into a meaningful totality, Barthes argues that such details resist
recuperation of this sort. The Barthesian detail then, is a signifier that has
been emptied of meaning, confronting us with its "brute" materiality.

Similarly, in photographs, there sometimes appear details that have
no necessary connection with that which is being pictured. These details
are unintentional, appearing inadvertently and quite independently of
the conscious will of the photographer, and are not in the service of the
meaning or message of the photograph.[5] As Schor puts it: "[The Barthesian
detail] is always supplementary, marginal, de-centered" (1987, 91). As such,
it appears as a luxurious extra that participates in an "economy of excess."
Thus, just as with the modernist conception of ornament as "purposeless"
and incidental to the functioning of that which it adorns, so Barthes' detail
appears as an intentionless and "extravagant" addendum, extraneous to the
meaning of the whole.

Another distinguishing feature of the "detail" for Barthes is that it is not
affectively neutral, but is erotically charged. As he argues in *Camera lucida*,
the inadvertent detail in the photograph, or "*punctum*," as he terms it,
"pricks" the spectator, provoking a heightened emotional response. Rather
than appealing to the intellect and conscious will of the viewer, it operates
directly on the senses, soliciting a more bodily or visceral response, which
occurs unexpectedly and involuntarily. Here again, Barthes' concept of the
detail converges with the modernist notion of ornament, particularly as
defined by Loos, who, as we have seen, conceived of it as libidinal excess.
Like the modernist conception of ornament, for Barthes, the detail is "irrational," appealing primarily to the senses and defying interpretation. It is a
site for anarchic, prerational impulses, which threaten to disrupt the unity
of the whole. The only difference is that whereas for Loos, it was necessary to suppress such impulses, for Barthes, they should be liberated in an
unfettered profusion of detail that is no longer subservient to underlying
structures or systems of cultural representation.

Schor concurs with this evacuation of meaning from the detail by
Barthes. Her only objection is that at the same time as Barthes defends
the detail he degenders it. In this respect, the revaluation of the detail is
a somewhat Pyrrhic victory for feminism, according to Schor, since the

rescue from its previously secondary status has only occurred when it has been uncoupled from the feminine. As she writes:

> Though highly sexualized in Barthes, the detail/fragment paradigm is degendered, as the marks of sexual specification are erased from the textual, as well as the referential, contingent body of desire. By bringing his aesthetics, in his own words "closer to the body" and its "drift," Barthes has struck a decisive blow against idealist aesthetics and its devalorizing gendering of the detail. But it would appear that in transvaluating the detail, the feminine has vanished. (1987, 97)

In opposition to Barthes, then, she argues for the necessity of maintaining the connection of ornament with the feminine in the process of its revalorization so that the feminine does not, once again, become subsumed by the masculine and its prerogatives. To quote her, once more:

> Whether or not the detail *is* feminine . . . given Western culture's longstanding association of the order of the small, the finely wrought, and the *Heimlich* with the feminine sphere, the need to affirm the power and the positivity of the *feminine particular* cannot for the moment be denied. (1987, 97)

However, in upholding the femininity of ornament, Schor, like Broude, ultimately reinforces the stereotypical association of the feminine with the sensuous, rather than with the intellectual, since she continues to adhere to the modernist conception of ornament as "libidinal excess," which "undoes" meaning.

The perpetuation of the modernist emptying out of the meaning of ornament is also evident in the writings of a number of recent feminist theorists of fashion. In their book *Women and fashion: A new look* (1989), Evans and Thornton argue for a sartorial strategy that embraces, rather than eschews, artifice and decoration. In doing so, they present a challenge to earlier feminists and modernist theorists such as Loos, who criticized female fashion for its impracticality and frippery and advocated a plainer, more functional mode of dress. As they contend, the proponents of functional dress, in their advocacy of a less artificial mode of attire that revealed the body "as it truly was" in preference to the deceptive use of ornament to disguise imperfections, failed to recognize that there is no such thing as a "natural" body that preexists culture. "The 'natural look' in fashion," as they point out, "was not natural at all; it took as much labor as all the other 'looks'; its 'naturalness' was a function of the denial and concealment of that labor" (Evans and Thornton 1989, 13).

Given the inescapability of the cultural encoding of the body, they argue that the most appropriate form of bodily adornment is one that makes explicit, rather than seeks to disguise, its artificial nature. Instead of seeking to step outside of fashion in the chimerical search for an "authentic" self, untainted by culture, they propose that one should take advantage of the fashion industry's promotion of the idea that one's self-identity is forged through what one wears, and as such, is infinitely malleable. To quote them: "The feminine, whether artificial or 'natural' is constructed through a system of adornment . . . If it is fashion that sets out the terms of this control, then fashion may also be used to subvert it" (Evans and Thornton 1989, 14). It is in this context that they embrace the concept of dress as masquerade that foregrounds itself as something "stuck on," that is, as pure "surface" rather than organically connected to that which it adorns. Dress is not seen to reflect an identity that is already pre-given, but rather itself is constitutive of it. In their view, such a concept is emancipatory insofar as it highlights that one's self-identity is not fixed by biology, but is culturally constructed. Gender identity comes to be seen as the product of an infinite number of appearances divorced from biological sex.

Evans and Thornton see this idea of dress as masquerade epitomized by the fashion magazines of the 1980s, such as *i-D, The Face*, and *Blitz*, which promoted the idea of self-identity as the product of an infinitely variable series of changing guises. No longer regarded as reflective of the body it adorned, dress became a parodic play in which the body of the wearer was denaturalized. This involved the mixing together of decorative elements from a diverse range of past styles without any regard for consistency. Detached from any context beyond themselves, they became free-floating signs to be arranged and combined in an infinite myriad of different ways. Rather than being governed by a feeling of nostalgia that would imply a wish to recover the original meaning of that which was imitated, this practice was characterized by an attitude of ironic detachment in which delight was taken in being deliberately anachronistic, recontextualizing items of dress in ways that were quite at odds with their former meanings. Amongst the many fashion looks on the London fashion scene from the early to the mid-'80s, there were Pirates, Buffalo Girls, New Romantics, rockabilly, new psychedelia, Hassidic ringlets, white dreadlocks, bobtails, Victorian fetish wear, zoot suits, and Dickensian urchins. The 1930s, 1940s, 1950s, and even the 1960s, were cannibalized, recycled, refracted, and sprinkled with Third World and ethnic references.

While Evans and Thornton believe that this radical recontextualizing of styles opens up limitless possibilities for new meanings to emerge, I would argue that it ultimately robs them of their communicative potential by treating them purely as aesthetic forms empty of content. Torn from their moorings in history, they become denuded of meaning other than that of highlighting their artificially constructed nature. Not anchored in anything outside of themselves, their "meanings" become entirely arbitrary. Since they can potentially mean anything, they ultimately signify nothing. For the postmodern fashion habitué, the past is turned into a playground in which the surface appearance of various styles is imitated without engaging with their substance. It is in this sense that Hal Foster describes the postmodern "return to history" as profoundly "ahistorical" (Foster 1985, 16).[6]

Evans and Thornton acknowledge this emptying of meaning in their analysis of the operation of style in the punk movement. As they argue: "Punk was postmodern in its detachment of the signifier from the signified (for example in its use of the swastika), its insistence on the meaningless-ness of its icons, and in its use of pastiche and kitsch"(Evans and Thornton, 1989, 75). But they contend that it was this very "illegibility" that made Punk subversive. As they explain:

> The subversive potential of sub-cultural style lies in the indirectness of its utterances. The sub-cultural use of style as a system of signification is complex because it has to be: it is the mark of minorities that they establish their sub-cultural space by making their statements—verbal, sartorial and behavioral—*opaque* to the dominant culture [my emphasis] . . . Within this scheme of things dress is significant precisely because it is a means of indirect communication and as such can hit, so to speak, "below the belt." (1989, 74–75)

While they regard Punk's "insistence on blankness" as an oppositional stance, however, I would see this as a diminishing of the semiotic richness of ornament. By erasing, rather than critically engaging, the past meanings of the symbols it appropriated, the Punk movement prepared the way for their use as meaningless embellishments by the fashion industry. It was but a short step from the Punk's use of the swastika purely as a blank cipher to its employment by the fashion industry as an aesthetic emblem drained of meaning. Indeed, as Evans and Thornton themselves admit (1989, 31, 75), the Punk movement was very quickly and readily assimilated by the fashion industry, so that by the early '80s, its resistance to the dominant culture had been superseded by a symbiotic relation in which high fashion now looked toward subcultural style as a source for inspiration.

Finally, the evacuation of meaning from ornament is also repeated in Sawchuk's analysis of fashion. In her defense of decorative forms of attire, she argues that criticisms of female dress for its overly ornamental nature have often been tied to a Christian discourse that is intent on repressing women's potentially subversive sexuality and returning them to the confines of the domestic sphere. As she writes:

> [T]he dress reform movements of the early twentieth century were often less concerned with making women more comfortable than with returning them to the proper sphere of the home; they were part of the movement for social purity. Just as improper dress indicated a woman's lack of reason and her immorality, a proper form of dress was said to enhance her "natural" beauty, emphasizing her health and freshness and promising her fecundity. (Sawchuk 1987, 68)

Equating moral purity with simplicity, Christian dress reformers advocated a plainer form of dress that was regarded as being more "natural," and hence "truer," than the elaborate artifice of the women's fashion of the day. Sawchuk concludes that the argument for austerity in dress, and the return to more neutral forms, valorizes what is seen as characteristic of men—namely, their rationality—and reinforces the stereotypical conception of women as superficial, duplicitous, and in possession of a sexuality that, if not kept under control, poses a threat to men.

In her advocacy for the employment of decoration in dress, however, she unwittingly perpetuates the notion of ornament as surface embellishment rather than as vehicle of communication. This arises from her concern to discount conceptions of dress that seek to decode its meaning in a way analogous to the interpretation of symbols. In particular, she criticizes the analysis of dress in terms of the degree to which it "reflects" the social structure, insofar as it fails to consider the constitutive role that dress plays in fashioning our identity. As she writes: "[L]ike all forms of cultural production, fashion cannot be considered a mere expression of the current *Zeitgeist*, for it is a *constituent relational element* in the fabric of the social" (Sawchuk 1987, 73; my emphasis). She argues that dress does not merely reflect an identity that is already preformed, but actively contributes to the very constitution of that identity. In her desire to avoid a naive, reflectionist epistemology that sees dress merely as an expression of an already constituted identity, she goes so far as to argue that rather than seeking to "decode" fashion by showing how it is expressive of social inequalities, we should regard it as reflective of nothing other than itself. To assume that fashion is the mirror of some external social reality is fundamentally misconceived, since this presupposes that the self has an identity independent of fashion, when in fact it is constituted by it.

Rather than "decoding" the meaning of dress by showing what particular items of clothing signify, Sawchuk proposes a Derridean process of "deciphering," in which the signifying elements of dress are no longer seen to represent something existing independently of them, but gain their meaning only in relation to each other.[7] To quote her: "Feminist criticism must regard events, objects, images as cultural signs . . . which do not have one fixed or stable meaning, but which derive their significance . . . from their place in a chain of signifiers . . ." (1987, 67). Instead of searching for the meanings of items of dress, then, the task becomes that of demonstrating how mobile their meanings are. As she writes, whereas decoding "implies that there is a master system to which all signs can be returned; deciphering on the other hand, implies that we are cognizant of the instability of all meaning"(1987, 73). She likens the process of deciphering to Walter Benjamin's concept of allegory, whose basic characteristic is its absolute fluidity where "any person, any object, any relationship can mean absolutely anything else" (1987, 66). [8]For example, as Sawchuk points out (1987, 67), whereas once, the wearing of a crucifix almost certainly indicated the Christianity of its wearer, one cannot assume that a crucifix worn by Madonna is an expression of her Christian beliefs. Indeed, it is much more likely that Madonna is adopting such an icon ironically, deliberately misappropriating its traditional significance for the sake of fashion or in order to shock.

While the arguments of Sawchuk represent a salutary warning to those who would too readily seek to find a straightforward correlation between an item of bodily adornment and some aspect of the social world that it reflects, nevertheless, her alternative—that of "deciphering"—steers perilously close to undermining the interpretive endeavor altogether.[9] If, as this approach implies, the "language" of dress is totally malleable, having no connection to anything outside of itself, then how are we to make sense of the clothes we wear? All that we are left with is a mire of constantly fluctuating meanings whose significance it is impossible to interpret. Rather than opening up unlimited possibilities for meaning, such an approach renders ornament meaningless—an empty cipher drained of any content. Instead of allowing for the multiple reinterpretation of signs, it indefinitely defers the possibility of meaning.

## Conclusion

As can be seen, then, despite the transvaluation of ornament in recent feminist defenses of it, the modernist conception of ornament as sensuous embellishment devoid of meaning still persists. As long as ornament continues to be treated in this way, the celebration of it as a reassertion of the value of the feminine does little to unsettle patriarchal associations of femininity with the realm of appearance over essence and style over substance. A more fundamental challenge to the modernist dismissal of ornament requires rather that one recognizes its role as a communicator of cultural values and seeks to engage critically with the meanings that it once had, in a way that makes it relevant to the present.[10] To treat a sign as being a blank cipher, and therefore capable of being invested with any meaning whatsoever, is evidence of the "semiotic illiteracy" (to borrow a phrase from Nelson [1993, 5]) that was the legacy of modernism's reduction of ornament to senseless decoration. It is only in recognizing the semiotic functions of ornament that it can be rescued from its degradation by the advertising and fashion industries, where it has been stripped of substance and used merely for effect. But if we treat ornament as an empty signifier to be endlessly played with in a perpetual circular semiosis of stylistic variation, then its radical possibilities will never be unleashed, and the feminine will continue to be mired in the realm of artifice and the superficial.

One of the most significant aspects of the practice of pastiche in recent fashion has been its play with gender signifiers. This is the focus of the last chapter, which argues that the postmodern "gender carnival" has led not to an undermining of gender distinctions, as is claimed by its proponents, but rather, to their renegotiation. In the course of this analysis, the importance of adequately recognizing the groundedness of this "play" in the materiality of the body, and the structures of inequality that set its parameters, is underlined.

# 7

# The Postmodern
# Gender Carnival

One of the features of fashion in the postmodern era has been the increasing prevalence of gender border crossings, where elements of male and female dress are mixed together in apparently arbitrary ensembles irrespective of the "sex" of the wearer. This has been exemplified by the fashion spreads in *i-D* magazine and *The Face*, for instance, where both male and female models sport outfits combining a mélange of gender signifiers, such as bomber jackets teamed with tutus, and pink sleeveless tops juxtaposed with cycling shorts and Doc Martens boots. Likewise, in *haute couture*, designers such as Jean-Paul Gaultier have freely mixed gender signifiers, presenting outfits for men employing sensuous fabrics and colors normally associated with female dress, such as pink satin and gold lamé accompanied by "feminine" accoutrements such as handbags, gloves, and frills, on the one hand, and "masculine" style garments such as sailor suits for women, on the other. Other fashion designers such as Gianni Versace, Issey Miyake, Katherine Hamnett, Rei Kawakubo, and Calvin Klein have created androgynous style fashions where there is no longer a clear differentiation between male and female garments.[1] Beauty products such as perfume are now also being marketed for men and women without a clear differentiation between them, for instance, Calvin Klein's fragrance *One* for him and her. The great popularity of "gender-bending" celebrities such as Boy George, David Bowie, Grace Jones, Michael Jackson, Annie Lennox, kd lang, and Madonna is also testament to the growing occurrence of this freewheeling play with signifiers of gender.

While the phenomenon of gender border crossing in dress is not new, there are some features of the postmodern manifestation of this that distinguish it from examples in previous eras. In particular, whereas in the earlier part of the twentieth century, most border crossings involved the adoption of elements of male dress by women, trousers being the most notable example, increasingly, men are appropriating elements of female adornment, such as items of jewelry (including earrings and neck chains), as well as fragrances and skin care products that were once almost exclusively a female domain. More colorful and decorative elements are also entering into men's fashion, particularly in the area of leisurewear.

Accompanying this apparently greater reciprocity in the crossing of gender boundaries is a sense of gender markers as no longer being connected with particular "sexed" bodies. Rather, they emerge as arbitrary signs that bear no necessary relation to the "sex" of the body of the wearer who appropriates them. No longer signifying anything beyond themselves, they are treated as "free-floating" signifiers, which can be adopted or discarded at will and mixed together in a myriad of different combinations. The modern day consumer, conceived of or promoted as genderless by advertisers and the fashion industry, purchases for him- or herself an identity that can be assembled and reassembled from an apparently endless repertoire of signs. Gender becomes a "performance" that is not seen to represent anything beyond itself. As Evans and Thornton point out, in magazines such as *i-D* and *The Face*, which were aimed at both sexes, "sexual difference [is deployed] as a pure signifier, detached from biological difference. In such images, the play of clothing signifiers present[s] gender as just one term among many" (1989, 64). Detached from their referents, gender signifiers come to be seen as artificial constructs—that is, as artifacts of culture—rather than expressing essentialist biological categories.

A number of theorists, such as Baudrillard (1993b [1990]), Schwichtenberg (1993), Polhemus (1996), and Garber (1997), have interpreted this freewheeling play with signifiers of masculinity and femininity as indicative of a breakdown of the binary logic of gender distinctions. Jean Baudrillard, for instance, characterizes postmodernity as a "transsexual" era in which the dichotomous distinction between male and female has been replaced by the infinite convertibility of gender signifiers. As he writes:

> The sexual body has now been assigned a kind of artificial fate. This fate is transsexuality—"transsexual" not in any anatomical sense, but rather in the more general sense of transvestism, of playing with the commutability of the signs of sex—and of playing, in contrast to the former manner of playing on sexual difference, on sexual indifference: on lack of differentiation between the sexual poles, and on indifference to sex *qua* pleasure. (1993b [1990], 20)

However, in contrast to these above theorists, it will be argued in this chapter that the postmodern play with gender does not represent a transcendence of gender distinctions, but rather a renegotiation of those boundaries. That is, the recent play with gender signifiers is more about redefining masculinity and femininity than with collapsing the distinction between them. Indeed, as will be demonstrated, the more one seeks to blur gender boundaries, the more they keep reasserting themselves. Rather than disappearing, what constitutes each gender category is continuously being redefined.

Instead of regarding the cross gender borrowings in contemporary dress as being subversive of gender boundaries, they can more properly be seen as an inherent characteristic of fashion. As Fred Davis has pointed out in his discussion of androgyny in fashion, gender border crossings have been a constant feature of fashion since its inception in the fourteenth century (1992, 33). Throughout the history of Western fashion, as he demonstrates, the masculine/feminine dichotomy has constantly been renegotiated without the distinction between the two disappearing. Indeed, it is the continually shifting nature of the distinction that has been one of the primary motors driving the changes in fashion (Davis, 1992, 17).

## The Postmodern Gender Playground

Baudrillard is one of the foremost theorists who have drawn attention to the apparently "free-floating" nature of gender signifiers in postmodern fashion. He argues that, as with all other signs, the markers of gender have become increasingly subject to the process of infinite commutability in fashion, so that dress no longer signifies the gender and sexuality of the wearer in an unambiguous manner. According to Baudrillard, we live in a "transsexual" era in which the binary distinction between masculine and feminine has collapsed. In its place, we are surrounded by the constant circulation of signifiers of sexuality, which bear no necessary relation to the gender of those who adopt them as part of their sartorial "costume." Signifiers of masculinity and femininity are now treated simply as part of a repertoire of "looks" that individuals can adopt irrespective of their gender, as epitomized by celebrities such as Madonna, Michael Jackson, La Cicciolina, and Andy Warhol. Detached from the body, gender signs are employed as "masks" that can be adopted and discarded at will. For Baudrillard, the key figure of postmodernity is that of the *mannequin*, which, in French, signifies simultaneously a masculine, a feminine, and a neuter.[2] To quote him:

Abandoned to the signs of fashion, the body is sexually disenchanted, it becomes a *mannequin*, a term whose lack of sexual discrimination suits its meaning well. The mannequin is sex in its entirety, but sex without qualities. Fashion is its sex. Or rather, it is in fashion that sex is lost as difference but is generalized as reference (as simulation). Nothing is sexed any longer,

everything is sexualized. The masculine and the feminine themselves redis-
cover, having once lost their particularity, the chance of an unlimited second
existence. (1993a, 97)

Baudrillard is equivocal about whether this apparent implosion of gender distinctions in fashion is emancipatory or not. In his work *On seduction*, he celebrates it as the harbinger of a postgender utopia in which sexual
desire is no longer governed by the dichotomous logic of heterosexuality.
As he declares:

> . . . the decline of psychoanalysis and sexuality as strong structures . . . allows
> us to glimpse a parallel universe . . . which can no longer be interpreted in
> terms of psychical and psychological relations or in terms of repression and
> the unconscious but in terms of play, challenge, dual [*duelles*] relations and
> the strategy of appearances: in terms of seduction, not at all in structural
> terms or distinctive oppositions, but seduction as reversibility. . . . (1990b
> [1979], 130–31)

The manipulation of the signs of gender in the realm of "appearances,"
here, is interpreted as a subversive act that undoes the systems of meaning
and power. This is epitomized for Baudrillard by the figure of the transvestite. As he writes:

> . . . what transvestites love is the game of gender confusion. The spell they
> cast . . . comes from sexual wavering and not, as is customary, from the
> attraction of one sex for the other. They truly love neither men/men nor
> women/women, nor those who tautologically define themselves as distinct
> sexual beings. For a sex to exist, signs must redouble the biological being.
> But here signs are detached from the body—there is no sex strictly speaking,
> for what transvestites are enamored with is this game of signs, what excites
> them is *the seduction of the signs themselves.* Everything for them is makeup,
> theatre, seduction. (1990b [1979], 134)

Rather than seeking to overturn social inequalities in the "real" world,
the more effective strategy, according to Baudrillard in *On seduction*, is to
unravel the system of signification of gender difference, thereby ushering
in a polymorphous eroticism free from the strictures of Oedipal sexuality.
  Elsewhere, however, Baudrillard is less positive in his appraisal of the
postmodern play with gender. Thus, for instance, in *The transparency of
evil*, he laments the infinite exchangeability of gender signs as an *ersatz*
form of sexual liberation. In his view:

. . . the promised sexual utopia [has not] materialized. This was to have consisted in the self-negation of sex as a separate activity and its self-realization as total life. The partisans of sexual liberation continue to dream this dream of desire as a totality fulfilled within each of us, masculine and feminine at once, this dream of sexuality as an assumption of desire beyond the difference between the sexes. In point of fact sexual liberation has succeeded only in helping sexuality achieve autonomy as an undifferentiated circulation of the signs of sex. Although we are certainly in transition towards a transsexual state of affairs, this has nothing to do with a revolution of life through sex— and everything to do with a confusion and promiscuity that open the door to virtual indifference (in all senses of the word) in the sexual realm. (1993b [1990], 11–12)

In contrast with Baudrillard's equivocation, other analysts of postmodern fashion, such as Polhemus and Schwichtenberg, have embraced the recent "transvestism" in fashion wholeheartedly. Ted Polhemus, in his book *Style surfing* (1996, 115), praises it insofar as it challenges the apparent "naturalness" of the categories of "masculinity" and "femininity," thereby highlighting the constructedness of identity. As he writes:

While the transsexual seeks a physical solution to correct a "mistake of nature," the "drag artist" scoffs at the very idea of "The Natural"—delighting in artifice, exaggeration, the "off," always proudly proclaiming, "I am not what I seem." More "woman" than a real woman, more "man" than a real man, the male-to-female or female-to-male cross-dresser exhibits precisely those qualities (hyperreality, the dislocation of image and meaning, quotation, playful semantic cruising) that define . . . Post-Modernity. The ultimate Style Surfer, the transvestite cruises gender identity as well as all the other universes of style as meaning. (1996, 120)

For Polhemus, the sexual indeterminacy of the transvestite, who flaunts the artificial construction of the body, is what carries the greatest erotic charge in contemporary culture, rather than unambiguously sexed bodies.

In a similar vein, Cathy Schwichtenberg regards the freewheeling play with gender signifiers engaged in by celebrities such as Madonna as a liberation from the straightjacket of gender binaries. For her, Madonna's gender bending ". . . represent[s] a deconstruction of lines and boundaries that fragment[s] male/female gender polarities and pluralize[s] sexual practices. This is a postmodern, unbounded feminism that unifies *coalitionally* rather than foundationally" (1993, 132). In her analysis of this phenomenon, she draws on Judith Butler's concept of gender as performance.

As outlined by Butler in her book *Gender trouble*, "gender" is not a set of characteristics that individuals possess, but is rather the product of a series of actions that individuals perform, that is, gender is not something one "is," but is the product of what one "does." As such, it is not the expression of the identity of a subject who preexists the performance of gender. Rather, the identity of the subject is itself constituted by the gender performance. Gender then, should not be seen as a substantial thing or a static cultural marker, but rather as an incessant and repeated action. Gender is something that one becomes but can never be. As Butler writes:

> Gender is a complexity whose totality is permanently deferred, never fully what it is at any given juncture in time. An open coalition then, will affirm identities that are alternately instituted and relinquished according to the purposes at hand; it will be an open assemblage that permits of multiple convergences and divergences without obedience to a normative *telos* of definitional closure. (Butler 1990a, 16)

Because it is reliant on the continual reenactment of certain actions, behaviors, and modes of presentation deemed by culture to be "masculine" or "feminine," gender is inherently unstable. Since gender is dependent on the constant reinstantiation of socially defined norms of masculinity and femininity, rather than being an inherent property of the individual, there is always the possibility of the disruption of gender performances.

Similarly, "sex" is no more stable a category than "gender." While "sex" is frequently differentiated from "gender" on the grounds that the former is a biological distinction while the latter is a cultural construct, "sex" is just as much an artifact of culture as is gender. Drawing on Foucault, Butler argues that the category of "sex" and the binary division between male and female on which it is predicated is a discursive construct and not simply a biological datum preexisting discourse.[3] As she explains, it is culture that produces the concept of a "natural sex" as a "prediscursive" entity existing prior to culture (Butler 1990a, 91–97). For Foucault, the body is not "sexed" in any significant sense prior to its determination within a discourse through which it becomes invested with an "idea" of natural or essential sex.[4] The body gains meaning within discourse only in the context of power relations. Sexuality is a historically specific organization of power, discourse, bodies, and desire.

Once the constructed nature of gender and sex distinctions is acknowledged, then there is no reason to suppose that those designated as "male" will automatically take on masculine cultural characteristics, while those designated "female" will assume the culturally defined features of femininity, according to Butler. In theory, males could just as easily take on feminine characteristics and vice versa. Furthermore, there is no reason why gender categories should be limited to two, this being simply a product of cultural convention, having no necessary basis in fact.

Butler concludes that the binary distinction between male and female is a politically oppressive construct predicated on the regulation of sexual desire in terms of a compulsory heterosexuality. Only in a system of heterosexuality, she argues, is there a necessity for a clear-cut, unambiguous distinction between male and female, where individuals are unequivocally one or the other. Institutional heterosexuality both requires and produces the univocity of each of the gendered terms that constitute the limit of gendered possibilities within an oppositional, binary gender system. It is predicated on the assumption that there is a mimetic, rather than an arbitrary, relation between sex and gender in which gender is determined by one's anatomical sex. As Butler writes, the "disciplinary production of gender effects a false stabilization of gender in the interests of the heterosexual construction and regulation of sexuality" (Butler 1990b, 335).

In seeking to expose the essentially contingent nature of the relation between sex and gender, Butler turns to the phenomenon of drag, where there is a disjunction between the anatomy of the performer and the gender that is being performed. With cross dressing, there emerge three distinct dimensions—anatomical sex, gender identity, and gender performance—between which there are no natural or necessary correspondences. As Butler writes, cross-dressing

> reveals the distinctness of those aspects of gendered experience which are falsely naturalized as a unity through the regulatory fiction of heterosexual coherence . . . In the place of the law of heterosexual coherence, we see sex and gender denaturalized by means of a performance which avows their distinctness and dramatizes the cultural mechanism of their fabricated unity. (Butler 1990b, 338)

In Butler's view, transvestism denaturalizes the body, since the transvestite's external appearance bears no relation to the body beneath. Unlike transsexuals who undergo anatomical alterations so that their "biological" body corresponds with their external appearance, transvestites refuse to ground their identity in their anatomical body. They define themselves rather through the various guises that they adopt, whose constructed nature is made evident. For the transvestite, the concept of "sex" as a biological datum is displaced by the notion of gender as performance.

Furthermore, Butler interprets the practice of cross-dressing not simply as the parodic imitation of an original sexual identity conceived of as being "true," but rather, as involving a parody of the very notion of an original sexual identity. In her view, drag reveals that the original identity after which gender fashions itself, is itself an imitation without an origin. That is, sex and gender are both arbitrary cultural constructs, neither having any priority over the other. According to her, it is a mistake to see one's anatomical sex as constituting one's "true" identity and regarding gender identifications that are at odds with one's anatomical sex as "false," since both "sex" and "gender" are cultural fabrications (Butler 1990b, 337). To quote her, once again:

> The psychological language which purports to describe the interior fixity of our identities as men or women works to enforce a certain coherence and to foreclose convergences of gender identity and all manner of gender dissonance ... [It is necessary] to resist the myth of interior origins, understood either as naturalized or culturally fixed. Only then, gender coherence might be understood as the regulatory fiction it is.... (Butler 1990b, 339)

The example of drag suggests that changing gender identity is as easy as changing one's clothes. While Butler herself has resisted such a voluntaristic interpretation of gender as performance in her later writings,[5] nevertheless, many of those who have applied her ideas to the analysis of gender border crossings in postmodern fashion have treated gender as a kind of improvisational theater where different identities can be more or less freely adopted and explored at will.

Thus, Schwichtenberg interprets Madonna's play with the various signifiers of gender in her performances as a challenge to the foundational "truths" of sex and gender (1993, 7). Madonna's constantly shifting persona is seen as typifying the postmodern blurring of boundaries and polarities, such as those of male versus female. For Schwichtenberg, the radicality of Madonna's gender-bending performances lies in the fact that she detaches the signifiers of gender from their association with particular "sexed" bodies, treating them as theatrical masks whose artificial status is thereby highlighted. Rather than being seen as expressive of an "authentic" identity, gender is revealed to be a stylistic fabrication. To quote Schwichtenberg: "Madonna's body, caught in the flux of destabilized identities, deconstructs gender as a put-on . . . This imaginary construction of the body as fragments reflects on the artifice of gender" (1993, 135).

As well as playing fast and loose with gender signifiers, Madonna frequently hyperbolizes them, as exemplified for instance by her video *Material girl*, where she took on the appearance of the ultrafeminine Marilyn Monroe, exaggerating this to the point of parody. By putting the markers of gender in quotation marks, as it were, she draws attention to their culturally constructed and hence, essentially arbitrary, nature. As Sch-wichtenberg writes: "... Madonna bares the devices of femininity, thereby asserting that femininity is a device. [She] takes simulation to its limit in a deconstructive maneuver that plays femininity off against itself—a metafemininity that reduces gender to the overplay of style" (1993, 134).

The political implications that Schwichtenberg draws from Madonna's subversion of the categories of "sex" and "gender" is that a politics of "iden-tity," in which one mobilizes around a particular gender category such as "woman," is no longer the most effective way to combat inequalities arising from sexual difference, since it perpetuates, rather than problematizes, the binary logic of gender distinctions. Rather than continuing to identify with a particular gender category, individuals should embrace the dissolution of gender boundaries epitomized by figures such as Madonna. In Schwich-tenberg's view:

> ... the material power exerted through postmodern sex and gender rep-resentations, as practiced within the gay community and popularized by Madonna, can fracture the notion of "an identity" with a motley pastiche of interests, alignments and identities that intersect at decisive moments. Such provisional coalitions could present a formidable challenge to patriarchal moralism, which, lacking the presumed immanence of identity categories, would have a more difficult time maintaining social control over others aligned in a disparate unity. (1993, 140)

*Gender Still Matters*

However, is it really the case that gender distinctions are no longer relevant in the postmodern carnival of signs? While theorists of postmodern fash-ion such as Baudrillard, Polhemus and Schwichtenberg, present the play with gender codes as a freewheeling activity without limits, this occludes recognition of the fact that this "play" cannot be engaged in equally by everyone, but occurs in a context where gender inequalities persist. Indica-tive of the lack of a level "playing field" in the postmodern gender play-ground is the fact that there continues to be a marked asymmetry in gender border crossings that are governed by the dominance of the male principle. Contrary to the suggestion of reciprocity in gender borrowings in post-modern fashion, female appropriations of male items of attire continue to dominate. While it is certainly true that men are taking on more features of female body adornment than was the case in the first half of the twen-tieth century, it is still the case that the adoption of male items of attire by women is the more common occurrence.

As Fred Davis points out in his book *Fashion, culture, and identity* (1992, 33–7), ever since the nineteenth century, gender border crossings in dress have been predominantly one-way, involving the appropriation of male items of dress by women, notwithstanding some movement in the opposite direction in recent times. Where men have flirted with the possibility of adopting elements of feminine attire, such as the long hair and beads of the hippy movement during the 1960s or the so-called "peacock" revolution of the early 1970s, these forays have tended to be short-lived.[6] There is nothing comparable in male attire to the adoption of trousers, male styled shirts, and coats by women.

Typical of the reticence of men to appropriate feminine sartorial features was the largely negative response to the attempt by Jean-Paul Gaultier to introduce sarongs and pants-skirts in his fall 1984 men's collection.[7] As Davis points out (1992, 34), even as he introduced them, Gaultier stated he was not seeking to feminize men, declaring: "I'm not saying men and women should look alike. It won't be like the sixties where they had the same haircut and everything. They'll share the same wardrobe but they'll wear it differently. Men will stay masculine and women feminine."

Similarly, where male celebrities such as Boy George have feminized their appearance, their popularity has been greatest amongst female fans. As Evans and Thornton point out in their analysis of Boy George, it was the female rather than the male fans who sought to model their appearance on his. For his female fans, Boy George represented a "safe" femininity that was both sophisticated and innocent. They write that: "[Boy George] claimed to prefer tea to sex, he was cuddly and loveable." He was "like a geisha girl for girls, meticulously confected and designed to please. . . ." (1989, 48).

The imbalance in cross border traffic can be explained by the fact that it occurs in a context where gender inequalities still prevail. Since the nineteenth century, when male and female dress became sharply differentiated, male dress—particularly the business suit—has become a symbol of the power and authority enjoyed by men in a patriarchal society. First adopted by the emergent bourgeoisie to signal their rejection of the excessive opulence and indolence of the aristocratic lifestyle, the business suit has become emblematic of a serious-minded professionalism that commands respect. For women to appropriate elements of a sartorial costume that is invested with such qualities is a much more attractive option than for men to feminize their dress, which would imply a diminution of their status.

This explains why, despite the fact that men sacrificed the pleasures of color and ornament when they adopted the plainer and more austere "uniform" of the business suit, it has been far more common for women to seek to emulate male dress than vice versa. Flugel, in his book *The psychology of clothes* (1930, 110–13), described the adoption of the business suit as the "great masculine renunciation" in which men ceded to women the joys associated with elaborate and flamboyant modes of dress that had once also been a feature of male dress. However, at the same time, this was more than compensated for by the power and prestige associated with the sobriety of this new mode of dress. Thus, in spite of being deprived of the pleasures of sartorial decorativeness, men have been reluctant to embrace such elements from female dress, while women have been willing to forgo these pleasures in their adoption of male items of attire.

It is clear from this, then, that not only are female to male border crossings more frequent than the converse, but the significance of each is quite different. Not all gender border crossings are equivalent, as the postmodern gender playground suggests, but occur in a context that is structured by the dominance of the male principle in which menswear is taken as paradigmatic. As Anne Hollander points out (2000, 158–59), most examples of androgynous outfits in contemporary culture involve a feminization of male dress, rather than the reverse, whether the wearer is male or female. Where men take on feminine characteristics in their dress, it involves a variation on the basic items of male attire rather than a masculinization of female attire.[8]

If we examine work wear for women as compared to that worn by their male counterparts, the paradigmatic status of male dress is clear. During the 1970s and '80s, the "dress for success" look that was promoted to professional women, and continues to hold sway today, was a feminization of the masculine business suit. As women increasingly entered into professions that had previously been the preserve of men, they were advised to emulate the dress of their male colleagues in order to gain their respect. It was felt that by appropriating the insignia of male authority and power, women, too, would be imbued with these same qualities. The "feminine" version of the male business suit typically took the form of a tailored skirt with matching jacket, featuring padded shoulders and the same subdued colors as the male version. Today, tailored slacks may be worn instead of the skirt, but otherwise, it is largely unchanged.

In investing professional women with a sense of authority, this new "uniform" was designed so as not to draw attention to the contours of the body of the wearer. As Molloy, author of the power-dressing manual *Women: Dress for success* (1980), wrote, if a woman is to command the authority necessary in order to achieve success in her career, she needs to avoid looking too much like a "secretary," and therefore, not obviously "professional," and looking too "sexy." Thus, he advised women to wear jackets that were cut fully enough to cover the contours of the bust and were not pinched in at the waist. He also warned against the wearing of waistcoats for business since they drew attention to the bust.[9]

At the same time as women have emulated male dress in the workplace, it is precisely in this arena where the masculinity of male dress is most strictly guarded. While it is permissible for men to flirt with aspects of feminine adornment in their leisurewear, through the adoption of more brightly colored shirts or trousers or the wearing of neck chains, for instance, the inclusion of such elements in their professional dress is still very much taboo. For a man to countenance the incorporation of feminine elements into his work wear would most likely be detrimental to his career prospects, since it is seen to undermine his professional status and diminish the respect that he would otherwise command.

The privileging of the male principle applies not just to dress in the workplace, but also to leisurewear. As Hollander points out (2000, 154), one of the most significant occurrences of "androgynous" clothing in recent times can be seen in the adaptation of sportswear to casual dress. Tracksuits, shorts, T-shirts, zipped jackets, and joggers have become de rigueur for women and men alike. But while the male and female versions of these garments are often indistinguishable, nevertheless, they are modeled on what were once exclusively male items of dress.[10] This also applies to jeans, which have become standard casual wear for women as well as men.

On the occasions where men do incorporate feminine elements into their leisure clothes, such as brightly colored or patterned fabrics, and the wearing of jewelry such as neck chains or earrings, these serve more as embellishments of male garb rather than as the masculinization of feminine garments. Although women have taken on men's trousers and made them their own, there is no male version of the female skirt. The closest one comes to a "skirt" in male attire today is the sarong or kilt, but in both cases, they derive from cultural sources where such items were traditionally worn by men, rather than being based on an imitation of female dress.

Even in the case of the more adventurous gender transgressions engaged in by male celebrities such as Stephen Linard and Leigh Bowery during the late 1970s and early '80s, the dominance of the male principle is still evident. As Evans and Thornton point out, although the "peacock" style, made popular in the London clubs by these celebrities, involved the adoption of the most extravagant elements of feminine dress, such as the use of sensuous fabrics and brightly colored and elaborately decorated garments, ultimately, it was male sexual power that was reasserted within this subculture. While men played freely with the signifiers of femininity, there was very little room left for women to experiment with these insignia. The play with gender was seen primarily as a male prerogative. As Evans and

Thornton write: "Generally, men's 'use' of femininity was exclusively theirs in that . . . it was addressed to other men. It was unfashionable to be a woman, fashionable to be a man and most fashionable to be a man dressed as a woman" (1989: 46). Thus, at the same time as Blitz culture and the peacock male in the early '80s put femininity on the map, men kept it in their own hands.

As the previously discussed examples attest, then, the postmodern vision of contemporary fashion as a realm characterized by the infinite commutability of the signifiers of gender obscures the continued existence of gender inequalities that significantly influence the nature of this play with gender identity. Gender border crossings are not completely reciprocal or interchangeable. Nor are gender signifiers of equal valence, even though they may be presented as such by the postmodern carnival of signs. In its treatment of gender markers as "free-floating" signifiers, postmodern fashion converts them into aesthetic categories where they are regarded as different "looks" without any connection to particular social and political realities, thereby occluding the persistence of gender inequalities. This is made quite explicit in Schwichtenberg's article on Madonna, where she writes that: "Gender play is the *mix and match of styles* that flirt with the signifiers of sexual difference, cut loose from their moorings. Such inconstancy underscores the fragility of gender itself as pure artifice" (1993, 134; my emphasis).

While it is all very well to behave, in the realm of the imagination, as if gender differences no longer matter, it is another to overcome them in actual social life. Although, in theory, it is possible to entertain the notion of a world no longer structured by the binary division between men and women, the fact remains that in practice, significant structural inequalities between the sexes remain. Blurring gender boundaries in the realm of appearances does not displace them in actuality. Notwithstanding Butler's argument that "sex" and "gender" are discursive constructs, the hierarchical organization of society on the basis of gender differentiation has a reality that transcends that of discourse. It is not simply a product of discourse that can be willed away simply by redefining the object of discourse. While, in theory, we may stop talking in terms of binary oppositions of male versus female, social reality continues to be organized along these lines. As Teresa Ebert writes:

> Gender and sexuality are not simply the result of discursive or signifying practices performed on the body but also, and more importantly, they are

> the effect of labor performed by, on, and through bodies as historically determined by the division of labor and the unequal access to economic and social resources. (1992–93, 40)

Thus, she concludes that

> to disrupt, undo, or exceed the gender binary requires a collective social struggle not only on the level of ideological constructions but, more importantly, against the systematic socioeconomic relations requiring and maintaining the specific forms of gender and sexual difference. (1992–93, 39)

In this light, the semiotic play with gender advocated by postmodern theorists, such as Schwichtenberg and Polhemus, can be seen to perpetuate such inequalities by falsely presenting the transcendence of gender distinctions as something that has already been achieved. Postmodern fashion, then, plays with the signs of sex, while leaving intact real gender inequalities.

Bordo makes a similar point when she argues that the rhetoric of "incalculable choreographies"[11] of gender employed by much recent postmodern theory treats the subject as being ungrounded in history and without social location. It is as if individuals are capable of embodying any combination of gender signifiers they choose, irrespective of their social position, and that all gender border crossings are commensurate with each other. Critical of those who uphold Madonna's chameleon-like transformations of identity as a model for a postmodern subjectivity, Bordo writes, "This abstract, unsituated, disembodied freedom . . . glorifies itself only through the effacement of the material praxis of people's lives, the normalizing power of cultural images, and the continuing social realities of dominance and subordination" (1993b, 275). In contrast to the postmodern gender playground where all are engaged in a dance of elusive, ever-changing subjectivity, Bordo argues for the necessity to recognize the subject's locatedness in history, which constrains and shapes the nature of their play with identity.

Once this is recognized, it becomes clear that the plea by postmodern theorists such as Schwichtenberg for male/female gender identifications to be abandoned in favor of a pluralistic play with gender boundaries is counterproductive. To behave as if gender distinctions no longer matter in a situation where gender inequalities still prevail only serves to perpetuate them. As Bordo notes, the postmodern celebration of a nomadic, fragmented, post-gendered subjectivity ultimately results in an effacement of the specificity of women's concerns. To quote her:

> Instead of distinctions, endless *differences* reign—an undifferentiated pastiche of differences, a grab bag in which no items are assigned any more importance or centrality than any others. This spectacle of difference defeats the ability to sustain coherent political critique. Everything is the same in its unvalenced difference. (1993b, 258)

To advocate the abandonment of the binary distinction between male and female in favor of the free play with gender identities obscures the unequal position that women occupy in relation to men in the context of the experimentation with gender markers. While, at first glance, it may appear that women have a greater freedom than men to play with gender identity in fashion, this play is structured by the dominance of the male principle as we have seen.

Furthermore, the apparent freedom accorded to women in the realm of fashion belies the fact that there continue to be fewer options open to women than men in most areas of social life. From this perspective, it could be argued that the comparatively greater license given to women, in the realm of dress, to adopt any guise they wish serves as a compensatory mechanism for the lack of options open to them in the other areas of social life. The postmodern celebration of post-gendered identities in the realm of fashion, then, in a context where economic, political, and cultural inequalities between the sexes remain, steers dangerously close to becoming a legitimizing ideology of patriarchal capitalism rather than providing a radical challenge to it. This is reiterated by Wernick, who writes that "[i]t is one thing for men and women to look and behave more nearly the same in the unencumbered leisure situations typically shown in [fashion] ads; quite another for their economic, cultural and political power to have actually become equal" (1991, 63).

As well as effacing the social locatedness of the subject, the play with gender in postmodern fashion presents a curiously disembodied view of the subject. In its treatment of gender signifiers as free-floating signifiers that are detached from their association with particular types of bodies, postmodern theorists of fashion perpetuate the mind/body distinction. It is as if the markers of gender have a life of their own, unrelated to the bodies of the individuals who appropriate them, while the body is treated as a *tabula rasa*, or neutral surface, onto which these signifiers are inscribed. As the relation between the outward "mask" and the body that wears it is entirely arbitrary, it makes no difference whether the body is "male" or "female." Since gender identity is seen as constituted by the mask that one adopts, the nature of the body wearing that guise is no longer considered relevant. The male transvestite is just as much a "woman" as the woman who dons the masque of femininity since there is no self apart from the one forged by our outward appearance.

However, as Sweetman points out, clothes are not just semiotic signs whose meaning depends simply on their relation to other signs, but are integrally related to the body that wears them. The body one has is not immaterial in this play with gender signifiers, contrary to what postmodern theorists of fashion might presuppose. As Sweetman writes:

> Fashion . . . involves far more . . . than simply the symbolic manipulation of codes. When I wear a suit, I walk, feel and *act* differently, and not simply because of the garment's cultural connotations . . . but also because of the way the suit is cut and the way its sheer materiality both enables and constrains, encouraging or demanding a certain gait, posture and demeanor, whilst simultaneously denying me the full range of bodily movement that would be available were I dressed in jogging-pants and a loose-fitting t-shirt. (2001, 66)

Once the corporeal nature of our experience of wearing clothes is recognized, then it becomes clear that our ability to don whatever guise we desire is not as open-ended or flexible as the postmodern "carnival of signs" suggests. For, associated with the wearing of particular types of clothes is a certain body *habitus*—a form of comportment or way of holding and moving the body—that is deeply ingrained and not easily modified. As male transvestites are only too well aware, adopting the masque of femininity involves much more than simply putting on women's clothes, but also entails learning the deportment of the body appropriate for this "look." This leads Sweetman to conclude that

> [f]ashion should not be viewed as simply a symbolic process, and the fashionable body should not be read simply as a cultural text. We also need to attend to the experiential or affectual dimensions of fashionable behavior, and the ways in which fashion as a social process impacts upon the corporeal realities of those involved. (2001, 74)

Likewise, Entwistle points to the necessity to pay due heed to the body as a concrete, fleshly entity rather than simply a blank slate on which signs are imprinted (2001: 42–46). While it is true that the body is mediated by discourse, it is important to realize that it is not simply a discursive construct, but also has a materiality that exceeds this. Following Csordas, Entwistle advocates a shift away from a semiotic/textualist framework to a notion of embodiment and "being in the world," drawn from phenomenology.[12] Central to Merleau-Ponty's phenomenology is an awareness of the body not as the passive receptor of outside stimuli, but rather, as the medium through which we experience the world.[13] Far from being an inert object, our bodies are the sites through which we articulate our sense of self.

However, as Entwistle observes, despite his attention to the corporeality of the body, Merleau-Ponty fails to consider the body as gendered and how this may generate differential experiences of embodiment.[14] In this respect, he shares with post-structuralist theory its failure to acknowledge how the different physical nature of male and female bodies impacts on the way we experience our being-in-the-world. In order to give due weight to the materiality of the body and its gendered specificity, Elizabeth Grosz suggests that a more adequate way of conceiving of the operations of culture on the body is a model based on the process of etching rather than that of inscription. As she writes:

> The kind of model I have in mind here is not simply . . . a model of an imposition of inscription on a blank slate, a page with no 'texture' and no resistance of its own. As any calligrapher knows, the kinds of texts produced depend not only on the message to be inscribed, not only on the inscriptive tools—stylus, ink—used, but also on the quality and distinctiveness of the paper written upon. Perhaps, then, a more appropriate model for this kind of writing is not the writing of the blank page—but a model of etching, a model which needs to take into account the specificities of the materials being thus inscribed and their concrete effects in the kind of text produced. (1994, 191)

While the notion of gender as performance is celebrated as a liberation from fixed, essentialist notions of the self, what is occluded by this conception of the self is its dissociation from the body as fleshly, corporeal substance. In spite of her claims to put bodies center stage, Butler neglects to acknowledge the physicality of the body itself as it becomes reduced to an effect of discourse. Though we are certainly not determined by our biology, neither can we totally transcend it into a free-floating carnival of signs. Our experience of who we are is unavoidably mediated through the physical presence of our bodies, and not to recognize this is to perpetuate the disassociation of the mind from the body, which has been so prevalent in Western culture. In upholding the transgendered body as quintessential, theorists such as Butler perpetuate the denial of gender specificity for which many male theorists of the body have been criticized.

Despite the fact that the bodies in the postmodern world of fashion are presented as genderless mannequins, the "sex" of the wearer does still matter and impacts on the way in which clothes are experienced, both by the wearer and by those around them. Thus, for example, as Entwistle points out (2001, 53–54), while the male business suit serves to "desexualize" the wearer by rendering the body underneath largely "invisible," a similar outfit worn by women produces a different effect. Though the intention here is also to neutralize the sexuality of the wearer, it is still seen as being more erotic than when worn by a man. This is because the bodies of women continue to be seen as more sexual than those of men. There is still a deeply ingrained cultural assumption that men are more capable than women of transcending their bodies to attain a "higher" plane of existence.

In its failure to acknowledge the significance of the body as a corporeal entity, the transgendered subject of postmodernity can be seen to be symptomatic of the heightened sense of alienation from the body that we experience today, despite our constant preoccupation with it. As Arthur and Marilouise Kroker argue (1987, 20–33), with the growing ubiquity of the virtual world of cyberspace and new biotechnologies that provide prosthetic substitutes for body parts and functions, we increasingly experience ourselves as disembodied subjects. They suggest that our contemporary preoccupation with the body can be seen as a "panic reaction" to our increasing sense of its obsolescence. The proliferation of images of the body in consumer culture masks the disappearance of the "natural" body and its replacement by technological devices. As they write:

> Everywhere today the aestheticization of the body and its dissolution into a semiurgy of floating body parts reveals that *we* are being processed through a media scene consisting of our own (exteriorized) body organs in the form of second-order simulacra . . . *Ideologically*, the body is inscribed by the mutating signs of the fashion industry as skin itself is transformed into a screen-effect for a last, decadent and desperate, search for desire after desire. (1987, 21)

While they write in somewhat hyperbolic terms of the absorption of the body in a simulacra of signs that substitute for the "real," nevertheless, their description is apt for the way the body has been presented by postmodern theorists of fashion as a semiotic playground with seemingly no material limits.

### Gender Renegotiation Rather than Gender Transcendence

In contrast to the view that the gender border crossings in postmodern fashion represent a transcendence of gender boundaries, I argue then, that these have not disappeared, but have simply been renegotiated. Despite the increasing frequency of gender border crossings in recent times, gender distinctions have not disappeared, but continue to reassert themselves, even if in slightly new forms. The result of such cross gender borrowings has not been the undermining of the categories of femininity and masculinity, but rather, their reconfiguration.

This can be seen, for instance, in the way in which fragrances have been marketed to men. While the marketing to men of what was once a quintessentially feminine item may seem indicative of the dissolution of gender boundaries, the promotion of male fragrances has been done in such a way as to reassure men of their masculinity.[15] Thus, such advertisements abound with signifiers of traditional masculinity to counter any fears of emasculation attendant upon the use of a traditionally feminine product. Firstly, the very designation of the product seeks to differentiate it from the female version, being commonly referred to as "fragrance," "cologne," "eau-de-toilette," or "aftershave," rather than "perfume." There is also careful styling of the container of the fragrance to give it a more masculine appearance. Generally speaking, cologne bottles for men tend to be chunkier in appearance than are the containers for women's perfumes, as well as having a more pared back, minimalist look. Even in the case of the recent trend toward the unisex marketing of fragrances such as Calvin Klein's *One*, the product continues to be "masculine" in its look (in this case, resembling a hip flask), so as not to alienate the male segment of the market.[16] Also, men's fragrances are frequently associated with traditionally manly outdoor activities, such as sailing or athletics, to reassure the man using the product of his masculinity, or are displayed in conjunction with a professional man in a business suit who radiates an air of authority and confidence in his masculinity, as exemplified by recent advertisements for Hugo Boss men's fragrance.[17]

Similarly, while there are an increasing number of advertisements promoting fashion and personal care products to the male consumer, in which men are portrayed in a quasi-feminine position as the object of the gaze, at the same time, this is counterbalanced by the inclusion of elements that remind us of the masculinity of the models depicted. This is exemplified by a number of recent Calvin Klein underwear advertisements.[18] In these advertisements, the demeanor of the male models is somewhat "feminine" in that they adopt body postures more commonly associated with the female nude–either reclining or standing languidly, with the body displaying a sinuous line calculated to invite the desirous gaze of the spectator. In these advertisements, the models do not stare at the viewer challengingly or belligerently, as do many of the models in earlier advertisements for male underwear, but have an averted or nonthreatening gaze. Their torsos are also smooth and hairless like a woman's body. At the same time, however, signs of traditional masculinity are still present to reassure us of their masculinity. Thus, the models are typically well muscled, projecting an air of strength and solidity, despite their apparent passivity. They are also well endowed, as the body hugging underwear makes clear, and their hair is often slightly disheveled, indicating a rugged masculinity that is not overly narcissistic.[19]

Even in advertisements where there seem to be a more overtly ironic play with the signs of masculinity, as in some of the fashion spreads in *The Face*, ultimately, the masculinity of the subject is never in doubt. For example, in a fashion spread from *The Face* (1985b, 34), a young male model is depicted exhibiting a combination of boyishness and a "tough," assertive masculinity. The styling of the clothes brings together a collision course of signifiers in which cycling shorts are teamed up with "feminine" elements, including a pink, sleeveless top, pink cap, and white gloves. However, while the mixing up of conventional signifiers of masculinity and femininity suggests an ironic play with the conventional signs of gender, ultimately what is presented is a variant of masculinity rather than a transcendence of it. This is indicated by the emphasis on the muscularity and physicality of the model's body, which is posed in a quasi-boxing stance. The stubble on his face also gives him a look of rugged masculinity. Thus, despite the inclusion of some "feminine" elements, the look is still very masculine, "hard" and "street."[20]

This continues to be evident in more recent issues of *The Face*, for instance, the fashion spread, "Black Joe: He's the Driller Queen, Gunpowder and Gelatine, Dynamite with a Laser Beam," which appeared in the September 1999 issue, 128–29. Here, there is a disruption of traditional notions of masculinity, caused by the fact that the male model, who appears as a middle-aged oilrig worker named "Black Joe," is wearing designer dresses. However, despite this dramatic rupture of convention, ultimately, the images do not pose a serious threat to masculinity because of the hypermasculine context within which these garments are "modeled." Black Joe does not pose in a self-conscious way for the camera, but is depicted going about his daily business on the oilrig—an industry which is overwhelmingly masculine. As well as being depicted carrying out "manly" tasks, his physique is clearly masculine in its bulk, hairiness, and confident demeanor. The dresses themselves have the look of having suffered the consequences of the heavy labor in which the wearer has been engaged, with one in particular featuring numerous holes and torn and frayed edges. Furthermore, they are teamed with obviously male signifiers, such as heavy work boots, a hardhat, and safety goggles.

Conversely, despite the masculinization of aspects of women's appearance over the last few decades, this has not resulted in an undermining of femininity, but rather, in its modification to incorporate these new elements. Thus, for example, while slimness has been a long-standing ideal for women, in recent times, this has been modified to incorporate a firmer, well-toned look. As Bordo points out (1993a, 187–91), it is no longer considered sufficient for women to be slender, but they must also avoid being flabby—a look which can best be achieved by "working out" or engaging in some form of athletic activity. Whereas in the past, it was considered "unfeminine" for women to engage in strenuous physical activity, now such exercise is no longer a male prerogative. Developing one's muscle tone is now acceptable for women, though the degree of muscle bulk considered appropriate for women is still less than that deemed attractive in men. Thus, while women's bodies are, in some respects, becoming more like men's through fitness training (which not only increases muscle tone but can also decrease the size of the breasts), gender distinctions are still maintained through the different amount of muscle bulk allowable in each case.[21]

Likewise, while women have incorporated masculine elements into their dress, this has, in many instances, been seen to actually enhance their femininity rather than detract from it. As Steele (1985) points out, androgynous touches have traditionally been employed in fashion to heighten, not to desexualize, the erotic allure of women's clothing. A case in point was the adoption of top hat and tails by Marlene Dietrich during the 1930s in films such as *Morocco*. This was later taken up by Yves Saint Laurent in several of his collections during the 1960s, '70s, and '80s, where female models donned men's formal, black-tie evening wear, teamed with frilly lace, crêpe, or see-through chiffon blouses.[22] A clear indication of the erotic allure associated with the female tuxedo can be seen in a recent example that appeared in *Vogue Australia*, December 2007, where the commentary suggests that while ". . . a frock invites cooing compliments from other women . . . in a tux, the frank invitation of a sliver of naked décolletage framed by black satin revers will render men speechless" (2007, 78).

Even in situations where the intention has been to downplay a woman's sexuality through the masculinization of her dress, as in the adoption of the business suit by women, the result has not been a loss of femininity on the part of the wearer. For at the same time as women have taken on the sobriety of the professional male's garb, they frequently "soften" its masculinity through the incorporation of more "feminine" elements, such as a frilly blouse made of sensuous material, a colorful scarf, jewelry, and high-heeled shoes.[23]

Likewise, the Annie Hall look popular during the 1970s, where women dressed themselves in oversized male-styled garments did not undermine their femininity. As Davis points out (1992, 42–44), at the same time as the garments constituting this "look" were masculine in their style and choice of materials, the fact that they were grossly oversized served to undercut any serious claims to masculinity. Dwarfed by such large garments, women were imbued with the appearance of childlike innocence and vulnerability combined with an element of clownishness as the look suggested a small child playing dress-up.

## Conclusion

More recently, the adoption of the trench coat by women, pioneered by Burberry fashion designer Christopher Bailey, has not diminished the femininity of its wearers since it is accompanied by traditional signifiers of femininity, such as fishnet stockings and stiletto heels.[24] Ralph Lauren's inclusion of blazers, jodhpurs, and male-styled shirts into the female wardrobe, likewise, has resulted in a refeminization of these items rather than in a masculinization of the wearer. Again, in the fashion spreads where these items are featured, this is achieved through the inclusion of numerous emblems of femininity, such as jewelry, long hair, red fingernails, and makeup.[25]

Thus, as the above examples indicate, gender distinctions still remain in place within contemporary culture, despite the greater frequency of gender border crossings. Contrary to postmodern theorists who see the recent play with gender identity as indicative of a transcendence of gender distinctions, it can more accurately be seen as involving a renegotiation of those boundaries in which what constitutes masculinity and femininity is constantly being redefined. Furthermore, rather than being an exceptional situation, this can be seen as inherent to the dynamic of fashion itself. As Fred Davis argues, gender ambivalence has been one of the key driving forces of fashion ever since it originated in the fourteenth century. To quote him:

> . . . fashion has repeatedly, if not exclusively, drawn upon certain recurrent instabilities in the social identities of Western men and women. Among the more prominent ambivalences underlying such fashion-susceptible instabilities are the subjective tensions of . . . masculinity versus femininity. . . .
> (1992, 17–18)

Likewise, Hollander questions the claim of postmodern theorists, such as Garber, that male and female sartorial exchange undermines gender distinctions, arguing that "[f]ashion has always contained transvestism; indeed, it has largely invented it for the modern world" (2000, 166). Rather than being indicative of a "crisis" in gender identity, sexual ambiguities in dress are a recurrent feature of fashion.

Throughout the history of fashion, the distinction between masculinity and femininity in dress has constantly been renegotiated, as each side of the gender divide has made cross border incursions. While the frequency and nature of these incursions has varied over time, what has remained constant has been the persistence of gender distinctions despite their continual redefinition. Male dress has always been defined in relation to female dress and vice versa.[26] Even in instances where men and women have worn the same type of garment, gender differences have usually still been subtly indicated by, for example, using different material for the male and female versions or putting the buttons on the left-hand side for women's blouses and on the right hand side for men's shirts, as Kidwell points out (1989, 129). Truly unisex clothing has never existed. The postmodern play with gender identity, then, is just the latest manifestation of the renegotiation of gender boundaries that has characterized the whole history of fashion. Lipovetsky makes a similar point when he writes that:

> Homogenization of men's and women's fashions exists only at the level of the superficial survey; in reality, fashion has not stopped incorporating differentiating signs . . . Examples abound: men and women alike wear pants, but the cuts and often the colors are different; shoes have nothing in common; a woman's shirt is easy to tell from a man's; the shapes of bathing suits differ, and so do those of underwear, belts, pocket-books, watches, and umbrellas. More or less everywhere, fashion articles reinscribe difference in appearance by way of "little nothings." (1994, 109)

The persistence of gender distinctions, despite their constant redefinition, reveals their essentially contradictory nature. While on the one hand, their never-ending mutations suggest they are unsustainable, on the other, the fact that they continually reassert themselves indicates their intractability. Gender border crossings in fashion thus highlight both the impossibility and the unavoidability of the binary logic of gender. At the same time that we strive to transcend gender distinctions, the more impossible this seems to be. Though this may be disappointing for those who have a utopian vision of a post-gendered future, the recognition of the unstable and tenuous nature of these distinctions holds the promise of more radical reconfigurations of masculinity and femininity in the future.

# Notes

## Introduction

1. Although Davis provides a guarded defence of cosmetic surgery, she concedes that it is an option often taken up by women who have few, if any, other alternatives.

## Chapter 1

1. Douglas Kellner (1993) has a useful discussion of the "problem" of identity in postmodernity.
2. See Charles Baudelaire (1978 [1863], 26–29) for a discussion of dandyism.
3. Arthur Marwick (1988, 13–22) also argues that physical appearance is accorded a greater importance today than ever before, though he fails to see this as being in any way problematic.
4. See Bonnie English (2007, 28–42) for a more detailed account of the democratization of fashion in the early twentieth century.
5. Also indicative of the importance accorded to appearance in contemporary culture is the huge expenditure on cosmetics and other body care products, as Synnott points out (1993, 74–75).
6. Richard Sennett (1976, 162–76) goes on to argue that the advent of this notion of outward appearance as an expression of the personality of the wearer paradoxically resulted in clothing becoming more homogeneous and neutral, as people were afraid of revealing too much of themselves in public. This meant that those seeking to read someone's personality through their clothes had to search for clues in the small details of dress, much in the manner of the detective undertaking a forensic investigation. While I concur with Sennett's observation about the homogenization of appearance, I argue in this chapter that this is rather due to the increasing difficulty that individuals have in forging, for themselves, a meaningful sense of identity through the fashioning of their physical appearance.
7. Hilary Radner (1989) draws attention to this in her discussion of the changing nature of cosmetics advertising directed at women.
8. Rosalind Coward (1987, 55–60) notes the growing prevalence of the defiant pout in women's fashion advertising and points out that while, at first glance, it appears to present a more assertive image of female sexuality, it is

no less problematic than the ingratiating smile characteristic of earlier fashion models.

9. See Malcolm Barnard (1996, 166–69) for a discussion of this concept in relation to postmodern fashion. However, while I am using the terms "pastiche" and "*bricolage*" interchangeably, Barnard seeks to distinguish the latter from the former, suggesting that *bricolage* is less nihilistic than pastiche.

10. Heike Jenß (2004) discusses a recent trend to resurrect the style of the 1960s, in which the aim is to be as "authentic" as possible. This is at odds with the predominant trend in postmodern culture of mixing styles from the past in an eclectic way, but even here, as she demonstrates, '60s enthusiasts combine contemporary clothes made in a '60s style with actual garments from that period. Furthermore, their appropriation of '60s style is very much determined by their contemporary cultural context. Thus, they are quite selective in what they have chosen to revive, favoring those items that correspond with their current cultural context and bodies.

11. See Goffman (1959) for an elaboration of his performative notion of the self.

12. See Susan Kaiser (1997, 515–18) for a further discussion of this.

13. See Charlotta Kratz and Bo Reimer (1998) for a further discussion of this.

14. See Gilles Lipovetsky (1994, 107–9) for a further discussion of this.

15. Alison Clarke and Daniel Miller analyze this phenomenon (2002). As they argue, in contemporary culture, where there is no single dominant fashion but rather a multiplicity of different styles, individuals face increasing anxiety about what to wear. In response to this, there is a tendency to retreat into forms of dress that are less individualizing or expressive in order to avoid possible social embarrassment. Even in instances where individuals are knowledgeable about fashion and style, they are often at a loss as to what is most appropriate for them to wear.

## Chapter 2

1. While there were dissenting voices within the Women's Movement as discussed, for example, by Wilson (1987, 230–37), this was the predominant feminist dress code at the time.

2. Shilling (1994, 63–67) provides a useful discussion of Orbach and Chernin in this regard.

3. See Oakley (1981, 83) for a description of feminist garb in the 1970s.

4. Similarly, Holliday and Sanchez Tayor argue that the "natural" aesthetic championed by feminists conceals its operations—looking natural is not the same as being natural. They go on to argue that "the feminist acceptance of only a naturally beautiful body in fact endorses certain modes of cultivation—such as the gym—while arbitrarily dismissing others such as the beauty industry, interpreting the former as active and chosen and the latter as passive and consumed" (2006, 185).

5. Holliday and Sanchez Taylor (2006, 184) make a similar point.

6. See Giroux (1993–94) for a development of this argument. See also Bordo (1993b), who points out the similarity between postmodern notions of the body and self-identity and those promoted by the fashion and advertising industry.

7. A similar criticism applies to Peiss's and Holliday's and Sanchez Taylor's defense of the cultivation of appearance by black and working class women as a means of social advancement. According to Peiss (1996, 330), the employment of beautification techniques by Afro-American women was a tool of empowerment insofar as it challenged stereotypical conceptions of the black woman as ugly and unkempt and conferred on them a sense of dignity and pride. The production of cosmetics for Afro-American women also opened up opportunities of employment for such women, giving them a greater economic independence than they would otherwise have enjoyed. Similarly, Holliday and Sanchez Taylor positively appraise the fact that working class women, such as shop assistants and office workers, who adopted a "lady-like" appearance, which belied their working class origins, were able to command greater respect (2006, 184). In these ways, these authors claim, the cultivation of appearance challenged race and class hierarchies among women, opening up new economic opportunities for black and lower class women, and giving voice to their claims for cultural legitimacy. In making such claims, however, Peiss and Holliday and Sanchez Taylor fail to address the social structures of inequality that necessitated such a strategy in the first place. It was only because such women were denied access to power through legitimate means that they were forced to resort to beautification as the only way of achieving their aims.

8. For instance, as Hollander (1994, 25–26) points out, there was a precedent for the big-shouldered look in old Hollywood movies, where it was worn with short skirts and long hair, not long pants and shingled hair.

## Chapter 3

1. Georg Simmel makes a similar point in his article, "The aesthetic significance of the face," where he writes (1959, 278) that: "The face strikes us as the symbol, not only of the spirit, but also of an unmistakable personality. This feeling has been extraordinarily furthered in the period since the beginning of Christianity by the covering of the body. The face was the heir of the body; for in the degree to which nakedness was the custom, the body presumably had its share in the expression of individuality."

2. Craik (1994, 153–75) has a useful discussion of the contrasting nature of cosmetic practice in Western and non-Western cultures.

3. Andrew Strathern quotes one Mt Hagener tribesman who commented: "If the men's faces can be seen too clearly, we say, 'Oh, we went to that dance and even from a distance we were able to recognize the men early, it was no good.' So they put on a lot of charcoal to make their faces really dark as night and

prevent their recognition, so that people will praise them. They say, 'Hey, we can't recognize these men, this is a good dance performance'" (1987, 29).

4. Grosz (1994, chap. 6) provides a useful discussion of Lingis's analysis of body markings.

5. See Mercurio and Morera (2004) for examples of Andy Warhol's portraiture.

6. See Bell et al. (1994, 42–43) for a useful discussion of this style.

7. In a later article where she reconsiders her earlier position on masquerade, Doane acknowledges the conservative nature of the professional woman's masquerade of femininity as discussed by Rivière. However, she still maintains that it is possible to read such a performance "against the grain," arguing that "Rivière's patient, looking out at her own male audience, with impropriety, throws the image of their own sexuality back to them as 'game' or 'joke,' investing it, too, with the instability and the emptiness of masquerade" (1988, 52–53). The question still remains, however, to what extent the audience will see the "joke" being played by the woman who parades the artificiality of her femininity.

8. See Craik (1989, 12–14) for a discussion of this book.

9. This image also appears in *All the Rage: A history of fashion and trends* (1992): 66.

10. See *Marie Claire Australia*, November 2006, 1–2, for an example of this Estée Lauder advertisement. Another Estée Lauder advertisement in a similar vein from 2002 can be viewed at http://www.advertisingarchives.co.uk, no. 30518988

11. Wilson (1987, 110–11) also notes that when visible cosmetics were first promoted in the early twentieth century, they were seen as a sign of emancipation rather than of bondage by women.

12. See Peiss (1998, 249–51) for a discussion of this ad campaign. The Revlon Fire and Ice advertisement from 1952 can be viewed at http://www .advertisingarchives.co.uk, no. 30523066.

13. Revlon also introduced names such as *Fatal Apple, Paint the Town Pink*, and *Where's the Fire?* for its lipstick range to heighten such connotations. See Merskin (2007, 595) for a discussion of this.

14. In this regard, Peiss (1998, 268) mentions a Cincinnati distributor calling herself FeyKay (a play on Mary Kay cosmetics) whose "Go Grrrl! Cosmetics for Queers," "the first lesbian on-line cosmetics service," surfaced on the Internet in 1994.

15. Radner (1989), who offers an opposing point of view to this, seems to accept, uncritically, the claims of the advertising industry that making up is primarily an act of self-gratification.

16. See Goldstein (1995), who points out in her analysis of makeover videotapes that while they address each viewer as an individual in order to convey the impression that she is being instructed in a routine that has been specially tailored to her needs, in fact what is being promoted is a standardized set of beauty rituals. As she writes: "Makeup advertising . . . constructs women as objects while appealing to them as subjects" (1995, 312).

17. See also Wolin (1986) for further criticisms of this "aesthetics of existence."
18. Some Moslem women, however, claim that wearing the veil liberates them from attracting unwanted sexual attention from men, and also represents a symbol of rebellion against the West (Chapkis 1988, 43).

## Chapter 4

1. See for example Lakoff and Scherr (1984, 169–74).
2. Significantly, Davis, in an article entitled "'A dubious equality'" (2003, 117–31), pays much more attention to the social structures of gender inequality within which the technologies, practices, and discourses of cosmetic surgery operate than in her book *Reshaping the female Body: The dilemma of cosmetic surgery (1995)*.
3. This is something which Holliday and Taylor (2006, 189–91) tend to downplay in their claim that, today, aesthetic surgery is increasingly about standing out rather than blending in. However, despite their celebration of aesthetic surgery as an instrument of differentiation and distinction rather than of normalization, even they ultimately acknowledge that the negotiation between women and their surgeons is a profoundly asymmetrical one in which the surgeon's judgement about what is "suitable" generally prevails (192).
4. Indeed, she is critical of this, as revealed in Davis (1997, 176–80).
5. Haraway has in mind, here, eco-feminists such as Carolyn Merchant, Susan Griffin, Audre Lorde, and Adrienne Rich. See Haraway (1991, 154, 174).
6. Deleuze and Guattari (1983, chap. 1) also advocate a similar reconceptualization of the self. Like Haraway, they are opposed to the notion of the body as a unified organism, instead proposing the concept of the "body without organs" (following Artaud), where the body is no longer experienced as an integrated whole that is centrally organized, but as a series of non-hierarchically linked parts that are constantly entering into linkages with other loosely connected assemblages—both human and nonhuman, animate and inanimate. In contrast with the notion of the organism with hermetically sealed boundaries, they propose a conception of a body that is forever open to new connections and is constantly reconfiguring itself. In a world where there are no longer seen to be distinct entities with clearly defined boundaries, the old binary oppositions between the human and the non-human, the animate and the inanimate, subject and object and so on, are no longer relevant. All have the same ontological status. For them, a liberated practice is one that opposes all coagulations and rigidifications into a stable and unified entity. The aim should be to transcend identity and subjectivity, fragmenting and freeing up lines of flight, "liberating" multiplicities, corporeal and otherwise, that identity subsumes under the one.
7. Hirschhorn (1996, 110–34) provides a useful account of Orlan's practice.
8. In her later operations, Orlan employed a female cosmetic surgeon because, unlike the male surgeon who wanted to keep her "cute," the female surgeon was more prepared to do her bidding as is pointed out in O'Bryan (2005, 19).

9. Griggers (1997, 29–30) makes this point.
10. Orlan is not entirely consistent on this point. As Davis points out (1997, n. 11, 180), while Orlan has been cited as a model for postmodern notions of identity, she still, at some points, continues to operate with a notion of the sovereign subject, more akin to the existentialist concept of self than that of Butler.
11. Elsewhere in the same article (1999, 167), Goodall puts forward a somewhat different argument suggesting that Orlan's rhetoric about transcending bodily limits should not be taken at face value, since the rhetoric is belied by her actual performances, which strip the dream of a "post-biological" world of its appeal through the grotesque display of the body's interior. But if this was Orlan's intention, why does she seek to glamorize her performances with lavish costumes and props and to emphasize her apparent lack of suffering during her operations?
12. As Clarke herself acknowledges later in her article (1999, 195), while on the one hand, Orlan stresses corporeality by using her own body as the material for her art, on the other, she disavows it through her recreation of her body as text.
13. Curiously, earlier on in the same article (1991, 29), where Morgan is developing her critique of mainstream cosmetic surgery, she seems much more concerned about the risks associated with such a practice.
14. The fact that Orlan has had one botched operation is also glossed over by her.
15. As pointed out in Ayers (1999, 180).
16. While Orlan's most recent work involves computer manipulations of her image rather than actual physical operations, she has indicated in an interview with Ayers (1999, 182–84) that she intends to undergo further operations.
17. Best and Kellner (1991, 211, 290) develop this point further.

## Chapter 5

1. See Baudrillard (1993a, 87–95) for a discussion of this.
2. Crossley (2005, 30) argues that while many forms of body modification are used today as a sign of individuality, they are not all the same in nature, some being socially endorsed, while others, such as tattooing, are still regarded as not quite socially acceptable. I would suggest that it is this very unacceptability that commends itself to those whose primary purpose is to establish their distinctiveness through the fashioning of their appearance, i.e., tattoos, even more so than other forms of body modification, such as dieting or cosmetic surgery, for instance, are particularly appropriate as a way of signalling one's uniqueness because of their past association with those outside of the mainstream.
3. Generally, there were no facial and hand tattoos since they are prohibited in the military.

4. The term "queer," employed here by Pitts, came into vogue in the 1990s when it was used in positive self-identification by many individuals of a sexuality traditionally regarded as deviant, including homosexuals and transsexuals.
5. See Rubin (1988), where the meanings of body marking practices in many different cultures from around the world are discussed.
6. See Eubanks (1996) and Klesse (1999) for a more detailed critique of "modern primitivism."
7. This is particularly evident in those magazines promoting a "new laddism," i.e., a resurgence of old style masculine values. See Benyon (2002, 108–14) for a further discussion of the "new laddism."
8. Though, as Edwards (1997, 41–54) points out, the range of masculinities is still limited—for instance, it excludes older men, those who are not trim and fit, and rural men.
9. See Bell et al. (1994, 34–38) for a discussion of more recent versions of the "masculine" look in gay sartorial strategies.
10. The two Jean-Paul Gaultier advertisements discussed here can be viewed at www.advertisingarchives.co.uk, image nos. 30533850 and 30524118.
11. Jean-Paul Gaultier derived his figure of the sailor from Fassbinder's film based on Jean Genet's book, *Le querelle de brest*. In using the figure of the sailor, Gaultier was exploiting the fact that the well-built sailor out for a night on the town has become not only a standard piece of port mythology, but also a staple of gay iconography, as McDowell (2001, 57) points out.
12. In 1997 and 1998, Gaultier designed outfits for men in which he used decorative patterning to simulate tattoos—see McDowell (2001, 127). Here, the resemblance between tattoos and decorative lacework was even more explicit.
13. These Calvin Klein jeans advertisements can be viewed at www.davidtoc.com/ck. One features model David Silveria Korn in an ad for Dirty Denim jeans, the second Butch Walker, and the third Ryan Shuck in an ad for Rinse Denim jeans.
14. This image can be viewed in the *The Face*, No. 86, November 1995b, 18–19
15. This image can be viewed in *The Face*, No. 85, October1995a, 6–7

## Chapter 6

1. See Lévi-Strauss (1969) for more on his analysis of the significance of face-painting among the American Indians.
2. See Kandinsky (1947, 67–68) where he outlines his views on the decorative.
3. See Greenberg (1952, 148) where he seeks to distance Matisse's work from the decorative.
4. See Meyer and Schapiro (1978, 66–69) for a discussion of Schapiro's concept of "femmage."
5. See Barthes (1981, part 1) for a discussion of this.
6. Similarly, Frederic Jameson describes the practice of postmodern pastiche as "blank parody," in which styles of the past are imitated, not in order to mock them (which would involve an engagement with their previous meanings) but

simply to highlight their fabricated nature. As he puts it: "Pastiche is, like parody, the imitation of a peculiar or unique style, the wearing of a stylistic mask, speech in a dead language: but it is a neutral practice of such mimicry, without parody's ulterior motive, without the satirical impulse . . ." (1983, 114).

7. See Derrida (1981, 26) for a discussion of his concept of "deciphering."

8. See Benjamin (1977) for a discussion of his concept of "allegory."

9. Sawchuk herself, at one point (1987, 72) draws back from the implications of her adoption of Derrida's approach of deciphering, arguing that meaning is never absolutely arbitrary in any text. If this is accepted, however, then this undermines the fundamental premise of Derrida's project of deciphering— namely, the emancipation of signifiers from any external referents.

10. This is not to suggest that the communicative function of ornament exhausts all of its other functions. As Paul Sweetman points out in his discussion of fashion (2001, 59–74), ornament has an important affective dimension as well—something which semiotic approaches tend to neglect in their treatment of ornament as a disembodied text that can be decoded like a language.

## Chapter 7

1. Mendes and de la Haye (1999) have a useful discussion of the work of these designers.

2. As pointed out by the translator of *Symbolic exchange* (1993a, 100, fn 7), *mannequin* in French refers to a man with no strength of character who is easily led, as well as to a woman employed by a large coutourier to present models wearing its new collection, and finally, to an imitation human.

3. Laquer and Gallagher (1987) make a similar point when they argue that the notion of two biologically opposite sexes only originated in the eighteenth century. Up until this time, women were regarded simply as a variation of the male sex rather than being diametrically opposed to it.

4. See Foucault (1981) for an elaboration of his discursive concept of sexuality.

5. See, for instance, her argument concerning drag in Butler (1993) and also her interview (Osborne and Segal, 1997). Butler argues here that although gender is the result of a series of actions by a subject, the performance is not simply the product of the will or intentions of the subject, since individuals are always constituted by social norms and cultural conventions that preexist them. Furthermore, the operations of the unconscious mean that there is much that is not under the conscious control of the subject. Moya Lloyd (1999) has a useful analysis of Butler's notion of performativity and how it has been taken up by other postmodern theorists.

6. As Paoletti and Kidwell point out (1989, 159), even when such apparently feminine symbols were borrowed, justification was offered by citing examples of men's earlier use of the style. For instance, those men who adopted long hair in the 1960s often justified it with reference to the fact that prior to the

nineteenth century, it was customary for men to have long hair or to wear wigs.

7. McDowell (2000) provides a useful survey of Jean-Paul Gaultier's work that demonstrates his preoccupation with playing with gender signifiers, including the introduction of skirts for men.

8. See Lipovetsky (1994, 110), who also makes a similar point. As he writes, "While women can allow themselves to wear virtually anything, can include items of masculine origin in their wardrobe, men for their part are subject to a restrictive code based on the exclusion of feminine emblems . . . [U]nder no circumstances may men wear dresses or skirts, or use makeup . . . Dress and makeup are, at least for now, the property of the feminine; they are strictly forbidden to men. Here is proof that fashion is not a system of generalized commutation in which everything is exchanged in the indeterminacy of codes, in which all signs are 'free to commutate and permutate without limits.'"

9. Entwistle (2002, 187–91) has a useful discussion of power dressing.

10. Hollander (2000, 154–57) argues further that such garments derive originally from children's clothing and are suggestive of a form of eroticism free from adult responsibilities.

11. This phrase comes from Derrida and McDonald (1982) who use it as a way of describing postmodern subjectivity.

12. See Csordas (1993) for an elaboration of this.

13. See Merleau-Ponty (1976) for an elaboration of this.

14. Iris Marion Young (1990, 141–44) makes a similar critique of Merleau-Ponty in her book *Throwing like a girl and other essays*, where she develops a phenomenological theory of female embodiment.

15. See Haug (1986, 78–87) for further discussion of the marketing of body care products and fashion to men.

16. An image of the fragrance bottle for Calvin Klein's *One* can be viewed at www .advertisingarchives.co.uk, no. 30544001.

17. Examples of such advertisements can be viewed at www.advertisingarchives .co.uk, nos. 30551444, 30511668, 30551442, 30555625, and 30552455.

18. See www.advertisingarchives.co.uk for examples, nos. 30553500, 30553281, 30533010, and 30532934

19. See Bordo (1999b, 168–225) for examples of these advertisements. In this chapter, she provides a useful discussion of other examples of similar advertisements.

20. This is reiterated by Evans and Thornton, who write that the fashion pages of *The Face* and *Blitz* magazines during the mid 1980s "marketed not a play on gender but an image of entrenched masculinity." (1989, 52). While men became objects of desire, these images were addressed primarily to a male audience (both heterosexual and homosexual) and still presented models with the sort of physique associated with the traditional masculinity of the 1950s. This was reinforced by captions such as: "Portrait of a Buffalo Boy looking hard in the yard" (quoted from *The Face* [1985a, 73]).

21. As Dworkin (1998, 252) found in her study of women who work out, most of them expressed an awareness of an upper limit on the quest for muscular size and strength, and tailored their exercises so as not to exceed these limits.
22. See Yves Saint Laurent (1982) for images of these outfits.
23. See Davis (1992, 50–51) for a further discussion of this.
24. See www.advertisingarchives.co.uk, no. 30553288 for an example of this.
25. See www.advertisingarchives.co.uk, no. 30548602.
26. See Hollander (1994, 7–13), where she develops this point further in her discussion of the evolution of male and female dress in the twentieth century.

# References

Anger, Jenny. 1996. Forgotten ties: The suppression of the decorative in German art and theory, 1900–1915. In *Not at home: The suppression of domesticity in modern art and architecture*, ed. Christopher Reed, 130–46. London: Thames and Hudson.

Ayers, Robert. 1999. Serene and happy and distant: An interview with Orlan. *Body & Society* 5 (2–3): 171–84.

Baker, Nancy C. 1984. *The beauty trap*. New York and Toronto: Franklin Watts Press.

Balsamo, Anne. 1996. *Technologies of the gendered body: Reading cyborg women*. Durham and London: Duke University Press.

Barnard, Malcolm. 1996. *Fashion as communication*. London and New York: Routledge.

Barthes, Roland. 1981. *Camera lucida: Reflections on photography*, trans. Richard Howard (Orig. pub. 1980)

Bartky, Sandra L. 1988. Foucault, femininity, and the modernization of patriarchal power. In *Feminism and Foucault*, ed. Irene Diamond and Lee Quinby, 61–86. Boston: Northeastern University Press.

Baudelaire, Charles. 1978. The painter of modern life. In *The painter of modern life and other essays*. Selected and trans. Jonathan Mayne, 1–40. New York and London: Garland Publishing. (Orig. pub. 1863)

Baudrillard, Jean. 1981. *For a critique of the political economy of the sign*. St. Louis: Telos Press. (Orig. pub. 1972.)

———. 1984. The ecstasy of communication. In *The anti-aesthetic: Essays on post-modern culture*, ed. Hal Foster, 126–34. Port Townsend, WA: Bay Press.

———. 1990a. *Seduction*. London: MacMillan Education.

———. 1990b. The ecliptic of sex. In *Jean Baudrillard: Revenge of the crystal, selected writings on the modern object and its destiny, 1968–1983*, ed. and trans. Paul Foss and Julian Pefanis, 129–62. Sydney: Pluto Press (Orig. pub. 1979).

———. 1993a. *Symbolic exchange and death*. London: Sage. (Orig. pub. 1976.)

———. 1993b. *The transparency of evil*. London: Verso. (Orig. pub. 1990.)

Bauman, Zygmunt. 1997. From pilgrim to tourist—or a short history of identity. In *Questions of cultural identity*, ed. Stuart Hall and Paul du Gay, 18–36. London: Sage Publications.

Bell, David, Jon Binnie, Julia Cream, and Gill Valentine. 1994. All hyped up and no place to go. *Gender, Place and Culture* 1 (1): 31–47.

Benjamin, Walter. 1977. *The Origin of German Tragic Drama*, trans. John Osborne. London: New Left Books

Benson, Susan. 2000. Inscriptions of the self: Reflections on tattooing and piercing in contemporary Euro-America. In *Written on the body*, ed. Jane Caplan, 234–54. London: Reaktion Books.

Benyon, John. 2002. *Masculinities and culture*. Buckingham and Philadelphia: Open University Press.

Best, Steven, and Douglas Kellner. 1991. *Postmodern theory: Critical interrogations*. London: MacMillan.

Bordo, Susan. 1993a. Reading the slender body. In *Unbearable weight: Feminism, Western culture, and the body*, ed. Susan Bordo, 185–212. Berkeley: University of California Press.

———. 1993b. "Material girl": The effacements of postmodern culture. In *Unbearable weight: Feminism, Western Culture, and the body*, ed. Susan Bordo, 245–75. Berkeley: University of California Press.

———. 1993c. Introduction: Feminism, Western culture, and the body. In *Unbearable weight: Feminism, Western Culture, and the body*, ed. Susan Bordo, 1–42. Berkeley: University of California Press.

———. 1999a. Gay men's revenge. In *The male body*, ed. Susan Bordo, 153–67. New York: Farrar, Straus and Giroux.

———. 1999b. Beauty (re)discovers the male body. In *The male body*, ed. Susan Bordo, 168–225. New York: Farrar, Strauss, and Giroux.

Broude, Norma. 1982. Miriam Schapiro and "femmage": Reflections on the conflict between decoration and abstraction in twentieth century art. In *Feminism and art history: Questioning the litany*, ed. Norma Broude and Mary D. Garrard, 315–29. New York: Harper & Row.

Brownmiller, Susan. 1984. *Femininity*. New York: Linden Press, Simon and Schuster.

Butler, Judith. 1990a. *Gender trouble: Feminism and the subversion of identity*. London: Routledge.

———. 1990b. Gender trouble, feminist theory, and psychoanalytic discourse. In *Feminism/Postmodernism*, ed. Linda Nicholson, 324–40. New York: Routledge.

———. 1993. Critically queer. In *Bodies that matter*, ed. Judith Butler, 223–42. London: Routledge.

Carboni, Massimo. 1991. Infinite ornament. *Artforum* 30 (September): 106–11.

Chapkis, Wendy. 1988. *Beauty secrets: Beauty and the politics of appearance*. London: The Women's Press.

Chernin, Kim. 1983. *Womansize: The tyranny of slenderness*. London: The Women's Press.

Clark, Danae. 1991. Commodity lesbianism. *Camera Obscura* 25 (6): 181–201.

Clarke, Alison, and Daniel Miller. 2002. Fashion and anxiety. *Fashion Theory* 6 (2): 191–213.

Clarke, John, Stuart Hall, Tony Jefferson, and Brian Roberts. 1977. Subcultures, Cultures and Class. In *Resistance through rituals: Youth subcultures in post-war Britain*, ed. Stuart Hall and Tony Jefferson, 9–74. London: Hutchinson.

Clarke, Julie. 1999. The sacrificial body of Orlan. *Body & Society* 5 (2–3): 185–207.

*Cleo*, January, 2008.

Coe, Kathryn, Mary P. Harmon, Blair Verner, and Andrew Tonn. 1993. Tattoos and male alliances. *Human Nature* 4 (2): 199–204.

Cole, Shaun. 2000. "Macho man": Clones and the development of a masculine stereotype. *Fashion Theory* 4 (2): 125–40.

Connor, Steven. 2001. Mortification. In *Thinking through the skin*, ed. Sara Ahmed and Jackie Stacey, 36–51. London and New York: Routledge.

Constable, Catherine. 2000. Making up the truth: On lies, lipstick and Friedrich Nietzsche. In *Fashion cultures: Theories, explorations and analysis*, ed. Stella Bruzzi and Pamela C. Gibson, 191–200. London and New York: Routledge.

Corson, Richard. 1981. *Fashions in makeup*. London: Peter Owen.

Coward, Rosalind. 1984. *Female desire: Women's sexuality today*. London: Paladin.

Craik, Jennifer. 1989. "I must put my face on": Making up the body and marking out the feminine. *Cultural Studies* 3 (1): 1–24.

———. 1994. *The face of fashion*. London and New York: Routledge.

Crossley, Nick. 2005. Mapping reflexive body techniques: On body modification and maintenance. *Body & Society* 11 (1): 1–35.

Csordas, Thomas J. 1993. Somatic modes of attention. *Cultural Anthropology* 8 (2): 135–56.

Curry, David. 1993. Decorating the body politic. *New Formations* 19: 69–82.

Davis, Fred. 1992. *Fashion, culture and identity*. Chicago: University of Chicago Press.

Davis, Kathy. 1995. *Reshaping the female body: The dilemma of cosmetic surgery*. New York and London: Routledge.

———. 1997. "My body is my art": Cosmetic surgery as feminist Utopia? In *Embodied practices: Feminist perspectives on the body*, ed. Kathy Davis, 168–81. London: Sage Publications.

———. 2003. "A dubious equality": Men, women, and cosmetic surgery. In *Dubious equalities and embodied differences: Cultural studies on cosmetic surgery*, ed. Kathy Davis, 117–31. Lanham: Rowman & Littlefield.

De Beauvoir, Simone. 1975. *The second sex*. Middlesex: Penguin. (Orig. pub. 1949.)

Deleuze, Gilles, and Felix Guattari. 1983. *Anti-oedipus: Capitalism and schizophrenia*. London: The Athlone Press.

———. 1988. *A thousand plateaus*. London: The Athlone Press.

DeMello, Margo. 2000. *Bodies of inscription*. Durham and London: Duke University Press.

Derrida, Jacques. 1981. *Positions*, trans. Alan Bass. Chicago: University of Chicago Press.

Derrida, Jacques, and Christie V. McDonald. 1982. Choreographies. *Diacritics* 12 (2): 66–76.

Di Stefano, Christine. 1990. Dilemmas of difference: Feminism, modernity, and postmodernism. In *Feminism/Postmodernism*, ed. Linda J. Nicholson, 63–82. New York and London: Routledge.

Doane, Mary A. 1988. Masquerade reconsidered: Further thoughts on the female spectator. *Discourse: Journal for Theoretical Studies in Media and Culture* 11 (1): 42–54.

———. 1990. Film and the masquerade: Theorizing the female spectator. In *Issues in feminist film criticism*, ed. Patricia Erens, 41–57. Bloomington and Indianapolis: Indiana University Press. (Orig. pub. 1982.)

Dutton, Kenneth R. 1995. *The perfectible body: The Western ideal of physical development*. London: Cassell.

Dworkin, Shari. 1998. "Holding back": Negotiating a glass ceiling on women's muscular strength. In *The politics of women's bodies*, ed. Rose Weitz, 240–56. New York: Oxford University Press.

Eastlake, Charles. 1971. *Hints on household taste*. New York: Benjamin Blom. (Orig. pub. 1872.)

Ebert, Teresa. 1992–93. Ludic feminism, the body, performance and labour: Bringing materialism back into feminist cultural studies. *Cultural Critique* 23: 5–50.

Editors of Time-Life Books. 1992. *All the rage: A history of fashion and trends*. London: Caxton Publishing Group.

Edwards, Tim. 1997. *Men in the mirror*. London: Cassell.

English, Bonnie. 2007. *A cultural history of fashion in the twentieth century*. Oxford: Berg.

Entwistle, Joanne. 2001. The dressed body. In *Body dressing*, ed. Joanne Entwistle and Elizabeth Wilson, 33–58. Oxford and New York: Berg.

———. 2002. *The fashioned body*. Cambridge and Oxford: Polity Press.

Eubanks, Virginia.1996. Zones of dither: Writing the postmodern body. *Body & Society* 2 (3): 73–88.

Evans, Caroline, and Minna Thornton. 1989. *Women and fashion: A new look*. London: Quartet Books.

———. 1991. Fashion, representation, femininity. *Feminist Review* 38: 56–66.

*The Face*. 1985a, January 57: 73.

*The Face*. 1985b, June 62: 34.

*The Face*. 1995a, October 85: 6–7.

*The Face*. 1995b, November 86: 18–19.

*The Face*. 1999, September 32: 128–29.

Faunthorpe, Rev. J. P., ed. 1895. *Household science: Readings in necessary knowledge for girls and young women*. London: Edward Stanford. (Orig. pub. 1879)

Featherstone, Mike. 1991a. The body in consumer culture. In *The body: Social process and cultural theory*, ed. Mike Featherstone, Mike Hepworth, and Bryan S. Turner, 170–96. London: Sage Publications. (Orig. pub. 1982.)

———. 1991b. *Consumer culture and postmodernism*. London: Sage Publications.

Felski, Rita. 1995. *The gender of modernity*. Cambridge and London: Harvard University Press.

Finkelstein, Joanne. 1991. *The fashioned self*. Oxford: Polity.

Flax, Jane. 1991. *Thinking fragments: Psychoanalysis, feminism, and postmodernism in the contemporary West*. Berkeley, Los Angeles, and Oxford: University of California Press.

Flugel, John C. 1930. *The psychology of clothes*. London: Hogarth Press.

Forty, Adrian. 1992. *Objects of desire: Design and society since 1750*. London: Thames and Hudson.

Foster, Hal. 1985. *Recodings: Art, spectacle, cultural politics*. Port Townsend, WA: Bay Press.

Foucault, Michel. 1981. *The history of sexuality*. vol. 1: *An introduction*. Harmondsworth: Penguin.

Freedman, Rita. 1986. *Beauty bound*. Lexington, MA: Lexington Books.

Gadamer, Hans-Georg. 1975. *Truth and method*. New York: Seabury Press.

Garber, Marjorie. 1997. *Vested interests: Cross dressing and cultural anxiety*. New York: Routledge.

Giddens, Anthony. 1991. *Modernity and self-identity*. Cambridge: Polity Press.

Gill, Rosalind, Karen Henwood, and Carl McLean. 2005. Body projects and the regulation of normative masculinity. *Body & Society* 11 (1): 37–62.

Gilman, Sander. 1999. *Making the body beautiful*. Princeton: Princeton University Press.

Giroux, Henry A. 1993–94. Consuming social change: The "united colors of Benetton." *Cultural Critique* Winter: 5–32.

Goffman, Erving. 1959. *The presentation of self in everyday life*. New York: Anchor Books.

Goldstein, Judith. L. 1995. The female aesthetic community. In *The traffic in culture: Refiguring art and anthropology*, ed. George E. Marcus and Fred R. Myers, 310–29. Berkeley and Los Angeles: University of California Press.

Gombrich, Ernst. 1980. *The sense of order: A study in the psychology of decorative art*. Oxford: Phaidon.

Goodall, Jane. 1999. An order of pure decision: Un-natural selection in the work of Stelarc and Orlan. *Body & Society* 5 (2–3): 149–70.

Griggers, Camilla. 1997. The despotic face of white femininity. In *Becoming-woman*, ed. Camilla Griggers, 1–35. Minneapolis: University of Minnesota Press.

Grosz, Elizabeth. 1994. *Volatile bodies: Toward a corporeal feminism*. Sydney: Allen & Unwin.

Hanson, Karen. 1993. Dressing down dressing up: The philosophic fear of fashion. In *Aesthetics in feminist perspective*, ed. Hilde Hein and Carolyn Korsmeyer, 229–41. Bloomington: Indiana University Press.

Haraway, Donna J. 1991. A cyborg manifesto: science, technology, and socialist feminism in the late twentieth century. In *Simians, cyborgs, and women: The reinvention of nature*, ed. Donna Haraway, 149–81. New York: Routledge.

Haug, Wolfgang F. 1986. *Critique of commodity aesthetics*. Cambridge: Polity Press.

Haweis, Mary E. 1878. *The art of beauty*. London: Chatto and Windus.

———. 1879. *The art of dress*. London: Chatto and Windus.

Hill, Andrew. 2005. People dress so badly nowadays: Fashion and late modernity. In *Fashion and modernity*, ed. Christopher Breward and Caroline Evans, 66–77. Oxford and New York: Berg.

Hirschhorn, Michelle. 1996. Orlan: Artist in the post-human age of mechanical reincarnation: Body as ready (to be re-)made. In *Generations and geographies in the visual arts: Feminist readings*, ed. Griselda Pollock, 110–34. London and New York: Routledge.

Hollander, Anne. 1993. *Seeing through clothes*. Berkeley: University of California Press.

———. 1994. *Sex and suits: The evolution of modern dress*. New York: Alfred A. Knopf.

———. 2000. *Feeding the eye*. Berkeley: University of California Press.

Holliday, Ruth, and Jacqueline Sanchez Taylor. 2006. Aesthetic surgery as false beauty. *Feminist Theory* 7 (2): 179–95.

Ince, Kate. 2000. *Orlan: Millenial female*. Oxford: Berg.

Jameson, Frederic. 1983. Postmodernism and consumer society. In *The anti-aesthetic: Essays on postmodern culture*, ed. Hal Foster, 111–25. Port Townsend, WA: Bay Press.

Jensen, Robert, and Patricia Conway. 1982. *Ornamentalism*. New York: Clarkson N. Potter.

Jenß, Heike. 2004. Dressed in history: Retro styles and the construction of authenticity in youth culture. *Fashion Theory* 8 (4): 367–404.

Johnson, Pauline. 1994. *Feminism as radical humanism*. Sydney: Allen & Unwin.

Kaiser, Susan B., Richard H. Nagasawa, and Sandra S. Hutton. 1991. Fashion, postmodernity and personal appearance: A symbolic interactionist formulation. *Symbolic Interaction* 14 (2): 165–85

Kaiser, Susan B. 1997. *The social psychology of clothing: Symbolic appearances in context*. 2nd rev. ed. New York: Fairchild.

Kandinsky, Wassily. 1947. *Concerning the spiritual in art*. New York: Wittenbom, Schultz.

Kellner, Douglas. 1993. Popular culture and the construction of postmodern identities. In *Modernity and identity*, ed. Scott Lash and Jonathan Friedman, 141–77. Oxford: Blackwell Publishers.

———. 1994. Madonna, fashion, and identity. In *On fashion*, ed. Shari Benstock and Suzanne Ferriss, 159–82. New Brunswick, NJ: Rutgers University Press.

Kidwell, Claudia B. 1989. Gender symbols or fashionable details? In *Men and women: Dressing the part*, ed. Claudia B. Kidwell and Valerie Steele, 125–43. Washington, DC: Smithsonian Institution Press.

Klein, Naomi. 1999. *No logo: Taking aim at the brand bullies*. New York: Picador.

Kleinert, Sylvia. 1992. Deconstructing "the decorative": The impact of Euro-American artistic traditions on the reception of aboriginal art and craft. In *Craft in society*, ed. Noris Ioannou, 115–30. South Fremantle, Western Australia: Fremantle Arts Centre Press.

Klesse, Christian. 1999. "Modern primitivism": Non-mainstream body modification and racialized representation. *Body & Society* 5 (2–3): 15–38.

Kratz, Charlotta, and Bo Reimer. 1998. Fashion in the face of postmodernity. In *The postmodern presence*, ed. Arthur A. Berger, 193–211. London: Sage Publications.

Kroker Arthur, and Marilouise Kroker. 1987. Theses on the disappearing body in the hyper-modern condition. In *Body invaders: Panic sex in America*, eds. Arthur Kroker and Marilouise Kroker, 20–34. New York: St. Martin's Press.

Lakoff, Robin T., and Raquel L. Scherr. 1984. *Face value: The politics of beauty*. Boston and London: Routledge & Kegan Paul.

Laquer, Thomas, and Catherine Gallagher. 1987. *The making of the modern body: Sexuality, society and the 19th century*. London: University of California Press.

Le Corbusier. 1987. The decorative art of today. In *The decorative art of today*, ed. Le Corbusier, 83–99. London: Architectural Press. (Orig. pub.1925.)

Lemoine-Luccioni, Eugénie. 1983. *La robe: Essai psychoanalytique sur le vêtement*. Paris: Editions du Seuil.

Lentini, Paul. 1999. The cultural politics of tattooing. *Arena Journal* 13: 31–50.

Lévi-Strauss, Claude. 1966. *The savage mind*. London: Weidenfeld and Nicolson.

———. 1969. The art of Asia and America. In *Structural anthropology*, ed. Lévi-Strauss, 245–68. London: Allen Lane.

Lingis, Alfonso. 1983. Savages. In *Excesses: Eros and culture*, ed. Alfonso Lingis, 18–46. Albany: State University of New York Press.

Lipovetsky, Gilles. 1994. *The empire of fashion: Dressing modern democracy*. Princeton, NJ: Princeton University Press.

Lloyd, Moya. 1999. Performativity, parody, politics. *Theory, Culture & Society* 16 (2): 195–213.

Loos, Adolf. 1966. Ornament and crime. In *Adolf Loos, pioneer of modern architecture*, ed. Ludwig Munz and Gustav Kunstler, 226–31. New York: Praeger. (Orig. pub. 1908.)

———. 1982. Ladies' fashion. In *Spoken into the void: Collected essays, 1897–1900*. Selected and trans. Jane O. Newman and John H. Smith, 99–103. Cambridge: MIT Press. (Orig. pub. 1902.)

Lury, Celia. 1996. *Consumer culture*. Cambridge: Polity Press.

*Marie Claire Australia*, November, 2006 135: 1–2.

Marwick, Arthur. 1988. *Beauty in history*. London: Thames & Hudson.

Mascia-Lees, Frances E., and Patricia Sharpe.1992. Introduction. In *Tattoo, torture, mutilation and adornment: The de-naturalization of the body in culture and text*, eds. Frances E. Mascia-Lees and Patricia Sharpe, 1–9. Albany: State University of New York Press.

McDowell, Colin. 2001. *Jean Paul Gaultier*. New York: Viking Studio.

Mendes, Valerie and Amy de la Haye.1999. *20th Century Fashion*. London: Thames & Hudson.

Mercer, Kobena. 1992. Black hair/style politics. In *Marginalization and contemporary cultures*, ed. Russell Ferguson, Martha Gever, Trinh T. Minh-ha, and Cornel West, 247–64. Cambridge, MA: MIT Press.

Mercurio, Gianni and Daniela Morera. 2004. *The Andy Warhol Show*. Milan: Skira

Merleau-Ponty, Maurice. 1976. *The primacy of perception*. United States: Northwestern University Press.

Merskin, Debra. 2007. Truly toffee and raisin hell: A textual analysis of lipstick names. *Sex Roles* 56: 591–600.

Meyer, Melissa and Miriam Schapiro. 1978. Waste not/want not: Femmage. *Heresies: A feminist publication on art and politics.* 4: 66–9.

Modleski, Tania. 1991. *Feminism without women: Culture and criticism in a 'postfeminist' age.* London and New York: Routledge.

Molloy, John T. 1980. *Women: Dress for success.* New York: Peter H. Wyden.

Morgan, Kathryn. P. 1991. Women and the knife: Cosmetic surgery and the colonization of women's bodies. *Hypatia* 6: 25–53.

Mort, Frank. 1996. *Cultures of consumption: Masculinities and social space in late twentieth-century Britain.* London: Routledge.

Moss, Sue. 1999. Orlan's theatre of wound and word. Unpublished paper, School of English and European Languages, University of Tasmania.

Muggleton, David. 2004. *Inside subculture: The postmodern meaning of style.* Oxford and New York: Berg.

Nelson, Robert. 1993. *Ornament: An essay concerning the meaning of decorative design.* Fitzroy, Victoria: Craft Victoria.

Newton, Stella M. 1974. *Health, art, and reason: Dress reformers of the 19th century.* London: J. Murray.

Nixon, Sean. 1992. Have you got the look? Masculinities and shopping spectacle. In *Lifestyle shopping: The subject of consumption*, ed. Rob Shields, 149–69. London and New York: Routledge.

Oakley, Ann. 1981. *Subject women.* New York: Pantheon Books.

O'Bryan, C. Jill. 2005. *Carnal art: Orlan's refacing.* Minneapolis: University of Minnesota Press.

Orbach, Susie. 1978. *Fat is a feminist issue.* London: Arrow Books.

Osborne, Peter, and Lynne Segal. 1997. Gender as performance: An interview with Judith Butler. In *Identity and difference*, ed. Kathryn Woodward, 235–38. London: Sage. (Orig. pub. 1994.)

Paoletti, Jo B., and Claudia B. Kidwell. 1989. Conclusion. In *Men and women: Dressing the part*, ed. Claudia B. Kidwell and Valerie Steele, 158–61. Washington, DC: Smithsonian Institution Press.

Peiss, Kathy. 1996. Making up, making over: Cosmetics, consumer culture, and women's identity. In *The sex of things*, ed. Victoria de Grazia and Ellen Furlough, 311–36. Berkeley: University of California Press.

———. 1998. *Hope in a jar: The making of America's beauty culture.* New York: Metropolitan Books.

Pitts, Victoria. 2003. *In the flesh: The cultural politics of body modification.* New York: Palgrave Macmillan.

Polhemus, Ted. 1994. *Streetstyle.* London: Thames & Hudson.

———. 1996. *Style surfing.* London: Thames & Hudson

———. 2000. The invisible man. In *Material man: Masculinity, sexuality, style*, ed. Giannino Malossi, 44–51. New York: Harry N. Abrams.

Powell, Nelson and Brian Humphreys. 1984. *Proportions of the Aesthetic Face.* New York: Thième-Stratton

Quant, Mary. 1986. *Quant on make-up*. London: Century Hutchinson.

Radner, Hilary. 1989. "This time's for me": Making up and feminine practice. *Cultural Studies* 3 (3): 301–22.

Rivière, Joan. 1986. Womanliness as a masquerade. In *Formations of fantasy*, ed. Victor Burgin, J. Donald, and Cora Kaplan, 35–44. New York: Methuen. (Orig. pub. 1929.)

Rose, Barbara. 1993. Is it art? Orlan and the transgressive act. *Art in America* February: 82–87, 125.

Rubin, Arnold, ed. 1988. *Marks of civilization*. Los Angeles: University of California Press.

Saint Laurent, Yves. 1983. *Yves Saint Laurent*. New York: The Metropolitan Museum of New York.

Saisselin, Remy G. 1985. *Bricabracamania: The bourgeois and the bibelot*. London: Thames & Hudson.

Salecl, Renata. 2001. Cut in the body: From clitoridectomy to body art. In *Thinking through the skin*, ed. Sara Ahmed and Jackie Stacey, 21–35. London and New York: Routledge.

Sawchuk, Kim. 1987. A tale of inscription/fashion statements. In *Body invaders: Panic sex in America*, ed. Arthur Kroker and Marilouise Kroker, 61–77. New York: St. Martin's Press.

Schopenhauer, Arthur. 1970. *Essays and Aphorisms*. London: Penguin.

Schor, Naomi. 1987. *Reading in detail: Aesthetics and the feminine*. New York and London: Methuen.

Schwichtenberg, Cathy. 1993. Madonna's postmodern feminism: Bringing the margins to the center. In *The Madonna connection*, ed. Cathy Schwichtenberg, 129–45. Boulder: Westview Press.

Scott, Linda M. 2005. *Fresh lipstick: Redressing fashion and feminism*. New York: Palgrave Macmillan.

Sennett, Richard. 1976. *The fall of public man*. Cambridge: Cambridge University Press.

Shilling, Chris. 1994. *The body and social theory*. London: Sage Publications.

Shusterman, Richard. 1988. Postmodernist aestheticism: A new moral philosophy? *Theory, Culture & Society* 5 (2–3): 337–55.

Silverman, Kaja. 1986. Fragments of a fashionable discourse. In *Studies in entertainment: Critical approaches to mass culture*, ed. Tania Modelski, 139–154. Bloomington and Indianapolis: Indiana University Press.

Simmel, Georg. 1959. The aesthetic significance of the face. In *Georg Simmel 1858–1918: A collection of essays*, ed. Kurt H. Wolff, 276–81. Columbia: Ohio State University Press.

———. 1971. Fashion. In *On individuality and social forms: Selected writings*, selected and trans. by Donald N. Levine, 294–323. Chicago: University of Chicago Press. (Orig. pub. 1904.)

Sontag, Susan. 1966. Notes on "camp." In *Against interpretation and other essays*, ed. Susan Sontag, 275–92. New York: Farrar, Straus & Giroux.

Sparke, Penny. 1995. *As long as it's pink: The sexual politics of taste*. London: Pandora.

Stannard, Una. 1971. The mask of beauty. In *Woman in sexist society*, ed. Vivian Gornick and Barbara K. Moran, 118–30. New York and London: Basic Books.

Steele, Valerie. 1985. *Fashion and eroticism*. New York: Oxford University Press.

Steiner, Wendy. 2001. *Venus in exile: The rejection of beauty in twentieth century art*. Chicago: University of Chicago Press.

Strathern, Andrew. 1987. Dress, decoration, and art in New Guinea. In *Man as art: New Guinea body decoration*, ed. Malcolm Kirk, 15–36. London: Thames & Hudson.

Strathern, Marilyn. 1979. The self in self-decoration. *Oceania* 48 (4): 241–57.

Sweetman, Paul. 2000. Anchoring the (postmodern) self? Body modification, fashion, and identity. In *Body modification*, ed. Mike Featherstone, 51–76. London: Sage Publications.

———. 2001. Shop window dummies? Fashion, the body, and emergent socialities. In *Body dressing*, ed. Joanne Entwistle and Elizabeth Wilson, 59–78. Oxford and New York: Berg.

Synnott, Anthony. 1990. Truth and goodness, mirrors and masks, part II: A sociology of beauty and the face. *British Journal of Sociology* 41 (1): 55–76.

———.1993. *The body social*. London and New York: Routledge.

Thevoz, Michel. 1984. *The painted body*. New York: Rizzoli.

Tickner, Lisa. 1984. Why not slip into something a little more comfortable? In *Spare rib reader*, ed. Marsha Rowe, 39–47. England: Penguin.

Tseëlon, Efrat. 1992. Is the presented self sincere? *Theory, Culture & Society* 9 (2): 115–28.

———. 1995. *The masque of femininity*. London: Sage.

Vale, V., and Andrea Juno, eds. 1989. *Re/search #12: Modern primitives. An investigation of contemporary adornment and ritual*. San Francisco: Re/Search Publications.

Veblen, Thortstein. 1970. *The theory of the leisure class*. London: Unwin Books. (Orig. pub. 1899.)

*Vogue Australia*, December, 2007.

Wernick, Andrew. 1991. *Promotional culture: Advertising, ideology, and symbolic expression*. London: Sage Publications.

Wilson, Elizabeth. 1987. *Adorned in dreams: Fashion and modernity*. London: Virago. (Orig. pub. 1985.)

———. 1990a. These new components of the spectacle: Fashion and postmodernism. In *Postmodernism and society*, ed. Roy Boyne and Ali Rattansi, 209–36. London: MacMillan Education.

———. 1990b. All the rage. In *Fabrications: Costume and the female body*, ed. Jane Gaines and Charlotte Herzog, 28–38. New York and London: Routledge.

———. 2000. A response to Llewellyn Negrin. *Theory, Culture & Society* 17 (5): 121–25.

Wolf, Naomi. 1991. *The beauty myth*. London: Vintage.

Wolin, Richard.1986. Foucault's aesthetic decisionism. *Telos* 67: 71–86.

Woolnough, Damien. 2008. Changing suit. *Vogue Australia*. February: 48.
Young, Iris M. 1990. *Throwing like a girl and other essays in feminist philosophy and social theory*. Bloomington: Indiana University Press.
———. 1994. Women recovering our clothes. In *On fashion*, ed. Shari Benstock and Suzanne Ferriss, 197–210. New Brunswick, NJ: Rutgers University Press.

## Films

Quine, Richard (director). 1960. *The World of Suzi Wong*. United States: Paramount Pictures
Von Sternberg, Joseph (director). 1930. *Morocco*. United States: Paramount Pictures.

# Author Index

# Subject Index